THE DAILY STUDY BIBLE

THE LETTERS
to
THE PHILIPPIANS, COLOSSIANS,
and THESSALONIANS

THE LETTERS

to

THE PHILIPPIANS, COLOSSIANS,

and

THESSALONIANS

Translated, with Introductions and Interpretations
by

WILLIAM BARCLAY

THE WESTMINSTER PRESS
PHILADELPHIA

First published by The Saint Andrew Press
Edinburgh, Scotland
Philippians, First Edition, 1957; Second Edition, 1959
Colossians, First Edition, 1957; Second Edition, 1959
I and II Thessalonians, First Edition, 1954; Second Edition, 1959

Library of Congress Catalog Card No. 59-10146

Typeset in Great Britain
Printed in the United States of America

To
J. K. AND H. C. M.
WHOSE SYMPATHY AND KINDNESS
WE WILL NOT FORGET

GENERAL INTRODUCTION

IT may truly be said that this series of Daily Bible Studies began almost accidentally. A series which the Church of Scotland was using came to an end, and another series was immediately required. I was asked to write a volume on *Acts*, and, at the moment, had no intention beyond that. But one volume followed another, until the demand for one volume became a plan to write on the whole New Testament.

The translation which is given in each volume claims no special merit. It was included in order that the reader might be able to carry both the text of the New Testament and the comments on it wherever he went, and that he might be able to read it anywhere. While I was making the translation, the translations of Moffatt, Weymouth, and Knox were ever beside me. *The American Revised Standard Version*, *The Twentieth Century New Testament*, and *The New Testament in Plain English*, by Charles Kingsley Williams, have been in constant use. Since its publication, I have consistently consulted *The Authentic New Testament*, translated by Hugh J. Schonfield.

I cannot see another edition of these books going out to the public without expressing my very deep and sincere gratitude to the Church of Scotland Publications Committee for allowing me the privilege of first beginning, and then continuing, this series. And in particular I wish to express my very great gratitude to the convener, Rev. R. G. Macdonald, O.B.E., M.A., D.D., and to the committee's secretary and manager, Rev. Andrew McCosh, M.A., S.T.M., for constant encouragement and never-failing sympathy and help.

As these volumes went on, the idea of the whole series developed. The aim is to make the results of modern scholarship available to the non-technical reader in a form that it does not require a theological education to understand; and then to seek to make the teaching of the New Testament books relevant to life and work to-day. The whole aim of these books is summed up in Richard of Chichester's famous prayer; they are meant to enable men and women to know Jesus Christ more clearly, to love Him more dearly, and to follow Him more nearly. It is my prayer that they may do something to make that possible.

vii

FOREWORD

ONCE again I should like to thank the Church of Scotland Publications Committee, and especially its Secretary and Manager, the Rev. Andrew M'Cosh, M.A., S.T.M., and its Convener, the Rev. W. M. Campbell, B.D., Ph.D., D.Litt., in the first place, for allowing me to write these volumes of Daily Bible Studies, and in the second place for now re-issuing them in this new edition.

This volume contains notes on the Letters of Paul to the Philippians, the Colossians, and the Thessalonians. Each of these letters has its own special importance. *Philippians* has been called " the Epistle of excellent things." It is not a difficult letter to understand, and for many it is the most charming and attractive letter that Paul ever wrote. *Colossians* is at once one of the greatest and one of the most difficult letters that Paul ever wrote. Nowhere does Paul reach such heights in his writing about the person and the work of Jesus Christ. Here is Pauline thought about Jesus Christ as its greatest and its highest. 1 and 2 *Thessalonians* are, with the possible exception of *Galatians*, Paul's earliest letters. They are of special importance in showing Paul's teaching to his earliest Churches, and in particular they contain some of his most definite teaching about the Second Coming. He who studies these three letters will see Paul's thought in many of its highest reaches and aspects. All these letters have been fortunate in their commentators.

No one can write on *Philippians* and *Colossians* without being deeply indebted to the great works of J. B. Lightfoot which rank among the greatest commentaries ever written. I have often gone back also to the commentaries of C. J. Ellicott. On *Philippians* the commentary of M. R. Vincent in *The International Critical Commentary* is of first-rate importance. On the English text of the letter the commentaries by H. G. C. Moule in the old *Cambridge Bible for Schools and Colleges*, by J. H. Michael in the *Moffatt*

Commentary, and the two devotional commentaries by H. G. G. Herklots and C. E. Simcox have much that is helpful.

On *Colossians* the volume by C. F. D. Moule in the new *Cambridge Greek Testament* is invaluable, and the volume in the *Moffatt Commentary* by E. F. Scott has all that writer's customary lucidity and helpfulness.

On the Greek text of 1 and 2 *Thessalonians* there are two very great commentaries, that by G. Milligan in the Macmillan Series of Commentaries, and that by J. E. Frame in the *International Critical Commentary*. These both rank among the greatest of all English New Testament Commentaries. On the English text the volume in the *Torch Commentary* and the volume in the *Moffatt Commentary* were both written by W. Neil, and are both excellent; and the volume by Leon Morris in the *Tyndale Commentary* is also helpful and illuminating.

The translation in this volume lays no claim to any special merit; it was originally produced simply in order that the reader might have translation and commentary in one handy pocket volume. I have always had by my side the translations by Moffatt and Weymouth, and that of J. B. Phillips; but I have found myself making more and more use of that most excellent, and not nearly well enough used, volume, *The New Testament in Plain English* by Charles Kingsley Williams, which I have always found meticulously accurate and notably illuminating.

As I have sent out all the other volumes in this series, so also I send out this one, with the prayer that it may do something to bring the New Testament alive for the modern reader.

WILLIAM BARCLAY.

TRINITY COLLEGE,
    GLASGOW.
        March, 1959.

CONTENTS

xi

CONTENTS

CONTENTS

I THESSALONIANS

xiii

2 THESSALONIANS

THE LETTER TO THE PHILIPPIANS

THE LETTER TO THE PHILIPPIANS

INTRODUCTION

WE are fortunate in one thing in our study of *Philippians*—there are practically no critical problems involved; for no reputable New Testament critic has ever doubted the genuineness of this epistle. Without argument, and without the labour of finding proofs, we can accept *Philippians* as undoubtedly an authentic and genuine letter of Paul.

Philippi
When Paul chose a place wherein to work and to preach the gospel, he always chose it with the eye of a strategist. He always chose a place which was not only important in itself, but which was the key point of a whole area. It has often been noted that, to this day, many of the places which Paul chose as preaching-centres are still great road centres and railway junctions. And such was Philippi. Philippi had at least three great claims to distinction.

(i) In the neighbourhood there were gold and silver mines, which had been worked as far back as the time of the Phoenicians. It is true that by the time of the Christian era they had become exhausted, but they had made Philippi a great commercial centre of the ancient world.

(ii) The city itself had been founded by Philip, the father of Alexander the Great, and it is his name that it bears. It was founded on the site of a place called *Krēnidēs*, a name which means The Wells or Fountains; and Krēnidēs was itself a very ancient city. Philip had founded Philippi for a very definite reason. There was no more strategic site in all Europe. There is a range of hills which divides Europe from Asia, the east from the west. Just at Philippi that chain of hills dips into a pass; and, therefore, Philippi commanded the road from Europe to Asia, for through the pass the road must go. It was for that reason that in 368 B.C. Philip had founded the city of Philippi to command the

3

road from the east to the west. And it was for that reason that one of the great decisive battles of history was fought much later at Philippi; for it was at Philippi that Antony defeated Brutus and Cassius, and thereby decided the whole future of the Roman Empire.

(iii) Not very long after Philippi attained to the dignity of becoming a Roman Colony. These Roman Colonies were amazing institutions. They were not colonies in the sense of being outposts of civilization in unexplored parts of the world. They had begun by having a military significance. It was the custom of Rome to send out parties of veteran soldiers, who had served their time, and who had been granted citizenship, and to settle them in strategic road centres. Usually these parties consisted of three hundred veterans with their wives and children. These colonies were the focal points of the great Roman road systems. The roads were so engineered that reinforcements could speedily be sent from one colony to another. They were founded to keep the peace, and to command the strategic centres in Rome's far-flung Empire. At first they had been founded in Italy; but soon they were scattered throughout the whole Empire, as the Empire grew. As we have seen, their original significance had been military, but in the later days the title of colony was given by the Roman government to any city which they wished to honour and to repay for faithful service.

These colonies had one great characteristic. Wherever they were they were little fragments of Rome, and their pride in their Roman citizenship was their dominating characteristic. The Roman language was spoken; Roman dress was worn; Roman customs were observed; their magistrates had Roman titles, and carried out the same ceremonies as were carried out in Rome itself. Wherever they were these colonies were stubbornly and unalterably Roman. They would never have dreamt of becoming assimilated to the people amidst whom they were set. They were parts of Rome, miniature cities of Rome, and they never

4

forgot it. We can hear the Roman pride breathing through the charge against Paul and Silas in *Acts* 16: 20, 21: " These men are Jews, and they are trying to teach and to introduce laws and customs which it is not right for us to observe—*for we are Romans.*" " You are a colony of heaven." Paul wrote to the Philippian Church (3: 20). Just as the Roman colonist never forgot in any environment that he was a Roman, so they must never forget in any society that they were Christians. Nowhere were men prouder of being Roman citizens than in these colonies. And such was Philippi.

Paul and Philippi

It was on the second missionary journey, about the year A.D. 52, that Paul first came to Philippi. Urged on by the vision of the man of Macedonia with the appeal to come over and help us, Paul had sailed from Alexandrian Troas in Asia Minor. He had landed at Neapolis in Europe, and thence he had made his way to Philippi.

The story of Paul's stay in Philippi is told in *Acts* 16; and an interesting story it is. There is no chapter in the New Testament which better shows the universality of the appeal of Christ. That chapter centres round three people— Lydia, the seller of purple, the demented slave girl, used by her masters to tell fortunes, and the Roman gaoler. It is an extraordinary cross-section of ancient life. These three people were of three different nationalities. Lydia was an *Asiatic*, and her name may well be not a proper name at all, but may simply mean " the Lydian lady." The slave-girl was a native *Greek*. The gaoler was a *Roman* citizen. The whole Empire was being gathered into the Christian Church. But not only were these three of different nationalities; they came from very different grades of society. *Lydia* was a dealer in purple, one of the most costly substances in the ancient world, and she was the equivalent of a *merchant prince*. The *slave-girl* was a *slave*, and, therefore, in the eyes of the law she was not a person at all, but a living tool. The *gaoler* was a Roman citizen, and member of the sturdy Roman *middle-class* from which the civil service was drawn. In these three the top, the bottom and middle of society are all represented. There is no chapter in the Bible which shows so well the all-embracing faith which Jesus Christ brought to men.

Persecution

Paul had to leave Philippi after a storm of persecution, and after an illegal imprisonment. That persecution was inherited by the Philippian Church. He tells them that they have shared in his bonds and in his defence of the gospel (I: 7). He bids them not to fear their adversaries for they are going through what he himself has gone through and is now enduring (I: 28-30).

True Friendship

There had grown up between Paul and the Philippian Church a bond of friendship closer than that which existed between him and any other Church. It was Paul's proud boast that he had never taken help from any man or from any Church, and that, with his own two hands, he had satisfied his needs. It was from the Philippians alone that Paul had agreed to accept a gift. Soon after he had left them, when he had moved on to Thessalonica, they had sent him a present (4: 16). When he had moved on and had arrived in Corinth by way of Athens, they alone had again remembered him with their gifts (2 *Corinthians* II: 9). " My brethren beloved and longed for," he calls them, " my joy and crown in the Lord " (4: I). Paul was closer to the Church at Philippi than to any other Church.

The Occasion of the Writing of the Letter

When Paul wrote this letter he was in prison in Rome, and he wrote it with certain definite objects.

(i)   It is a letter of thanks. The years had passed; it is

now A.D. 63 or 64 and once again the Philippians had sent him a gift (4: 10, 11).

(ii) The letter has to do with Epaphroditus. It seems that the Philippians had sent Epaphroditus, not only as a bearer of their gift, but that he might stay with Paul, and be his personal servant. But Epaphroditus had fallen ill. He was sick for home; and he was worried because he knew that the people at home were worried about him. So Paul sent him home. But Paul had the unhappy feeling that it was possible that the people in Philippi might think Epaphroditus a quitter, so he goes out of his way to give him a testimonial: " Receive him with all gladness, and hold such in reputation, because for the work of Christ he was nigh unto death " (2: 29, 30). There is something very moving in the sight of Paul, himself in prison and awaiting death, seeking to make things easier for Epaphroditus, when he was unexpectedly and unwillingly compelled to go home. Here is the very peak of Christian courtesy.

(iii) The letter is a letter of encouragement to the Philippians in the trials which they are going through (1: 28-30).

(iv) The letter is an appeal for unity. It is from that that there rises the great passage which speaks of the selfless humility of Jesus Christ (2: 1-11). In the Church at Philippi there were two women who had quarrelled and who were endangering the peace (4: 2); and there were false teachers who were seeking to lure the Philippians from the true path (3: 2); and this letter is an appeal to maintain the unity of the Church.

The Problem

It is just here that the one problem of Philippians arises. At 3: 2 there is an extraordinary break in the letter. Up to 3: 1 everything is serenity; the letter seems to be drawing gently to its close; then without any warning there comes the outburst: " Beware of dogs; beware of evil workers; beware of the concision." There is no connection with what goes before. All of a sudden this stern warning is introduced. Further, 3: 1 looks like the end. " Finally, my brethren," says Paul, " rejoice in the Lord." And having said *finally* he begins all over again! That, however, is not an unknown phenomenon in preaching!

Because of this break there are many scholars who think that *Philippians*, as we possess it, is not one letter, but two letters put together. They regard 3: 2—4: 3 as a letter of thanks and warning sent quite early after the arrival of Epaphroditus in Rome; and they regard 1: 1—3: 1 and 4: 4—4: 23 as a letter written a good deal later, and sent with Epaphroditus when he had to go home. On this view 3: 2—4: 3 is a letter of thanks and warning sent off as soon as Epaphroditus had arrived; 1: 1—3: 1 together with 4: 4—4: 23 is a later letter sent when Epaphroditus had to go back home. That is perfectly possible. We know that Paul almost certainly did, in fact, write more than one letter to Philippi, for Polycarp in his letter to the Philippian Church says of Paul, " when he was absent he wrote *letters* to you."

The Explanation

And yet it seems to us that there is no good reason for splitting this letter into two. The sudden break between 3: 1 and 3:2 can be explained in one of two ways.

(i) As Paul was writing, fresh news may have come of trouble at Philippi; and there and then he may have interrupted his line of thought to deal with it straight away·

(ii) But surely the simplest explanation is this. *Philippians* is a personal letter; a personal letter is never closely and logically ordered like a treatise. In such a letter we put things down as they come into our heads. In such a letter we chat on paper with our friends; and an association of ideas which may be clear enough to us may not be so obvious to anyone else. The simplest explanation is that Paul was writing a personal letter; and the sudden change of subject is just the kind of thing which might occur in any such letter.

THE LETTER TO THE PHILIPPIANS

The Lovely Letter

For many of us *Philippians* is the loveliest letter that Paul ever wrote. It has been called by two titles. It has been called *The Epistle of Excellent Things*—and so indeed it is; and it has been called *The Epistle of Joy*. Again and again the words *joy* and *rejoice* recur. " Rejoice," writes Paul, " and again I say unto you rejoice," even in prison directing the hearts of his friends—and directing our hearts—to the joy that no man taketh from us.

THE LETTER TO THE PHILIPPIANS

A FRIEND TO HIS FRIENDS

Philippians I: I, 2

> Paul and Timothy, slaves of Jesus Christ, write this
> letter to all those in Philippi who are consecrated to
> God because of their relationship to Jesus Christ,
> together with the overseers and the deacons.
> Grace be to you and peace from God, our Father,
> and from the Lord Jesus Christ.

THE opening sentence of this letter sets the tone of the
whole letter. It is characteristically a letter from a friend
to his friends. With the exception of the letter to the
Thessalonians and the little personal note, to Philemon
Paul begins every letter with a statement of his apostleship.
He begins, for instance, the letter to the Romans: " Paul,
a servant of Jesus Christ, *called to be an apostle* " (cp.
I *Corinthians* I:I; 2 *Corinthians* I:I; *Galatians* I:I;
Ephesians I:I; *Colossians* I:I). In the other letters he
begins with a statement of his official position, a statement
of why he has the right to write, and why the recipients have
the duty to listen. In the other letters he sets out his credentials in the first line. But he does not do that when he
writes to the Philippians. There is no need to. He does
not need to specify his authority and to demand that they
should listen; he knows that they will listen, and listen
lovingly. Of all his Churches, the Church at Philippi was
the Church to which Paul was closest; and he writes, not
as an apostle to members of the Church, but as a friend
to his friends.

Nonetheless, Paul does lay claim to one title; he claims
to be the servant (*doulos*) of Christ, as the Authorized
Version has it. *Doulos* is more than *servant*; it is *slave*.
A servant is free to come and go, and to attach himself to
another master; but a slave is the possession of his master
for ever. When Paul calls himself the slave of Jesus
Christ, he does three things. (i) He lays down that he is
the absolute possession of Christ. Christ has loved him,
and Christ has bought him with a price (I *Corinthians* 6:20),

and he can never belong to anyone but Christ. (ii) He lays it down that he owes an absolute obedience to Christ. The slave has no will of his own; his master's will must be his will, and his master's decisions must regulate his life. So Paul has no will but the will of Christ, and no obedience but to his Saviour and Lord. (iii) But there is a third thing here. In the Old Testament the regular title of the prophets is *the servants of God* (*Amos* 3:7; *Jeremiah* 7:25). That is the title which is given to Moses, to Joshua and to David (*Joshua* 1:2; *Judges* 2:8; *Psalm* 78:70; 89:3, 10). In point of fact, the highest of all titles of honour is *servant of God*; and when Paul takes this title, he humbly places himself in the succession of the prophets, and of the great ones of God. The Christian's slavery to Jesus Christ is no cringing and abject subjection. As the Latin tag has it: *Illi servire est regnare*, which may be freely translated: To be His slave is to be a king. To be the slave of Christ is the way to perfect freedom.

THE CHRISTIAN DISTINCTION

Philippians 1: 1, 2 (*continued*)

THE letter is addressed, as the Authorized Version has it, *to all the saints in Christ Jesus.* The word which is translated *saint* is the word *hagios*; and *saint* is a misleading translation. To modern ears the word *saint* paints a picture of almost unworldly piety. Its connection is rather with stained glass windows than with the market-place. Although it is easy to see the meaning of this word *saint*, it is hard to translate it.

The Greek word *hagios*, and its Hebrew equivalent *kadosh*, are most usually translated *holy*. In Hebrew thought, if a thing is described as *holy*, the basic idea is that it is *different* from other things; it is in some sense *set apart* from other things. The better to understand this, let us look at how this word *holy* is actually used in the Old Testament. When the special regulations regarding the priesthood are being laid down, it is written: " They shall be *holy* unto their God " (*Leviticus* 21: 6). The priests were to be *different* from other men, for they were set apart for a different and a special work and function. The tithe was the tenth part of all produce which was to be set apart for God, and it is laid down: " The tenth shall be *holy* unto the Lord, because it is the Lord's (*Leviticus* 27: 30, 32). The tithe was *different* from, and was used for different purposes from, other things which could be used as food. The central part of the Temple was the *Holy Place* (*Exodus* 26: 33). It was *different* from all other places and all other buildings. The word is specially used of the Jewish nation itself. The Jews are a *holy nation* (*Exodus* 19: 6). They are *holy* unto the Lord; God has severed them from other nations that they may be His (*Leviticus* 20: 26); it is they of all nations on the face of the earth whom God has specially known (*Amos* 2: 2). The Jews were different from all other nations, for they had a special place in the plan and the scheme and the purpose of God.

But the Jews refused to play the part in life and history which God meant them to play; when God's Son came into the world, they failed to recognize Him, and they rejected Him, and crucified Him. The privileges and the responsibilities they should have had were taken away from the nation of Israel and were given to the Church, which became the new and the true Israel, the real people of God. Therefore, just as the Jews had once been *hagios*, *holy*, *different*, so now the Christians must be *hagios*; the Christians are the holy ones, the different ones, as the Authorized Version has it, the *saints*. Thus Paul in his pre-Christian days was a notorious persecutor of the *saints*, the *hagioi* (*Acts* 9: 13). Peter goes to visit the *saints*, the *hagioi*, at Lydda (*Acts* 9: 32).

To say that the Christians are the holy ones—the saints

—means, therefore, that the Christians are *different* from other people. Wherein then does that difference lie?

Paul addresses his people as saints *in Christ Jesus*. No one can read Paul's letters without seeing how often the phrases *in Christ, in Christ Jesus, in the Lord* occur. In his letters the phrase *in Christ Jesus* occurs 48 times, *in Christ* 34 times, and *in the Lord* 50 times. Clearly to be *in Christ* was for Paul the very essence of Christianity. What did he mean? Marvin R. Vincent says that when Paul spoke of the Christian being in Christ, he meant that the Christian lives in Christ as a bird in the air, a fish in the water, the roots of a tree in the soil. To be *in Christ* is to live continually in the atmosphere and the Spirit of Christ; it is to live in a world where everything speaks to us of Him; it is to live a life where never for one moment do we feel separated from Him, and where we feel His presence and His strength and His power always around us and about us. That which makes the Christian different is that the Christian is always, everywhere, and for ever, conscious of the encircling presence of Jesus Christ.

So, then, when Paul speaks of *the saints in Christ Jesus* he means those who are different from other people, and who are consecrated to God, because of their special relationship to Jesus Christ—and that is what is possible for every Christian, and that is what every Christian should be.

THE ALL-INCLUSIVE GREETING

Philippians I: I, 2 *(continued)*

PAUL'S greeting to his friends is: Grace be to you and peace, from God the Father, and from our Lord Jesus Christ (cp. *Romans* I: 7; I *Corinthians* I: 3; 2 *Corinthians* 2: 2; *Galatians* I: 3; *Ephesians* I: 2; *Colossians* I: 2; I *Thessalonians* I: I; 2 *Thessalonians* I: 2; *Philemon* 3).

When Paul took and put together these two great words, *grace* and *peace*, *charis* and *eirēnē*, he was doing something very wonderful. He was taking the normal greeting phrases of two great nations and moulding them into one. *Charis* is the normal *Greek* greeting; it is the greeting with which Greek letters always began. *Eirēnē* is the normal Hebrew greeting, and was the greeting with which Jews met each other. Each of these words had its own flavour, and each of them was intensified and deepened and made infinitely more precious by the new meaning which Christianity poured into it.

Charis is a lovely word; the basic ideas in it are joy and pleasure, brightness and beauty; it is, in fact, connected with the English word *charm*. But with Jesus Christ there comes a new beauty to add to the beauty that was there. And that beauty is born of a new relationship to God—the relationship of *grace*. With Christ life becomes lovely because man is no longer the victim of the law of God; he has become the child of the love of God. With Christ there comes the supreme beauty of discovering God the Father.

Eirēnē is a great comprehensive word. We translate it *peace*; but it never means a negative peace; it never means simply the absence of trouble. It means total well-being, everything that makes for a man's highest good.

It may well be connected with the Greek word *eirein*, which means *to join, to weave, together*. And this peace has always got to do with personal relationships, a man's relationship to himself, to his fellow-men, and to God. It is always, as has been said, the peace that is born of reconciliation.

So, when Paul prays for grace and peace on his people he is praying that they should know the joy of knowing God as Father, and the peace of being reconciled to God, to men, and to themselves—and that grace and peace can only come through Jesus Christ.

THE MARKS OF THE CHRISTIAN LIFE

(i) THE CHRISTIAN JOY

Philippians 1: 3-11

> In all my remembrance of you I thank my God for you, and always in every one of my prayers, I pray for you with joy, because you have been in partnership with me for the furtherance of the gospel from the first day until now, and of this I am confident, that He who began a good work in you will complete it so that you may be ready for the day of Jesus Christ. And it is right for me to feel like this about you, because I have you in my heart, because all of you are partners in grace with me, both in my bonds, and in my defence and confirmation of the gospel. God is my witness how I yearn for you all with the very compassion of Christ Jesus. And this I pray, that your love for each other may continue to abound more and more in all fulness of knowledge and in all sensitiveness of perception, that you may test the things which differ, that you may be yourselves pure and that you may cause no other to stumble, in preparation for the day of Christ, because you have been filled with the fruit which the righteousness which comes through Jesus Christ produces, and which issues in glory and praise to God.

IT is a lovely thing when, as Ellicott puts it, remembrance and gratitude are bound up together. In all our personal relationships it is a great thing to have nothing but happy memories; and that was how Paul was with the Christians at Philippi. To remember brought no regrets, but only happiness.

Here in this passage there are set out the very marks of the Christian life.

There is *Christian joy*. It is with joy that Paul prays for his friends. The Letter to the Philippians has been called *The Epistle of Joy*. Bengel in his terse Latin commented: "*Summa epistolae gaudeo — gaudete.*" "The whole point of the letter is I do rejoice; do you rejoice." Let us look at the picture of the Christian joy, which this letter paints.

(i) Here in this passage (1: 4) there is the joy of *Christian prayer*, the joy of bringing those we love and who are dear to us to the mercy seat of God. George Reindrop in his book *No Common Task* tells how a nurse once taught a man to pray, and in doing so changed his whole life, until a dull, disgruntled and dispirited creature became a man of joy. Much of the nurse's work was done with her hands, and she used her hand as, as it were, a scheme of prayer. Each of her fingers stood for someone. Her thumb was nearest to her, and it reminded her to pray for those who were nearest and closest and dearest to her. The second finger is used for pointing ; those who teach us point to us with it when they would ask us a question; therefore her second finger stood for all her teachers in school and in the hospital. The third finger is the tallest and it stood for the V.I.P.'s, the leaders in every sphere of life, and in every party. The fourth finger is the weakest finger, as every pianist knows; and it stood for those who were weak, and in trouble, and in pain. The little finger is the smallest and the most unimportant, and to the nurse it stood for herself. That indeed is a lovely scheme of prayer. There must always be a deep joy and peace in bringing our loved ones, and all mankind, to God in prayer.

(ii) There is the joy that *Jesus Christ is preached* (1: 18). When a man enjoys a great blessing surely his first instinct must be to share it; and there is joy in thinking of the gospel being preached all over the world, so that another and another and another is brought within the love of Christ.

(iii) There is the joy of *faith* (1: 25). If Christianity does not make a man happy, it will not make him anything at all. There is a certain type of Christianity which is always a tortured and agonized affair. The Psalmist said, " They looked to him and were radiant ". When Moses came down from the mountain top his face shone. Christianity is the faith of the happy heart and the shining face.

17

(iv) There is the joy of seeing *Christians in fellowship together* (2: 2). As the Psalmist sang (*Psalm* 133: 1):

> Behold how good a thing it is,
> And how becoming well,
> Together such as brethren are
> In unity to dwell!

There is peace for no one where there are broken human relationships and strife between man and man. There is no lovelier sight than a family linked in love to each other, and a Church whose members are one with each other because they are one in Christ Jesus their Lord. Only in Christ can there be the loveliness of perfect human relationships.

(v) There is the joy of *suffering for Christ* (2: 17). In the hour of his martyrdom in the flames Polycarp prayed and said, " I thank Thee, O Father, that Thou hast judged me worthy of this hour." To suffer for Christ is a privilege, for it is an opportunity to demonstrate beyond mistake where our loyalty lies, and to have a real opportunity to share in the upbuilding of the Kingdom of God.

(vi) There is the joy of *news of the loved one* (2: 28). Life is full of separations, and there is always joy when news comes to us of those whom we love and from whom we are for a time separated. A great Scottish preacher once spoke of the joy that any man can give with a two-pence halfpenny stamp. It is worth remembering how easily we can bring joy to those who love us, and how easily we can bring anxiety to them, by keeping in touch or failing to keep in touch with them.

(vii) There is the joy of *Christian hospitality* (2: 29). There is the home of the shut door, and there is the home of the open door. The shut door is the door of unchristian selfishness; the open door is the door of the Christian welcome and the Christian love. It is a great thing to have a door from which the stranger and the one in trouble know that they will never be turned away.

(viii) There is the joy of *the man in Christ* (3: 1; 4: 1). We have already seen that to be in Christ is to live in His presence as the bird lives in the air, the fish in the sea, and the roots of the trees in the soil. It is human nature to be happy when we are with the person whom we love; and Christ is the lover and the loved one from whom nothing in time or eternity can ever separate us.

(ix) There is the joy of *the man who has won one soul for Christ* (4: 1). The Philippians are Paul's joy and crown, for he was the means of bringing them to Jesus Christ. It is the joy of the parent, the teacher, the preacher to bring others, especially the child, into the love of Jesus Christ. Surely he who enjoys a great privilege cannot rest content until he shares that privilege with his family and his friends. For the Christian evangelism is not a duty; it is a joy.

(x) There is the joy *in a gift* (4: 10). The joy in a gift does not lie so much in the gift; it is the joy of being remembered, the joy of realizing that some one cares and that someone has not forgotten. It is not the value of the gift that matters; it is the gift itself. That is a joy that we could bring to others far oftener than we do.

THE MARKS OF THE CHRISTIAN LIFE

(ii) THE CHRISTIAN SACRIFICE

Philippians 1: 3-11 *(continued)*

IN verse 6 Paul says that it is his confidence that God who has begun a good work in the Philippians will continue it and complete it, so that they will be ready for the day of Christ. There is a picture here in the language of the Greek, which it is not possible to reproduce in translation. The point is that the word which Paul uses for *to begin* is *enarchesthai*, and the word he uses for *to complete* is *epitelein*, and both are technical terms for the beginning and the ending of a sacrifice.

There was an initial ritual in connection with a Greek

sacrifice. A torch was lit with the fire on the altar; the blazing torch was then dipped into a bowl of water; the sacred flame thus cleansed the water, and with the purified water the victim and the people were sprinkled to make them holy and clean. Then there followed what was known as the *euphēmia*, the sacred silence, in which the worshipper was meant to make his prayers to his god. Then finally a basket of barley was brought, and some grains of the barley were scattered on the victim, and on the ground round about it. These actions were the *beginning* of the sacrifice, and the technical term for making this beginning was the verb *enarchesthai*, the verb which Paul uses here. The verb used for completing the whole ritual of sacrifice, and for carrying out the sacrifice perfectly in every smallest detail was the verb *epitelein*, which again is the verb which Paul uses here for *to complete*. The whole sentence, as Paul wrote it, moves in an atmosphere of sacrifice and thinks in terms and pictures of sacrifice.

So Paul is seeing the life of every Christian as a sacrifice prepared to offer to Jesus Christ. It is the same picture as he draws in *Romans*, when he writes to the Romans to present their bodies a living sacrifice, holy and acceptable to God (*Romans* 12: 1).

On the day when Christ comes it will be like the coming of a king. On such a day the king's subjects are bound to present him with gifts to mark their loyalty and to show their love. And the only gift which Jesus Christ desires from us is ourselves and our lives. So, then, the supreme task of life is nothing less than to make life fit to take it and to offer it to Jesus Christ. Only the grace of God can enable us to do that. From the moment we start out upon the Christian way God's grace begins to fit us to be the perfect offering to offer to Jesus Christ, and if we continue to allow His grace to work upon us, His grace will complete its work, and we ourselves will be a fit offering to offer to Him.

THE LETTER TO THE PHILIPPIANS

THE MARKS OF THE CHRISTIAN LIFE

(iii) The Christian Partnership

Philippians 1: 3-11 (*continued*)

In this passage the idea of *Christian partnership* is strongly stressed. There are certain things which Christians share in partnership and in fellowship together.

(i) Christians are *partners in grace*. Christians are people who have shared in a common gift of the grace of God. Christians are people who are drawn together because they owe a common debt to the goodness and the grace of God.

(ii) Christians are *partners in the work of the gospel.* Christians do not only share a gift; they also share a task; and that task is the furtherance of the gospel. Paul uses two words to express the work of the Christians for the sake of the gospel; he speaks of the *defence* and the *confirmation* of the gospel. The defence (*apologia*) of the gospel means the defence of the gospel against the attacks which come from outside; it is the defence of the gospel against the arguments and assaults of the enemies of Christianity. The Christian has to be ready to be a defender of the faith, and to give a reason for the hope that is in him. The confirmation (*bebaiōsis*) of the gospel is the building up of the strength of the gospel from within the edifying and the establishing in the faith of fellow-Christians within the Church. The Christian must further the gospel by defending it against the attacks of its enemies, and by building up and strengthening the faith and devotion of its friends.

(iii) Christians are *partners in suffering for the gospel.* The Philippians were partners in Paul's bonds. Whenever the Christian is called upon to suffer for the sake of the gospel, he must find strength and comfort in the memory that he does not suffer alone, but that he is one of a great fellowship, who in every age and every generation and every land have suffered for Christ rather than deny their faith.

(iv) Christians are *partners with Christ*. In verse 8 Paul has a very vivid saying. He says, " I yearn for you with the bowels of Jesus Christ." The Greek word for bowels is *splagchna*. The *splagchna* were the upper intestines, the heart, the liver, and the lungs. These the Greeks believed to be the seat of the emotions and the affections. So what Paul is saying is this: " I yearn for you with the very compassion of Jesus Christ Himself. I love you as Jesus loves you." The love which Paul feels towards his Christian friends is nothing other than the love of Christ Himself. J. B. Lightfoot, writing on this passage says, " The believer has no yearnings apart from his Lord; his pulse beats with the pulse of Christ; his heart throbs with the heart of Christ." When we are really one with Jesus, His love goes out through us to our fellow-men, the men whom He loves, and the men for whom He died. The Christian is nothing less than a partner in the love of Christ.

THE MARKS OF THE CHRISTIAN LIFE

(iv) THE CHRISTIAN PROGRESS AND THE CHRISTIAN GOAL

Philippians I: 3-11 (*continued*)

IT was Paul's prayer for his people that their love would grow greater every day (verses 9 and 10). And that love was not merely a sentimental thing. It was a love which was to grow more and more in knowledge, and more and more in sensitive perception, so that they would be more and more able to distinguish between right and wrong. Love is always the way to knowledge. If we love any subject, we want to learn more and more about it; if we love any person, we want to learn more and more about him or her; if we love Jesus, we will want every day to learn more and more about Him and about His truth. Love is always sensitive to the mind and the heart of the one it loves. If love blindly and blunderingly hurts the feelings of the one it claims to love, then it is not love at all. If we really love Jesus, we will be sensitive to His will and His desires; the more we love Him the tenderer our conscience will become; the more we will instinctively shrink from what is evil and desire that which is right. Real love leads to knowledge and obedience increasingly every day. The word which Paul uses for *testing* the things that differ is the word *dokimazein*, and that is the word which is used for testing metal, or for testing a coin, to see that the metal is genuine, pure and unalloyed, and not false. Real love is not blind; it is real love which will enable always to see the difference between the false and the true.

So, then, the Christian will become sincere and without offence, as the Authorized Version has it; he will become himself pure and he will cause no other to stumble. The word which is used for *pure* is an interesting word. It is the word *eilikrinēs*. The Greeks themselves were not sure of its derivation. They suggested two possible derivations, each of which has a vivid picture. It may come from *eilē*, which means *sunshine*, and *krinein* which means to *judge*, and it may describe that which is able to stand the test of the sunshine, that which can be exposed to the sun, held up to the light of the sun, without any flaw appearing. If that be the meaning of the word, it means that the Christian character can stand any light that is turned upon it. But *eilikrinēs* may be derived from *eilein* which means to whirl round and round as in a sieve and so to sift until every impurity is extracted. If that is the meaning, it means that the Christian character is cleansed and sifted of all evil until it is altogether pure. But not only is the Christian himself pure; he is also *aproskopos*, that is to say, he never causes any other person to stumble. There are people who are themselves faultless, but who are so hard and harsh and austere that they in the end drive people away from Christianity. There are people who are good, but they are so critical of others that they repel other people from goodness. The Christian is himself pure, but his love and his gentleness are such that he attracts others to the Christian way and never repels them from it.

Finally, Paul sets down the Christian aim. The Christian aim is to live such a life that the glory and the praise are given to God. Christian goodness is not meant to win praise and credit and honour and prestige for a man himself; it is meant to win praise for God. The Christian never points at himself; he always points at God; for he knows, and he witnesses, that he is what he is, not by his own unaided efforts, but only by the grace of God.

THE BONDS DESTROY THE BARRIERS

Philippians I: 12-14

> I want you to know, brothers, that what has happened to me has resulted rather in the advancement of the gospel, because it has been demonstrated to the whole Praetorian Guard and to all the others that my imprisonment is borne for Christ's sake and in Christ's strength; and the result is that through my bonds more of the brothers have found confidence in the Lord the more exceedingly to dare fearlessly to speak the word of God.

PAUL was a prisoner, and that fact might have seemed to be an end to his missionary activity; but so far from his imprisonment ending his missionary activity it actually expanded it for himself and for others. It was, in fact, the case that the bonds destroyed the barriers. The word that Paul uses for the *advancement*, the *furtherance* of the gospel is a vivid word. It is the word *prokopē*; this is the word which is specially used for the progress of an army or an expedition. It is the noun from the verb *prokoptein*, which means *to cut down in advance*. It is the verb which is used for cutting away the trees and the undergrowth, and removing the barriers which would hinder the progress of an army; it is the word which is used for clearing away the obstacles which would hinder an advance. Paul's imprisonment, so far from shutting the door, opened the door; so far from being a barrier, it opened the way to new spheres of work and activity, into which he would never otherwise have penetrated. Let us see just what the state of Paul was.

Paul, seeing that there was no justice for him in Palestine, had appealed to Caesar, as every Roman citizen had the right to do. In due time he had been despatched to Rome under military escort, and, when he had arrived there, he had been handed over to " the captain of the guard," and had been allowed to live by himself under the care of a soldier who was his guard (*Acts* 28: 16). Ultimately, although still under guard, he had been allowed to have his own hired lodging (*Acts* 28: 30), which was open to all who cared to come to see him.

Now, in the Authorized Version, we read that Paul said that his bonds were manifest in all the *palace*. The word that is translated *palace* is the word *praitōrion*. This word *praitōrion* can mean either a place, or a body of people. When it has the meaning of a place, it has three meanings. (i) Originally it meant *a general's headquarters in camp*, the tent from which he gave his orders and directed his campaign. (ii) From that it very naturally moved on to mean a general's residence; it could, therefore, mean the Emperor's residence, that is, his palace, although examples of it in that meaning are very rare. (iii) By another natural extension it came to mean a large house or villa, the residence of some wealthy or influential man. Now it is quite clear that here *praitōrion* cannot have any of these meanings, for *Acts* is clear that Paul stayed in his own hired lodging (*Acts* 28: 30), as we have seen, and it is not possible that Paul's hired lodging was in the Emperor's palace. That does not make sense.

So we turn to the other meaning of *praitōrion*, its meaning when it denotes a body of people. In this meaning it means the *Praetorian Guard*, or very much more rarely, the barracks where the Praetorian Guard were quartered. The second of these meanings we can leave on one side, for Paul would not likely have a hired lodging in a Roman barracks.

The Praetorian Guard were the Imperial Guard of Rome. They has been instituted by Augustus, and they were a body of ten thousand picked troops. Augustus had kept them dispersed throughout Rome and the neighbouring towns. Tiberius had concentrated them in Rome in a specially built and fortified camp. Vitellius had increased their number to sixteen thousand. They served for twelve, and later for sixteen, years. At the end of their term they received the citizenship and a grant of more than £250. In the end they became very nearly the Emperor's private bodyguard; and in the end they became very much a problem. They were concentrated in Rome, and there came a time when the Praetorian Guard became nothing less than king-makers; for inevitably it was their nominee who was made Emperor every time, since they could impose their will by force, if need be, upon the populace. It was to the Prefect of the Praetorian Guard, to their commanding officer, that Paul was handed over when he arrived in Rome.

Now Paul repeatedly refers to himself as a *prisoner* or as being *in bonds*. He tells the Roman Christians that, although he had done no wrong, he was delivered a *prisoner* (*desmios*) into the hands of the Romans (*Acts* 28: 17). In *Philippians* he repeatedly speaks of his *bonds* (*Philippians* 1: 7, 13, 14). In *Colossians* he speaks of being in bonds for the sake of Christ, and bids the Colossians to remember his bonds (*Colossians* 4: 3, 18). In *Philemon* he calls himself a prisoner of Jesus Christ, and speaks of the bonds of the gospel (*Philemon* 9, 13). In *Ephesians* he again calls himself the prisoner of Jesus Christ (*Ephesians* 3: 1). Now there are two passages in which these bonds are more closely defined. In *Acts* 28: 20 he speaks of himself as *being bound with this chain*; and he uses the same word (*halusis*) in *Ephesians* 6: 20, when he speaks of himself as *an ambassador in bonds*. It is in this word *halusis* that we find our key. The *halusis* was the short length of chain by which the wrist of a prisoner was bound to the wrist of the soldier who was his guard, so that escape was impossible. The situation was this. Paul had been delivered to the captain of the Praetorian Guard, to await trial before the Emperor. He had been allowed to arrange a private lodging for himself; but night and day in that private lodging there was a soldier to guard him, a soldier to whom he was chained by his *halusis* all the time. There would, of course, be a rota of guardsmen assigned to this duty; and in the long two years one by one the guardsmen of the Imperial Guard would be on duty with Paul. What a chance was there! These soldiers would hear Paul preach and talk to his friends. Is there any doubt that in the long hours Paul would open up a discussion about Jesus with the soldier to whose wrist he was chained? Paul's imprisonment had opened the way for preaching the gospel to the finest regiment in the Roman army, the Imperial Guards. No wonder Paul declared that his imprisonment had actually been for the furtherance of the gospel. All the Praetorian Guard knew why Paul was in prison; many of them were touched for Christ; and the very sight of all this gave to the brethren at Philippi fresh courage to preach the gospel and to witness for Christ.

Paul's bonds had removed the barriers, and given him access to the flower of the Roman army, and Paul's bonds had been the medicine of courage to the brethren at Philippi.

THE LETTER TO THE PHILIPPIANS

THE ALL-IMPORTANT PROCLAMATION

Philippians 1: 15-18

> Some in their preaching of Christ are actuated by
> envy and strife; some by goodwill. The one preach
> from love, because they know that I am lying here for
> the defence of the gospel; the other proclaim Christ
> for their own partisan purposes, not with pure motives,
> but thinking to make my bonds gall me all the more.
> What then? The only result is that in every way,
> whether as a cloak for other purposes, or whether in
> truth, Christ is proclaimed. And in this I rejoice—
> yes, and I will rejoice.

HERE indeed the great heart of Paul is speaking. His
imprisonment has been an incentive to preaching. That
incentive worked in two ways. There were those who loved
him; and, when they saw him lying in prison, they redouble-
ed their efforts to preach, and to spread the gospel, so
that the gospel would lose nothing because of Paul's
imprisonment. They knew that the best way to delight
his heart was to see that the work did not suffer because
of his unavoidable absence. But there were others. They
were moved by what Paul calls *eritheia*. They preached
for their own partisan motives. The word *eritheia* is an
interesting word. Originally *eritheia* was not a bad word
at all; it simply meant *working for pay*, working for hire.
But the man who works solely for pay works from a very
low motive. He is out solely to benefit himself, and to
advance himself and his own gains and prestige above
others. So the word came to describe a man who is a
careerist, the man who is out for office to magnify himself.
So the word come to be connected with politics, and it
came to mean *canvassing for office*; it came to describe
self-seeking and selfish ambition; it came to describe the
personally ambitious, competitive spirit which was out
to advance itself, and which did not care to what methods
it stooped to attain its own ends. So there were those
who preached the harder now that Paul was in prison,
for his imprisonment seemed to them to present them

with a heaven-sent opportunity to advance their own influence, their own prestige, and their own Church party, and to lessen his. We are not to think of those who preach like that as being heretics, or Judaisers who wished to involve the Christians in Jewish legalism; Paul would never have approved of that. They were preachers who were out to enhance their own prestige and to undermine Paul's influence, when he was in prison.

There is a lesson for us here. Paul knew nothing of personal jealousy; he knew nothing of personal resentment. So long as Jesus Christ was preached Paul did not care who received the credit and the honour and the prestige. He did not care what other preachers said about him, or how unfriendly they were to him, or how contemptuous they were of him, or if they tried to steal a march upon him. All that mattered to him was that Christ was preached. All too often we resent it because someone else gains a prominence or a credit or a prestige which we do not receive. All too often we regard a man as an enemy because he has expressed some criticism of us or of our methods. All too often we think a man can do no good because he does not do things in our way. The intellectuals have no truck with the evangelicals, and the evangelicals impugn the faith of the intellectuals. Those who believe in the evangelism of education have no use for the evangelism of decision, and those who practise the evangelism of decision have no use for those who feel that some other approach will have more lasting effects. Paul is the great example. He was cleansed of self; he had lifted the matter beyond all personalities; all that mattered was that Christ was preached.

THE HAPPY ENDING

Philippians 1: 19, 20

> For I know that this will result in my salvation, because of your prayer for me, and because of the generous help the Holy Spirit of Christ

gives to me, for it is my eager expectation and my hope that I shall never on any occasion be shamed into silence, but that on every occasion, even as now, I shall speak with all boldness of speech, so that Christ will be glorified in my body, whether by my life or by my death.

IT is Paul's conviction that the whole situation in which he finds himself will result in his salvation. Even his imprisonment, and even the almost hostile preaching of his personal enemies will in the end turn out to his salvation. What does he mean by *his salvation*? The word is *sōteria*, and here there are three possible meanings. (i) It can mean *safety*, in which case Paul will be saying that he is quite sure that the whole situation will end in his release. But that can hardly be the meaning here, since Paul goes on to say that he cannot be sure whether he will live or die. (ii) It can mean *his salvation in heaven*. In that case Paul would be saying that his conduct in the opportunity which this situation provides will be his witness in the day of judgment. There is a great truth here. In any situation of opportunity or challenge, a man is acting not only for time, but also for eternity. In any situation he is earning not only the verdict of men, but also the verdict of God. A man's reaction to every situation, to every decision, to every opporunity, to every challenge in time is a witness for or against him in eternity. (iii) But *sōteria* can have a wider meaning than either of these first two meanings. It can mean *health*, *general well-being*. Paul may well be saying that all that is happening to him, in this very difficult situation, is the best thing for him both in time and in eternity. He may well be saying, " God put me in this situation; and God means it, with all its problems and its difficulties, to make for my happiness and usefulness in time, and for my joy and peace in eternity. This is meant for my welfare in this world, and in the world to come." We will do well to remember that any challenge is sent to us as a tonic and a strength-builder from God.

In this situation Paul knows that he has two great

supports. (i) He has the support of the prayers of his friends. One of the loveliest things in Paul's letters is the way in which he asks again and again for the prayers of his friends. " Brethren," he writes to the Thessalonians, " pray for us." " Finally, brethren," he writes, " pray for us, that the word of God may have free course " (1 *Thessalonians* 5: 25; 2 *Thessalonians* 3: 1, 2). He speaks of the Corinthians as " helping together by prayer for us " (2 *Corinthians* 1: 11). He writes to Philemon that he is sure that through Philemon's prayers he will be given back to his friends (*Philemon* 22). Before he sets out on his perilous journey to Jerusalem, he writes to the Church at Rome asking for their prayers (*Romans* 15: 30-32). Paul was never too big a man to remember that he needed the prayers of his friends. He never stood on a height looking down; he never talked to people as if he could do everything and they could do nothing; he always remembered that neither he, nor they, could do anything without the help of God. There is something to be remembered here. When people are in sorrow and their hearts are broken, one of their greatest comforts is the awareness that there are others who are bearing them to the throne of grace. When people have to face some back-breaking effort or some heart-breaking decision, there is a new strength in remembering that others are remembering them before God. When people go into new places, and when they are far from home, it is an upholding thing for them to know that the prayers of those who love them are crossing seas and continents and lands to bring them before the throne of grace. We cannot call a man our friend—and we cannot call ourselves his friend— unless we pray for him. (ii) Paul knows that he has the support of the Holy Spirit. The presence of the Holy Spirit is the fulfilment of the promise of Jesus that He will be with us to the end of the world.

In all this situation Paul has one expectation and one hope. The word he uses for *expectation* is very vivid; it

is an unusual word; no one uses it before Paul, and he may
well have coined it himself. It is the word *apokaradokia*.
Apo means *away from*; *kara* means *the head*; *dokein* means
to look. And *apokaradokia* means the eager, concentrated,
intense look, which turns its gaze away from everything
else to fix it on the one object of its desire. Paul's hope
is that he will never be shamed into silence. Two things
might shame him into silence. Cowardice might make him
keep silent when he should have spoken. And ineffective-
ness and futility of work might take from him the right to
speak. Paul is certain that in Christ he will find courage
never to be ashamed of the gospel; and that through the
Christ his labours will be made effective for all men to see.
Paul's expectation is that there will be given to him boldness of speech. J. B. Lightfoot writes, " The right of
free speech is the badge, the privilege, of the servant of
Christ." To speak the truth with boldness is not only the
privilege of the servant of Christ; it is also at all times his
duty.

So, then, if Paul courageously and effectively seizes this
opportunity, the result will be that Christ will be glorified
in him. It does not matter how things go with him. If
he dies, his will be the martyr's crown. If he lives, his will
be the privilege still to preach and to witness for Christ.
As Ellicott nobly puts it, Paul is saying, " My body will be
the theatre in which Christ's glory is displayed." Here
is the terrible responsibility of the Christian. Once we
have chosen Christ, once we have become members of His
Church, by our life and by our conduct we bring either
glory or shame to Christ. A leader is always judged by
his followers; and Christ is judged by us.

IN LIFE AND IN DEATH

Philippians I: 21-26

For living is Christ to me, and death is gain. And
yet—what if the continuance of my life in the flesh

would produce more fruit for me? What I am to choose is not mine to declare. I am caught between two desires, for I have my desire to strike camp and to be with Christ, which is far better; but for your sake it is more essential for me to remain in this life. And I am confidently certain of this, that I will remain, and I will be with you and beside you all to help you along the road, and to increase the joy of your faith, so that you may have still further grounds for boasting in Christ because of me, when once again I come to visit you.

SINCE Paul was in prison awaiting trial, he had to face the fact that it was quite uncertain whether he would live or die; and to him it made no difference.

" Living," he says, in his great phrase, " is Christ to me." For Paul, Christ had been the *beginning* of life, for on that day on the Damascus road it was as if Paul had been born again and had begun life all over again. For Paul, Christ had been the *continuing* of life; there had never been a day when Paul had not lived in His presence, and in the frightening moments Christ had been there to bid him be of good cheer (*Acts* 18: 9, 10). And for Paul, Christ was the *end* of life, for it was towards the eternal presence of Christ that life ever lead. For Paul, Christ was the *inspiration* of life; Christ to him was the dynamic, the motive power of life. To him Christ had given the *task* of life, for it was Christ who had made him an apostle and who had sent him out as the evangelist of the Gentiles. To him Christ had given the *strength* for life, for it was Christ's all-sufficient grace that was made perfect in his own weakness. And for him Christ was the *reward* of life, for to Paul the only reward of life was closer and closer fellowship with his Lord. If Christ were to be taken out of life, for Paul there would be nothing left in life. To him Christ was nothing less than life itself.

" For me," said Paul, " death is gain". Death was only entrance into Christ's nearer presence. There are passages in which Paul seems to regard death as a sleep, from which all men at some future general resurrection shall be wakened (I *Corinthians* 16: 51, 52; I *Thessalonians* 4: 14, 16), but at the moment when the breath of death was on him Paul thought of death, not as a falling asleep, but as an immediate entry into the presence of his Lord. If we believe in Jesus Christ, death for us is *union* and *reunion*, union with Christ and reunion with those whom we have loved and lost awhile.

The result of this was that Paul was swayed between two desires. " I am caught," he says, " between two desires." As the Authorized Version has it: " I am in a strait betwixt two." The word Paul uses is *senechomai*, and that is the word which would be used of a traveller in a narrow, rocky defile, with a wall of rock on one hand and a wall of rock on the other, unable to turn aside either way, and only able to go straight on. For himself he would desire to depart and to be with Christ; for the sake of his friends and of what he could do with them and for them he would desire to be left in this life. And then there comes to him the thought that the choice is not his but God's, and that it is not given to him to say what he will do, for he can only do what God wills him to do.

" Having a desire to depart," says Paul, and the phrase is very vivid. The word he uses for *to depart* is *analuein*. Behind that word there can be three pictures. (i) It is the word for striking camp, loosening the tent ropes, pulling up the tent pins and going on. Death is moving on. It is said that in the terrible days of the war, when the Royal Air Force stood between this country and destruction, and when the lives of its pilots were being sacrificially spent, they never spoke of a pilot as having been killed; they always spoke of him as having been " posted to another station." Each day's march is a day's march nearer home, until in the end camp in this world is for ever struck and exchanged for permanent residence in the world of glory. (ii) It is the word for loosening the mooring ropes, pulling up the anchors and setting sail. Death is a setting sail, a launching out into the deep, a departure on that voyage to the everlasting haven and to God. (iii) It is the word for solving problems. Death brings life's solutions. There is some place where all earth's questions will be answered, where the torturing problems will find their solution, where the broken things will be mended and the lost things found, and where those who have waited will in the end understand.

It is Paul's conviction that, as the Authorized Version has it, he will *abide* and *continue* with them. Here there is a word-play in the Greek that is not reproducible in the English. The word for to abide is *menein*; and the word for to continue is *paramenein*. Lightfoot suggests the translation *bide and abide*. That keeps the word-play, but does not give the meaning. The point is this; *menein* simply means *to remain with*; but *paramenein* (*para* is the Greek for *beside*) means to wait beside a person to be ready to help and to help all the time; *paramenein* means not only to *wait*, but to wait ever ready, ever willing and ever able to help. Paul's desire to live is not for his own sake, but for the sake of those whom, by living, he can continue to help and to serve.

So, then, if Paul is spared to come and see them again they will have in him grounds to boast in Jesus Christ. That is to say, they will be able to look at Paul and to see in him what Christ can do for the man who trusts Him wholly, for Paul will be a shining example of how, through Christ, a man can face the worst, and come through it erect and unafraid. It is the duty of every Christian so to trust and so to live that men will be able to see what Christ can do for the man who has given his life to Him.

CITIZENS OF THE KINGDOM

Philippians 1: 27-30

One thing you must see to whatever happens—live a life that is worthy of a citizen of the Kingdom and of the gospel of Christ, so that whether I come and see you, or whether I go away and hear how things go with you, the news will be that you are standing fast, united in one spirit, fighting with one soul the battle of the gospel's faith, and that you are not put into fluttering alarm by any of your adversaries. For your steadfastness is a proof to them that they are doomed to defeat, while you are destined for salvation—and that from God. For to you has been given the privilege of doing something for Christ—the privilege of not only believing in Him, but also of suffering for Him, for you have the same struggle as that in which you have seen me engaged, and which now you hear that I am undergoing.

ONE thing is essential—no matter what happens either to them or to Paul the Philippians must live worthily of their faith and profession. Paul chooses his words very carefully. The Authorized Version has it: " Let your conversation be as it becometh the gospel of Christ." Nowadays this is misleading. To us *conversation* means *talk*; but *conversation* is derived from the Latin word *conversari*, which means *to conduct oneself* or *to behave oneself*. In the seventeenth century a person's *conversation* was not only his way of speaking and talking to other people; it was his whole life and conduct in word and in action and in behaviour. The phrase means: " Let your whole behaviour be worthy of those who are pledged to Christ." But on this occasion Paul uses a word which he very seldom uses to express his meaning, and to paint his picture. Normally the word which Paul uses for to behave oneself or to conduct oneself in the ordinary affairs of life is *peripatein*, which literally means *to walk about*; here he uses the word *politeuesthai*, which means *to be a citizen*; *politēs* is the Greek for *a citizen*. Paul was writing from the very centre of the Roman Empire, from Rome itself; it was the fact that he was a Roman citizen that had brought him there at all. Philippi was a Roman colony; and Roman colonies were little bits of Rome planted throughout the world. In Roman colonies the Roman citizens never forgot that they were Romans. They spoke the Latin language, wore the Latin dress, called their magistrates by the Latin names, insisted on being stubbornly Roman, however far they might be from Rome. So what Paul is saying is this, " You and I know full well the privileges and the responsibilities of being a Roman citizen. You know full well how even in Philippi, so many miles from Rome, you must still live and act as a Roman does. Well then, remember that you have an even higher duty than that. Wherever you are you must live as befits a citizen of the Kingdom of God; you must never forget the privileges and the responsibilities of citizenship, not this time of Rome, but of the Kingdom of God." So, then, a Christian must ever remember the Kingdom of which he is a citizen, and his conduct must befit his citizenship.

What then does Paul expect from them? He expects them *to stand fast*. The world is full of Christians on the retreat, Christians who, when Christianity is difficult, conceal, or at least play down, their Christianity. The true Christian stands fast, unashamed in any company. He expects *unity*; they are to be bound together in one spirit like a band of brothers. Let the world strive and quarrel and argue and differ; Christians must be one. He expects a certain *unconquerability*. They must never give up the struggle of the faith. Often evil seems beyond defeating; often it seems impossible for the Christian to cleanse the evil and to fight against the sin of the world. The Christian must never abandon hope or give up the struggle. The Christian must fight on, for ever undiscouraged, for Christ. He expects a *cool, calm courage*. In times of crisis others may be fluttering and nervous and afraid. At such a time the Christian is still serene and master of himself and the situation.

If they can be like that, they will set such an example that the pagans will be disgusted and revolted with their own way of life, and will realise that Christians have something which they do not possess, and will seek for very self-preservation to share it.

Paul does not suggest that this will be an easy way. When Christianity first came to Philippi, they saw him fight his own battle. They saw him scourged and imprisoned for the faith (*Acts* 16: 19). They know what he is now going through. But let them remember that any general chooses his best soldiers for his hardest tasks, and that it is an honour to suffer something for Christ. There is a French tale which tells how a veteran French soldier came in a desperate situation upon a young recruit trembling with fear. " Come, son," said the veteran, " and you and I will do something fine for France." So Paul says to the Philippians: " For you and for me the battle is on; let us do something fine for Christ."

THE CAUSES OF DISUNITY

Philippians 2: 1-4

> If the fact that you are in Christ has any power to influence you, if love has any persuasive power to move you, if you really are sharing in the Holy Spirit, if you can feel compassion and pity, complete my joy, for my desire is that you should be in full agreement, loving the same things, joined together in soul, your minds set on the one thing. Do nothing in a spirit of selfish ambition, and in a search for empty glory, but in humility let each consider the other better than himself. Do not be always concentrating each on your own interests, but let each be equally concerned for the interests of others.

THE one danger which threatened the Philippian Church was the danger of disunity. There is a sense in which that is the danger of every healthy Church. It is when people are really in earnest, when their beliefs really matter to them, when they are eager to carry out their own plans and their own schemes, that they are apt to get up against each other. The greater their enthusiasm, the greater the danger that they may collide. It is against that danger that Paul wishes to safeguard his friends.

In verses 3 and 4 he gives us the three great causes of discord and disunity. There is *selfish ambition*. There is always the danger that people should work, not to advance the work, but to advance themselves. It is an extraordinary thing how time and again the great princes of the Church almost fled from office in the agony of the sense of their own unworthiness. Ambrose was one of the great figures of the early Church. He was a great scholar; he was the Roman governor of the province of Liguria and Aemilia, and he governed with such loving care that the people regarded him as a father. The bishop of the district died, and the question of his successor arose. In the midst of the discussion suddenly a little child's voice arose: " Ambrose—bishop! Ambrose—bishop! " The whole crowd took up the cry. To Ambrose it was unthinkable. He fled by night to avoid the high office the Church was offering to him; and it was only the direct intervention and command of the Emperor which made him agree to become bishop of Milan. When John Rough, the preacher, publicly, from the pulpit in St. Andrews, summoned John Knox to the ministry, John Knox was appalled. In his own *History of the Reformation* he writes: " Thereat the said John, abashed, burst forth in most abundant tears, and withdrew himself to his chamber. His countenance and behaviour, from that day until the day that he was compelled to present himself in the public place of preaching, did sufficiently declare the grief and trouble of his heart. No man saw in him any sign of mirth, nor yet had he pleasure to accompany any man, for many days together." So, far from being filled with ambition, the great men were filled with a sense of their own unworthiness and inadequacy to hold high office at all.

There is the desire for *personal prestige*, the desire for empty glory. It is in many ways true to say that prestige is for many people an even greater temptation than wealth. To be admired, to be respected, to have a platform seat, to have one's opinion sought, to be known by name and appearance, to be listened to, to have a certain degree of fame, and even to be flattered, are for many people most desirable things. But the aim of the Christian is not self-display, but self-obliteration. When he does good deeds, he does them, not that men may glorify him, but that they may glorify his Father who is in heaven. The Christian desires, not to focus men's eyes upon himself, but to focus them on God. He shines with a light, but the light is not his own light, but the light of God shining through him.

And, lastly, there is *concentration on self*. If a man is for ever concerned first and foremost with his own interests, then he is bound to collide with others. If for any man life is a competition whose prizes he must win, if he for ever regards life as a struggle to overcome, to surpass, and to conquer others, then he will always think of other human beings as enemies, or at least as opponents who must be pushed out of the way. Concentration on self inevitably means elimination of others; and the object of life becomes, not to help others up, but to push them down.

Where there is selfish ambition, where there is the desire for personal prestige, where every man concentrates on his own interests, there cannot be anything else but disunity.

THE CURE OF DISUNITY

Philippians 2: 1-4 *(continued)*

IN face of this danger of disunity Paul sets down five considerations or appeals, which ought to prevent all discord and disharmony.

(i) The fact that we are all in Christ must keep us in unity one with another. No man can walk in disunity with his fellow-men and in unity with Christ. If a man has Christ as the companion of his way, he is inevitably the companion of every fellow wayfarer. No man can live in the atmosphere of Christ, and at the same time live in bitterness with his fellow-men. A man's relationships with his fellow-men are no bad indication of his relationship with Jesus Christ.

(ii) The power of Christian love will keep us in unity one with another. Christian love is that unconquered benevolence and good-will which will never know bitterness, and which will never seek anything but the good of others. This Christian love is not a mere reaction of the heart, as human love is; it is a victory of the will achieved by the help of Jesus Christ. It does not mean loving only those who love us; or those whom we like; or those who are lovable. It means an unconquerable good-will even to those who hate us; it means the power to love the people we do not like; it means the Christlike ability to love the unlovely and the unlovable. Herein is the very essence of the Christian life; and herein is that which affects us in time and in eternity. Richard Tatlock in *In My Father's House* writes: " Hell is the eternal condition of those who have made relationship with God and their fellows an impossibility through lives which have destroyed love . . . . . . Heaven, on the other hand, is the eternal condition of those who have found real life in relationships-through-love with God and their fellows." He who knows what Christian love is, and he who dwells in it, even if only in the most imperfect way, cannot live in disunity with his fellow-men.

(iii) The fact that they share in the Holy Spirit must keep Christians from disunity. The Holy Spirit is He who binds man to God, and man to man. It is the Spirit who reveals to us that which God wishes us to do; it is the Spirit who sheds abroad the love of God within our hearts; it is the Spirit who enables us to live the life of love, which is the life of God. If a man lives in disunity with his fellow-men, he has thereby given proof that the gift of the Spirit is not his.

(iv) The very existence of human pity and compassion should keep men from disunity. As Aristotle had it long ago, men were never meant to be snarling wolves, but to live in fellowship together. Disunity breaks the very structure of life.

(v) Paul's last appeal is the personal one. There can be no happiness for him so long as he knows that there is disunity in the Church which is dear to him. If they would complete his joy, let them complete their own fellowship. It is not with a threat that Paul speaks to the Christians of Philippi, for it is but seldom that the Christian pastor will threaten; it was with the appeal of love, which must ever be the accent of the pastor, as it was the accent of his Lord.

TRUE GODHEAD AND TRUE MANHOOD

Philippians 2: 5-11

> Have within yourselves the same disposition of mind as was in Christ Jesus, for He was by nature in the very form of God, yet He did not regard existence in equality with God as something to be snatched at, but He emptied Himself, and took the very form of a slave, and became like men. And when He came in appearance as a man for all to recognise, He became obedient even to the extent of accepting death, even the death of a cross. And for that reason God exalted Him, and granted to Him the name which is above every name, in order that at the name of Jesus every knee should bow, of things in heaven, and things upon the earth, and things below the earth, and that every tongue should confess that Jesus Christ is Lord to the glory of God the Father.

IT would be true to say that in many ways this is the greatest and the most moving passage that Paul ever wrote about Jesus. With Paul this passage states a favourite thought. The essence of it is in the simple statement which Paul made to the Corinthians that, although Jesus was rich, yet for our sakes He became poor (2 *Corinthians* 8: 9). But here that simple idea is stated with a fulness and a rich-ness which is without parallel. Paul is pleading with the

Philippians to live in unity and in harmony, to lay aside their disharmonies and their discords, to shed their personal ambitions and their pride and their desire for prominence and prestige, and to have in their hearts that humble, selfless desire to serve, which was the very essence of the life of Christ.   His final and unanswerable appeal for unity is to point at the example of Jesus Christ.

This is a passage which we must try fully to understand, because it has so much in it to awaken our minds to thought, and our hearts to wonder.   If we are to understand it more fully, we must in this case look closely at some of its great Greek words.

Greek is a far richer language than English.   Where English has one word to express an idea, Greek has often two or three or more. In one sense these words are synonyms, but they never mean entirely the same thing; they always have some special flavour, and some special significance. That is specially so of this passage.   In this passage every word is chosen by Paul with meticulous care to show two things—the reality of the manhood and the reality of the godhead of Jesus Christ.   Let us take the phrases one by one.   We will set them down in the Authorized Version translation and in our own translation, and then try to penetrate to the essential meaning behind them.

Verse 6: *Being in the form of God*; *He was by nature in the very form of God.*   Here two words are most carefully chosen to show the essential and unchangeable godhead of Jesus Christ.   The word which the Authorized Version translates *being* is from the Greek verb *huparchein*.   That word is not the common Greek word for *being*.   It describes that which a man is in his very essence, that which cannot be changed, that which he possesses inalienably and in such a way that it cannot be taken from him.   It describes the innate, unchangeable, unalterable characteristics and abilities of a man.   It describes that part of a man which, in spite of all the chances and the changes, and in any circumstances, remains the same.   So Paul begins by saying that Jesus was essentially, unalterably, and unchangeable God.

Then Paul goes on to say that Jesus was in the *form* of God. There are two Greek words for *form*. There is the word *morphē*, and there is the word *schēma*. They both mean *form*, and they have both to be translated by the word *form*, because there is no other English word by which to translate them, but they do not mean the same thing. *Morphē* is the essential form of something, which never alters; *schēma* is the outward form which changes from time to time and from circumstance to circumstance. For instance the essential *morphē* of any human bring is manhood; the fact of his manhood is constant, and never changes; but a person's *schēma*, his outward form will be continually changing. A baby, a child, a boy, a youth, a man of middle age, an old man always have the *morphē* of manhood, but the outward *schēma* changes all the time. Roses, daffodils, tulips, chrysanthemums, primroses, dahlias, lupins all have the one *morphē*; they are all flowers; but their outward form, their *schēma*, is different. Aspirin, penicillin, cascara, magnesia all have the one *morphē*; they are all drugs ; but their outward form, their *schēma*, is different. The *morphē* never alters; the *schēma* continually alters. Now the word Paul uses for Jesus being in the *form* of God is *morphē*; that is to say, Jesus is unalterably in the form of God; His essence, His unchangeable being is divine. However His outward *schēma* might alter, He remained in essence and in being divine.

In the same verse Paul goes on to say that Jesus *did not think it robbery to be equal with God*; *He did not regard existence in equality with God as something to be snatched at.* The word that Paul uses for *robbery*, and which we have translated *a thing to be snatched at* is *harpagmos*. *Harpagmos* comes from a verb which means *to snatch*, or *to clutch*. This phrase can mean one of two things, both of which are at the heart of them the same. (*a*) It can mean that Jesus did not need to snatch at equality with God, because He had it as a right. It was His, and there was no need for Him to try to snatch at it. (b) It can mean that Jesus did not clutch at equality with God, as if to hug it jealously to Himself, and to refuse to let it go. He laid it willingly down, for the sake of men. However we take this, and both meanings are perfectly possible, it once again stresses the essential unchangeable godhead of Jesus Christ.

Verse 7: *He emptied Himself; He made Himself of no reputation.* The Greek word is the verb *kenoun.* It means quite literally *to empty.* It can be used to removing things from a container, until the container is empty; of pouring something out, until there is nothing left. Here Paul uses the most vivid possible word to make clear to us *the sacrifice of the Incarnation.* The serenity, the peace, the glory of divinity—Jesus gave them up, voluntarily and willingly, in order to become man. He emptied Himself of His deity to take upon Himself His humanity. It is useless to ask how; we can only stand in awe at the sight of Him, who is almighty God, in hunger and in weariness and in tears. Here in the last reach of human language is the great saving truth that He who was rich for our sakes became poor.

Paul goes on to say that *He took upon Him the form of a servant; He took the very form of a slave.* The word which Paul uses for *form* is *morphē,* which we have seen means the essential form. What Paul means is that when Jesus became man it was no play-acting; it was reality. He was really and truly man. He was not like the Greek gods, who sometimes, so the stories ran, became men, but kept their divine privileges. Jesus really and truly became man in the sense of true human manhood. *But* there is something more here. *He was made in the likeness of men; He became like men.* The word which the Authorized Version translates *made* and which we have translated *became* is a part of the Greek verb *gignesthai.* This verb describes *a state which is not a permanent state.* The whole idea of it lies in the idea of *becoming*, not of being permanently made something. It describes a changing phase, which is completely real, but which passes and moves on. That is to say, the manhood of Jesus was not permanent; He *became* man, but only for a time; He is essentially divine; but He was for a time human. His manhood was utterly real, but it was something which passed; His godhead was also utterly real, but it is something which abides for ever.

Verse 8: *He was found in fashion as a man*; *He came in appearance as a man for all to recognise.* Here again Paul makes the same point. The word the Authorized Version has translated *fashion*, and which we have translated *appearance* is *schēma*, and we have seen that that is the word which translates the idea of a form which alters, and changes. Jesus came in the true form of a servant, really like man, but for Him that was a stage and a temporary thing, to which He came out of deity, and from which He returned to deity.

Verses 6-8 form a very short passage; but there is no passage in the whole New Testament which so movingly sets out the utter reality of the godhead and the manhood of Jesus Christ, and which makes so vivid the inconceivable sacrifice that Christ made when He laid aside His godhead and took manhood upon Him. How it happened, we cannot tell. The end is mystery, but it is the mystery of a love so great that we can never fully understand it, although we can blessedly experience it and adore it.

HUMILIATION AND EXALTATION

Philippians 2: 5-11 (*continued*)

It is always to be remembered that when Paul thought and spoke about Jesus, his interest and his aim and his intention were never primarily intellectual and speculative; they were always practical. To Paul theology and action were always bound together. Any system of thought for him must necessarily become a way of life. In many ways this passage is one of the greatest reaches of theological thought in the New Testament, but its whole aim was to persuade and to compel the Philippians to live a life in which disunity, discord, and personal ambition were dead.

So, then, Paul says of Jesus that He humbled Himself and became obedient unto death, even the death of a cross. The great characteristics of Jesus' life were humility, obedience, and self-renunciation. He did not desire to dominate men; He desired only to serve men. He did not desire His own way; He desired only God's way. He did not desire to exalt Himself; He desired only to renounce all His glory for the sake of men. Again and again the New Testament is sure that only the man who humbles himself will be exalted (*Matthew* 23: 12; *Luke* 14: 11; 18: 14). If humility, obedience, and self-renunciation were the supreme characteristics of the life of Jesus Christ, then they must also be the hall-marks of the Christian, for the Christian must ever be as his Lord. Christian greatness and Christian fellowship alike depend on the renunciation of self, and are destroyed by the exaltation of self. Selfishness, self-seeking and self-display destroy our likeness to Christ and our fellowship with each other.

But the self-renunciation of Jesus Christ brought to Him the greater glory. It brought Him the wondering worship of the whole universe. It meant that some day soon or late, every living creature in all the universe, in heaven, in earth and even in hell would worship him. Now it is to be carefully noted whence that worship comes. *It comes from love.* Jesus won the hearts of men, not by blasting them with power, but by showing them a love, a self-sacrifice, a self-renunciation, which cannot but move the heart. At the sight of this person who laid His glory by for men, and loved them to the extent of dying for them on a cross, men's hearts are melted and men's resistance is broken down. When men worship Jesus

Christ, they do not fall at his feet in broken submission, but in wondering love. A man does not say " I cannot resist a might like that," He says, " Love so amazing, so divine, demands my life, my soul, my all." A man does not say, " I am battered into surrender." He says, " I am lost in wonder, love and praise." It is not the might of Christ which reduces a man to defeated surrender; it is the amazing love of Christ which makes him kneel before Christ in wondering love. Worship is founded, not on fear, but on love.

Further, Paul says that, as a consequence of His sacrificial love, and His self-renunciation, God gave Jesus the name which is above every name. One of the common biblical ideas is the giving of a new name to mark a new and definite stage in a man's life. Abram became Abraham when he received the promise of God (*Genesis* 17: 5). Jacob became Israel when God entered into the new relationship with him (*Genesis* 32: 28). The promise of the Risen Christ to both Pergamos and to Philadelphia is the promise of a new name (*Revelation* 2: 17; 3: 12). The new name is the mark of a new stage. What then is the new name which was given to Jesus Christ? We cannot be quite certain what exactly was in Paul's mind, but most likely the new name is *Lord*. The great title by which Jesus came to be known in the early Church was the title *kurios*, which we translate by the English word *Lord*. Jesus became specifically and characteristically the *Lord Jesus*. This word *kurios* has an illuminating history. (i) It began by meaning *master* or *owner*; and was always a title of repect. (ii) It became the official title of the Roman Emperors; the Roman Emperor was in Greek *kurios*, in Latin *dominus*, master and lord. (iii) It became the title of the heathen gods; every heathen god had the title *kurios*, *lord*, prefixed to his name. (iv) It was the Greek word by which the Hebrew word *Jehovah* was translated in the Greek version of the Hebrew scriptures. So, then, when Jesus was called *kurios*, *Lord*, it meant that he was the Master and the Owner of all life; He was the King of kings, and the Lord of emperors; He was the Lord in a way in which the heathen gods and the dumb idols could never be. He was nothing less than divine. The new name of Jesus, the name by which the whole universe is one day to call Him, is the name Lord.

ALL FOR GOD

Philippians 2: 5-11 (*continued*)

PHILIPPIANS 2: 11 is one of the most important verses in the New Testament. In it we read that the aim of God, the dream of God, the purpose of God, is a day when every tongue will confess that *Jesus Christ is Lord.* These four words were the first creed that the Christian Church ever had. To be a Christian was to confess that Jesus Christ is Lord (cp. *Romans* 10: 9). It is a simple creed; yet it is an all-embracing creed. It may well be that we would do well to go back to that creed. In the later days men tried to define more closely what it meant, and, when they did so, they argued and quarrelled about it, and called each other heretics and fools. But it still remains true that if any man can say, " For me Jesus Christ is Lord," he is a Christian. If he can say that, he means that for him Jesus Christ is unique; that he is prepared to give to Jesus an obedience he is prepared to give to no one else; that he is prepared to give to Jesus a love, a loyalty, an allegiance that he will give to no other person in all the universe. It may be that he cannot put into words who and what he believes Jesus to be; but, so long as there is in his heart this wondering love, and in his life this unquestioning obedience, he is a Christian, because Christ-ianity consists less in the mind's understanding than it does in the heart's love.

So we come to the end of this passage; and, when we come to the end of it, we come back to the beginning of it.

The day will come when men will call Jesus Christ Lord, but they will do so *to the glory of God the Father.* The whole work of Jesus, the whole life of Jesus, the whole aim of Jesus, is not His own glory, but the glory of God. Paul is completely clear about the lonely and ultimate supremacy of God. In the first letter to the Corinthians he writes that in the end the Son Himself shall be subject unto Him that put all things under Him, that God may be all in all (I *Corinthians* 15: 28). Jesus draws men unto Himself that He may draw them unto God. In the Philippian Church there were men whose one aim was to gratify a selfish ambition; the one aim of Jesus was to serve others, no matter what depths of self-renunciation that service might cost. In the Philippian Church there were those whose one aim was to focus men's eyes upon themselves; the one aim of Jesus was to focus men's eyes upon God. So the follower of Christ must think always, not of himself but of others, not of his own glory but of the glory of God.

CO-OPERATION IN SALVATION

Philippians 2: 12-18

So then, my beloved, just as at all times you obeyed, not only as in my presence, but much more, as things now are, in my absence, carry to its perfect conclusion the work of your own salvation with fear and trembling; for it is God, who, that He may carry out His own good pleasure, brings to effect in you both the initial willing and the effective action. Do all things without murmurings and questionings, that you may show yourselves blameless and pure, the spotless children of God in a warped and twisted generation, in which you appear like lights in the world, as you hold forth the word which is life, so that on the day of Christ it may be my proud claim that I have not run for nothing and that I have not toiled for nothing. But if my own life is to be poured out on the sacrifice and service of your faith, I rejoice and I do rejoice with you all. So also do you rejoice, and share my rejoicing.

PAUL'S appeal to the Philippians is more than an appeal merely to live in unity and harmony in a given human situation; it is an appeal to live a whole life which will lead to the salvation of God in time and in eternity.

Nowhere in the New Testament is the work of salvation more succinctly and epigrammatically stated. As the Authorized Version has it in verses 12 and 13: " Work out your own salvation with fear and trembling, for it is God which worketh in you, both to will and to do of His own good pleasure." As is always the case with Paul, the words are carefully and meticulously chosen. *Work out* your own salvation, says Paul; the word he uses for *to work out* is the Greek verb *katergazesthai*, which always has the idea of bringing to completion, to a full and complete and perfect accomplishment and conclusion. It is as if Paul said: " Don't stop halfway; don't be satisfied with a partial salvation. Go on until the work of salvation is fully and finally wrought out in you." No Christian can be satisfied with anything less than the total benefits of the gospel. Then Paul goes on to say, " For it is God which *worketh* in you both to will and *to do* of His good pleasure." The Greek word which Paul uses for *worketh* and *to do* in this sentence is the same verb. It is the verb *energein*. There are two significant things about that verb; it is always used of *the action of God*; and it is always used of *effective action*. The whole process of salvation is the action of God; and it is action which is effective because it is the action of God. God's action cannot be frustrated, nor can it remain half-finished, it must be fully effective.

As we have said, here in this passage is the perfect example of the mode of salvation.

(i) Salvation is of God. It is God that works in man. (a) It is God that works in us the will and the desire to be saved. It is God who wakens the desire for Himself within our hearts. It is true that " our hearts are restless till they rest in Him," and it is also true that " we could not even begin to seek Him unless He had already found us."

The desire for the goodness of God, the desire for the peace of God, the desire for the salvation of God is not a desire kindled by any human emotion; it is kindled by God Himself within our hearts. The beginning of the process of salvation is not dependent on any human desire; it is awakened by God. (b) The continuance of that process is dependent on God. Without the help of God there can be no progress in goodness; without His help no sin can be conquered and no virtue achieved. It is through His help, and His help alone, that we receive power to overcome evil and to do the right. (c) The end of the process of salvation is with God, for the end of the process of salvation is friendship with God, in which we are the Beloved's and the Beloved is ours. It is, therefore, true to say that the work of salvation is begun, continued and ended in God.

(ii) But there is another side to this. Salvation is of man. " Work out your own salvation," Paul demands. Without the co-operation of man even God Himself is helpless. The fact is that any gift and any benefit have to be taken and received. A man may be ill; the doctor may be well able to cure him; the drugs and the techniques of healing may be there for the taking; but the man will never be healed and cured until he takes them; and he may stubbornly refuse the invitation and the persuasion to take them. A man cannot learn without a teacher; but the teacher is helpless to teach, if the scholar stubbornly refuses to use the books, the equipment, the training and the discipline through which knowledge comes. It is so with salvation. The offer of God is there; without that offer there can be no such thing as salvation; God will even breathe into a man's heart, seeking to fill him with the desire for Himself. But that man can never receive salvation unless he answers to the appeal of God, and takes what God offers, and accepts what God gives and what God commands.

There can be no salvation without God, but what God

offers man must take. It is never God who withholds salvation; it is always man who robs himself of it.

THE SIGNS OF SALVATION

Philippians 2: 12-18 (*continued*)

BUT, further, when we examine the chain of thought in this passage, we see that Paul in it sets down five signs of salvation, as we may call them.

(i) There is the sign of *effective progress*. The Christian must give continual evidence in his daily life that he is indeed working out his own salvation; day by day it must be more fully accomplished, more completely perfected. The great tragedy of so many of us is that we are never really any further on. Our life is for ever marked by the same faults and mistakes. We continue to be victims of the same habits and slaves of the same temptations. We remain guilty of the same disloyalties and the same failures. The truly Christian life cannot stand in the same place; it must be a continual progress. It cannot be otherwise, for the Christian life is a journey towards God.

(ii) There is the sign of what Paul calls *fear and trembling*. This is not the fear and trembling of the slave cringing before his master. It is not the fear of and the trembling at the prospect of punishment. This fear and trembling comes from two things. It comes, first, from a sense of our own creatureliness, our own weakness, our own inadequacy, our own powerlessness to deal with life and temptation. That is to say, it is not the fear and trembling which drives us to seek to hide from God, and which separates us from God. It is rather the fear and trembling which drives us to seek God, and which brings us ever closer to God, in the certainty that without His help we cannot effectively face life at all. It comes, second, from the fear to grieve and to disappoint God. When we really love a person, we are not afraid of what

53

that person may do to us; we are afraid of what we may do to him or her. The fear of love is not the fear that we may be punished by the other person; it is the fear that we may wound the heart of the other person. The Christian's one fear is the fear to wound God, and to crucify Christ again.

(iii) There is the sign of *serenity and certainty*. The Christian will do all things without *murmurings* and *questionings*. The word which Paul uses for *murmurings* (*goggusmos*) is an unusual Greek word. In the Greek of the sacred writers it has one special and characteristic connection. It is the word which is used of the rebellious and faithless murmurings of the children of Israel in their desert journey. The people murmured against Moses (*Exodus* 15: 24; 16: 2; *Numbers* 16: 41). *Goggusmos*— pronounced *gongusomos*—is an onomatopoetic word. It describes the low, threatening, discontented muttering of a mob who distrust their leaders, and who are on the verge of a rebellion and an uprising against them. The word Paul uses for questionings is *dialogismos* which describes useless, and sometimes ill-natured, disputing and debating, and doubting and wavering. In the Christian life there is the serenity and the certainty of perfect submission and perfect certainty and perfect trust.

(iv) There is the sign of *purity*. Christians, as the Authorized Version has it, are to be *blameless* and *harmless* and without *rebuke*. Each one of these words has its own contribution to add to the idea of Christian purity. (*a*) The word which is translated *blameless* is *amemptos*, and expresses *what the Christian is to the world*. His life is of such purity that none can find anything in it to blame, or with which to find fault. It is often said in courts of law that justice must not only *be* just, but must *be seen* to be just. The Christian must not only be pure, but the purity of his life must be seen by all. (*b*) The word which is translated *harmless* is *akeraios*, and expresses *what the*

Christian is in himself. The word *akeraios* literally means *unmixed, unadulterated.* It is used, for instance, of wine or milk, which is pure and not mixed with water; it is used of metal which has no alloy in it. When used of people, it implies absolute *sincerity*, motives of action which are unmixed and clean and pure. The Christian purity must issue in a complete sincerity of thought and character. (c) The word which is translated *blameless* is in fact *amōmos*, and it describes *what the Christian is in the sight of God.* This word is specially used in connection with sacrifices. Of a sacrifice it means *spotless* or *unblemished* and therefore fit to be offered on the altar of God. The purity of the Christian must be such that it will stand even the scrutiny of God. The Christian life must be such that it can be offered like an unblemished sacrifice to God. Christian purity is blameless in the sight of the world, sincere within itself, and fit to stand the scrutiny of God.

(v) There is the sign of *missionary endeavour*. The Christian offers to all the word of life, that is to say, the word which gives life, and brings life. This Christian missionary endeavour has two aspects. (a) It is the offer of a message; it is the proclamation of the offer of the gospel in words which are clear and unmistakable. (b) It is the witness of a life. It is the witness of a life that is absolutely straight in a world which is warped and twisted and distorted. It is the offer of light in a world which is dark. Christians are to be lights in the world. The word which Paul uses for *lights* is *phōstēres*. It is the same word as is used in the creation story of the *lights*, the sun and the moon, which God set in the firmament of the heaven to give light upon the earth (*Genesis* I: 14-18). The Christian offers and demonstrates straightness in a twisted world, and light in a dark world. His missionary endeavour is the bringing of a message and the demonstration of a life.

THE LETTER TO THE PHILIPPIANS

THE PICTURES OF PAUL

Philippians 2: 12-18 (*continued*)

THIS passage concludes with two vivid pictures, which are typical of Paul's way of thinking and writing.

(i) Paul longs for the Christian progress and perfection of the Philippians so that at the end of the day he may have the joy of knowing that he has not run in vain or laboured in vain. The word he uses for *to labour* is *kopian*. There are two possible pictures in it. (*a*) It may paint a picture of the sternest and the most exacting toil. *Kopian* means to labour to the point of sweat and utter exhaustion; it describes the kind of labour into which a man puts the last ounce of strength and energy which he possesses. (*b*) It may be that *kopian* describes the toil of the athlete's training; and that what Paul is saying is, that he prays that all the discipline of training that he imposed upon himself, and the race he has run may not go for nothing.

One of the features of Paul's writing is his love of pictures from the life of the athlete. And there is little wonder. In every Greek city the gymnasium was far more than a mere physical training-ground. It was in the gymnasium that Socrates so often talked and discussed the eternal problems; it was in the gymnasium that the philosophers and the sophists and the wandering teachers and preachers so often found their audience. In any Greek city the gymnasium was not only the physical training-ground, it was also the intellectual club of the city. In the Greek world there were the great Isthmian Games at Corinth, the great Pan-Ionian Games at Ephesus, and, greatest of all, the Olympic Games. Once every four years they were held. The Greek cities were often at variance and frequently at war; but when the Olympic Games came round, no matter what dispute was raging, a month's armistice and a month's truce was declared that there might be a contest in fellowship between them. Not only did the athletes come, but the historians and the poets came to give readings of their latest works, and the sculptors, whose names are immortal, came to make their statues of the winners.

There can be little doubt that in Corinth and in Ephesus, Paul had been a spectator of these games. Where there were crowds of men, very certainly Paul would be there to seek to win men for Christ. But apart from the preaching there was something about these athletic contests which found an answer in the heart of Paul. He knows the contests of the boxers (I *Corinthians* 9: 26). He knows the foot-race, most famous of all the contests. He had seen the herald summoning the racers to the starting-line (I *Corinthians* 9: 27); he had seen the runners press along the course to the goal (*Philippians* 3: 14); he had seen the judge awarding the prize at the end of the race (2 *Timothy* 4: 8); he knew of the victor's laurel crown and of his exultation (I *Corinthians* 9: 24; *Philippians* 4: 1). He knew the rigorous discipline of training which the athlete must undertake, and the strict regulations and rules which must be observed (I *Timothy* 4: 7, 8; 2 *Timothy* 2: 5).

So Paul's prayer is that he may not be like an athlete whose training and whose effort has gone for nothing. For Paul the greatest prize in life was to know that through him others had come to know and to love and to serve Jesus Christ.

(ii) But in verse 17 Paul has another picture. Paul had a special gift for speaking in language that people could understand. Again and again he took his pictures from the ordinary affairs and activities of the people to whom he was speaking or writing. He has already taken a picture from the games; now he takes one from heathen sacrifice. One of the commonest kinds of heathen sacrifice was what was called *libation*. A libation was a cup of wine poured out as an offering to the gods. For instance, every heathen meal began and ended with such a libation, as a kind of grace before and after meat. So Paul, in verse 17, speaks of the sacrifice and the service of the faith of the Philippians. He looks upon their fidelity and their

Christian living and their faith as an offering and a sacrifice to God, as indeed it was. He knows that it may well be that for him death is not very far away, for he is writing to them when he is in prison and awaiting trial. So he says, as the Authorized Version has it, that he is quite ready " to be offered upon " their sacrifice. The word he used for *to be offered upon* is the word *spendesthai*, which means literally *to be poured out as a libation*. So what he says to the Philippians is: " Your fidelity and your Christian loyalty are already a sacrifice to God; and if death for Christ should come to me, I am willing and glad that my life should be poured out like a libation to the gods on the altar on which your sacrifice is being made."

For Paul to die for Christ was a privilege. He was perfectly willing to make his life a sacrifice and an offering to God; and, if that happened, to him it would be all joy, and he calls on them, not to mourn at the prospect, but rather to rejoice. To Paul every call to suffer, to sacrifice, to toil, was a call to his love for Christ, and therefore he met every such call, not with regret and complaint, but with joy.

THE FAITHFUL HENCHMAN

Philippians 2: 19-24

I hope in the Lord Jesus soon to send Timothy to you, that I may find out how things are going with you, and take heart. I have no one with a mind equal to his, for he is the kind of man who will genuinely care for your affairs; for all men are concerned with their own interests, and not with the interests of Jesus Christ. You know his tried and tested character, and you know that, as a child serves a father, so he has shared my service in the work of the gospel. So, then, I hope to send him, as soon as I see how things go with me. But I am confident in the Lord that I myself too will soon come to you.

SINCE Paul cannot himself come to Philippi, it his intention to send Timothy to the Philippians as his representative. There was no one so close to Paul as Timothy was. We know very little about Timothy in detail, but the very record of his service with Paul shows his fidelity.

Timothy was a native either of Derbe or of Lystra. His mother Eunice was a Jewess, and his grandmother's name was Lois. His father was a Greek, and, the fact that he was not circumcised would seem to show that Timothy was trained and educated in Greek ways (*Acts* 16: 1; 2 *Timothy* 1: 5). We cannot tell how or when Timothy was converted to Christianity, but on his second missionary journey Paul met Timothy, and Paul saw in Timothy one whom he could clearly use in the service of Jesus Christ.

From that time Paul and Timothy were very close together. Paul can speak of him as his son in the Lord (1 *Corinthians* 4: 17). Timothy was with Paul in Philippi (*Acts* 16); he was with him in Thessalonica and Berea (*Acts* 17; 1-14); he was with him in Corinth and in Ephesus (*Acts* 18: 5; 19: 21, 22); and he was with him in prison in Rome (*Colossians* 1: 1; *Philippians* 1: 1). Timothy was associated with Paul in the writing of no fewer than five of his letters—1 and 2 *Thessalonians*, 2 *Corinthians*, *Colossians* and *Philippians*; and when Paul wrote to Rome Timothy is also joined with him in sending greetings (*Romans* 16: 21).

But Timothy's great use was that, whenever Paul wished for information from some Church, or when he wished to send advice or counsel or encouragement or guidance or rebuke, and when he could not go himself, it was Timothy whom he sent. So Timothy was sent to Thessalonica (1 *Thessalonians* 3: 6); to Corinth (1 *Corinthians* 4: 17; 16: 10, 11); to Philippi, as we learn here (*Philippians* 2: 19). And in the end we know that Timothy too was a prisoner for the sake of Christ (*Hebrews* 13: 23).

The great use of Timothy was that Timothy was a man

who could be sent anywhere, and who was always willing to go. In the hands of Timothy a message was as safe as if Paul had delivered it himself. Others might be consumed with selfish ambition, and might be concerned with their own interests alone; but Timothy's one desire was to serve Paul and to serve Christ in Christ's Church. Timothy is the patron saint of all those who are quite content with the second place, so long as they can serve.

THE COURTESY OF PAUL

Philippians 2: 25-30

I think it necessary to send to you Epaphroditus, my brother, and fellow-worker, and fellow-soldier, your messenger and the servant of my need, because he is longing for you all, and he is very distressed because you heard that he had been ill, so ill that he nearly died. But God had pity on him, and not on him only, but on me too, that I might not have grief upon grief. So, then, I send him to you with the more despatch, that, when you see him, you may be glad again, and that I may be less grieved. Welcome him in the Lord with all joy, and hold such men in honour, because he came near to death because of his work for Christ, hazarding his life, that he might fill up that part of your service to me which you were personally unable to supply.

THERE is a whole dramatic story behind this. It may be reconstructed in some such way as this. When the Philippians heard that Paul was in prison, their warm hearts were moved to action. They sent a gift to him by the hand of Epaphroditus. That which they could not personally do, because distance prevented them from doing it, they delegated to Epaphroditus to do for them. Not only did they intend Epaphroditus to be the bearer of their gift; they also intended him to stay in Rome and to be Paul's personal servant and attendant. Clearly Epaphroditus was a brave man, for any man who proposes to offer himself as the personal attendant of a man awaiting trial on a capital charge is laying himself open to the very considerable risk of becoming involved in the same charge. In truth, Epaphroditus did risk his life to serve Paul.

In Rome Epaphroditus fell ill. Maybe it was with the notorious Roman fever which sometimes swept the city like an epidemic and a scourge. He was so ill that he was near to death. He knew that news of his illness had penetrated back to Philippi, and he was worried because he knew that his friends in Philippi would be worried about what was happening to him. God in His mercy spared the life of Epaphroditus and spared Paul yet more sorrow. But Paul knew that it was time that Epaphroditus went back home; and in all probability Epaphroditus was the bearer of this whole letter.

But there was one problem. The Philippian Church had sent Epaphroditus to stay with Paul, and if Epaphroditus came back home, there would not be lacking those who said that he was a quitter and a coward. Here Paul gives Epaphroditus a tremendous testimonial, which will silence any possible criticism of his return.

In this testimonial every word is carefully chosen. Epaphroditus was his brother, his fellow-worker, and his fellow-soldier. As Lightfoot puts it, Epaphroditus was one with Paul in sympathy, one with him in work, one with him in danger. Epaphroditus in truth had stood in the firing-line. Then he goes on to call Epaphroditus your *messenger* and the *servant* of my need. It is impossible to supply the flavour of these words in any translation. The word which Paul uses for messenger is no less than the word *apostolos*. It is true that *apostolos* literally means *anyone who is sent out on an errand*; but Christian usage had consecrated and ennobled the word, and by using it Paul, by implication, ranks Epaphroditus with himself and all the apostles of Christ, with the very spiritual élite of the faith. The word he uses for *servant* is the word *leitourgos*. In secular Greek this was a magnificent word. In the ancient days in the Greek cities there were men who, because they loved their city so much, out of their own resources and at their own expense undertook certain great civic duties. It might be to defray the expenses of an embassy, or the cost of putting on one of the great dramas of the great poets, or of training the athletes who would represent the city in the games, or of fitting out a warship and paying a crew to serve in the navy of the state. These were munificent gifts to the state; such men were the supreme benefactors of the state; and such men were known as *leitourgoi*. Here is the word which Paul takes and applies to Epaphroditus. He takes the great Christian word *apostolos*, and the great Greek word *leitourgos*, and applies them to Epaphroditus. " Give a man like that a welcome home," he says. " Hold such a man in honour, for a man like that hazarded his life for Christ."

Here we see Paul smoothing the way, and making it easy for Epaphroditus to go home. There is something very wonderful here. It is a very touching thing to think of Paul, himself in the very shadow of death, in prison and awaiting judgment, showing that perfect Christian courtesy and consideration for Epaphroditus. Paul was facing death, and yet it mattered to him that Epaphroditus should not meet with embarrassment when he went home. Paul was a true Christian in his attitude to others; for Paul was never so lost and immersed in his own troubles to have no time to think of the troubles of his friends.

There is one word here in this passage which later had a famous usage. The Authorized Version speaks of Epaphroditus *not regarding his life*; we have translated it *hazarding* his life. The word is the verb *paraboleuesthai*; it is the gambler's word; it means to stake everything on a turn of the dice. What Paul is saying is that for the sake of Jesus Christ Epaphroditus gambled with his life. He recklessly risked his life for the sake of Christ. In the days of the Early Church there was an association of men and women called the *parabolani*, the gamblers. It was their aim and object to visit the prisoners and the sick.

especially those who were ill with dangerous and infectious diseases. In A.D. 252 plague broke out in Carthage; the heathen threw out the bodies of their dead, and fled in terror. Cyprian, the Christian bishop, gathered his congregation together and set them to burying the dead and nursing the sick in that plague-stricken city; and by so doing they saved the city, at the risk of their lives, from destruction and desolation.

There should be in the Christian an almost reckless courage which is ready to gamble with its life to serve Christ and to serve men.

The Church always needs the *parabolani*, the gamblers of Christ.

THE INDESTRUCTIBLE JOY

Philippians 3: 1

> As for what remains, my brothers, rejoice in the Lord. It is no trouble to me to write the same things to you, and for you it is safe.

HERE Paul sets down two very important things.

(i) He sets down what we might call the indestructibility of Christian joy. He must have felt that he had been setting a high challenge before the Philippian Church. For them there was the possibility of the same kind of persecution, and even the same kind of death, as threatened himself. For them there was the struggle and the discipline of the Christian way. From one point of view it looked as if Christianity was a grim job. But in it and beyond it all there was joy. " Your joy," said Jesus, " no man taketh from you " (*John* 16: 22). There is a certain indestructibility in Christian joy; and it is so, because Christian joy is *in the Lord*. Its basis is that the Christian lives for ever in the presence and the company of Jesus Christ. He can lose all things, and he can lose all people, but he can never lose Christ. And, therefore, even in circumstances where joy would seem to be impossible, and even in conditions in which there seems to be nothing but pain and discomfort, the Christian joy remains, because not all the threats and terrors and discomforts of life can separate the Christian from the love of God in Christ Jesus his Lord (*Romans* 8: 35-39). In 1756 a letter came to John Wesley from a father who had a prodigal son. When the revival swept England the son was in York gaol. " It pleased God," wrote the father, " not to cut him off in his sins. He gave him time to repent; and not only so, but a heart to repent." The lad was condemned to death for his misdeeds; and the father's letter goes on: " His peace increased daily, till on Saturday, the day he was to die, he came out of the condemned-room, clothed in his shroud, and went into the cart. As he went on, the cheerfulness and composure of his countenance were amazing to all the spectators." The lad had found a joy which not even the scaffold could take away.

It often happens that men can stand the great sorrows and the great trials of life, but that they are undone and upset and irritated by what are almost minor inconveniences. But this Christian joy enables a man to accept even them with a smile. John Nelson was one of Wesley's most famous early preachers. He and Wesley carried out a mission in Cornwall, near Land's End, and Nelson tells about it. " All that time, Mr. Wesley and I lay on the floor: he had my greatcoat for a pillow, and I had Burkitt's notes on the New Testament for mine. After being here near three weeks, one morning about three o'clock Mr. Wesley turned over, and, finding me awake, clapped me on the side, saying: ' Brother Nelson, let us be of good cheer: I have one whole side yet, for the skin is off but on one side! ' " They had little enough even to eat. One morning Wesley had preached with great effect: " As we returned, Mr. Wesley stopped his horse to pick the blackberries, saying: ' Brother Nelson, we ought to be thankful that there are plenty blackberries; for this is the best country I ever saw for getting a stomach, but the worst I ever saw for getting food! ' " Christian joy made Wesley able to accept the great blows of life, and to greet the lesser discomforts with a jest. If the Christian walks with Christ, he must of necessity walk with joy.

(ii) Here also Paul sets down what we might call the necessity of repetition. He says that he proposes to write things to them that he has written before. This is interesting, for it must mean that Paul had written more letters than one to the Philippians, and these letters are lost. When we think about it, this is nothing to be surprised at. Paul was writing letters from A.D. 48 to A.D. 64, for sixteen years, and we possess only thirteen of them. Unless there were long years, and periods of years, when he never put pen to paper there must have been many more of them, which have gone lost. There is nothing to be surprised at in the fact that Paul refers back to letters to the Philippians which we no longer possess.

Like any good teacher, Paul was never afraid of repetition. It may well be that one of the mistakes we make is our desire for novelty. The great saving truths of Christianity do not change. We cannot hear them too often. We do not tire of the foods which are the essentials of life. We expect to eat bread and to drink water every day in life. Therefore, we must listen again and again to the truth which is the bread of life and the water of life. No teacher must find it a trouble to go over and over again the great basic truths of the Christian faith; for that is the way to ensure the safety of his hearers. We may like the " fancy things " at meal times, but it is the basic foods on which we live. Preaching and teaching and studying the side-issues may be attractive, and has its place, but the fundamental truths can neither be spoken nor heard too often for the safety of our souls.

THE EVIL TEACHERS

Philippians 3: 2, 3

> Be on your guard against the dogs; be on your guard against the evil workers; be on your guard against the party of mutilation; for we are the truly circumcised, we who worship in the Spirit of God; we whose proud boast is in Jesus Christ, we who place no confidence in merely human things.

QUITE suddenly Paul's accent changes to that of warning. Wherever Paul taught, the Jews followed him, and tried to undo his teaching. It was the teaching of Paul that we are saved by grace alone, that salvation is the free gift of God, that we can never earn it, and never deserve it, and that we can only humbly and adoringly accept what God has offered to us. Further, it was Paul's teaching that the offer of God was to all men, of all nations, and that none was excluded from it. It was the teaching of these Jews that, if a man wished to be saved he must earn credit in the sight of God by countless deeds of the law, that he must build up a credit balance in the sight of God, that he must put God in his debt by continuously carrying out these deeds of the law. Further, it was the teaching of these Jews that salvation belonged to the Jews and to no one else, and that, before God had any use for a man, the man must be circumcised and must, as it were, become a Jew. Paul offered free salvation by the grace of God to all men. The Jewish teachers said that salvation belonged only to the Jews, and must be earned by keeping the law. Paul opened salvation to the whole world; the Jews kept it for Jews. Paul made salvation dependent solely on the grace of God; the Jews made it dependent on the human efforts of men. Here Paul rounds upon these Jewish teachers who were seeking to undo all his work. He calls them three things; and the three things he calls them are carefully chosen, to throw their own claims back upon themselves.

(i) "Beware of the dogs", he says. With us the dog is a

well-loved animal, but it was not so in the East in the time of Jesus. The dog was the pariah dog, roaming the streets, sometimes in packs, hunting amidst the garbage dumps and the rubbish heaps, and snapping and snarling at all whom they met. J. B. Lightfoot speaks of " the dogs which prowl about eastern cities, without a home and without an owner, feeding on the refuse and filth of the streets, quarrelling among themselves, and attacking the passer-by." In the Bible the dog always stands for that than which nothing can be lower. When Saul is seeking to take the life of David, David's demand is: " After whom dost thou pursue? After a dead dog, after a flea? " (I *Samuel* 24: 14, cp. 2 *Kings* 8: 13; *Psalm* 22: 16, 20). In the Parable of the Rich Man and Lazarus, part of the torture of Lazarus in his sickness and his poverty is that the street dogs annoy him by licking his sores (*Luke* 16: 21). In *Deuteronomy* the Law brings together the price of a dog and the hire of a whore, and declares that neither must be offered to God (*Deuteronomy* 23: 18). In *Revelation* the word *dog* stands for those who are so impure that they are debarred from the Holy City (*Revelation* 22: 15). It was the same in Greek thought; the dog stood for everything that was shamelessly and audaciously unclean and impure. That which was holy must never be given to dogs (*Matthew* 7: 5). Now, it was by this name that the Jews called the Gentiles. There is a Rabbinic saying, " The nations of the world are like dogs."

So, this is Paul's answer to these Jewish teachers. He says to them, " In your proud self-righteousness, you call other men dogs; in your nationalistic pride in being a Jew, you call other nations dogs; it is you yourselves who are dogs, because you shamelessly pervert the gospel of Jesus Christ." Paul takes the very name the Jewish teachers would have applied to the impure and to the Gentiles and flings it back at themselves. A man must always have a care that he is not himself guilty of the very sins of which he accuses others.

(ii) He calls them evil workers, workers of evil things. The Jews would have been quite sure that they were workers of righteousness. It was their view that to keep the Law, to go on with the many details of it, to keep its countless rules and regulations was to work righteousness. But Paul was certain that the only kind of righteousness there is comes from casting oneself freely upon the grace of God. The effect of their teaching was to take men further away from God instead of to bring men nearer to God. They thought they were working good, but they were working evil. Any teacher or preacher must be more anxious to listen to God than to propagate his own opinions or he too will run the risk of being a worker of evil, even when he thinks that he is a worker of righteousness.

THE ONLY TRUE CIRCUMCISION

Philippians 3: 2, 3 *(continued)*

(iii) Lastly, he calls them, as the Authorized Version has it, the *concision*, or, as we have translated it, *the party of mutilation*. There is a pun here in the Greek which is not translatable into English. There are two Greek verbs which are very like each other. *Peritemnein* means *to circumcise*; *katatemnein* means *to mutilate*. *Peritemnein* describes the sacred sign and work of circumcision; *katatemnein*, as in *Leviticus* 21: 5, describes forbidden self-mutilation, such as castration and the like. So Paul says, " You Jews think that you are circumcised; in point of fact, you are only mutilated."

What is the point of this? According to Jewish belief, circumcision was ordained upon Israel in sign and symbol that they were the people with whom God had entered into a special covenant and a special relationship. The story of the beginning of that sign is in *Genesis* 17: 9, 10. When God entered into His special covenant and relationship with Abraham, circumcision was laid down as an eternal sign of the covenant. Now, circumcision is only a sign in the flesh. It is something which is done to a man's body. But if a man is to be in special relationship with God, if God is to be near to that man, and if that man is to be near to God, then something far more is needed than a mark in his body. He must have a certain kind of mind and heart and character of life. This is where at least some of the Jews made the mistake. They regarded circumcision *in itself* as being enough to set them apart specially for God. They regarded this merely physical badge as making them belong to God, and making everything else unnecessary. Long, long before this the great teachers and the great prophets had seen that circumcision of the flesh is by itself not nearly enough; that there is, what we can only call, a spiritual circumcision. In *Leviticus* the sacred law-giver says that the *uncircumcised hearts* of Israel must be humbled to accept the punishment of God (*Leviticus* 26: 41). The summons of the writer of *Deuteronomy* is: " Circumcise the foreskin of your heart and be no more stiff-necked " (*Deuteronomy* 10: 16). He says that the Lord will circumcise their hearts to make them love Him (*Deuteronomy* 30: 6). Jeremiah speaks of the uncircumcised ear, the ear that will not hear the word of God (*Jeremiah* 6: 10). The writer of *Exodus* speaks of uncircumcised lips (*Exodus* 6: 20). Always the great Jewish thinkers had seen that mere physical circumcision was nothing; it was consecration of mind and heart and lips that were necessary.

So what Paul says is, " If you have nothing to show but circumcision of the flesh, if all you have is a physical mark, then you are not really circumcised—you are only mutilated. For real circumcision is devotion of heart and mind and thought and life to God."

Because of all that, says Paul, it is the Christians who are the truly circumcised. They are circumcised, not with the outward badge and mark in the flesh, but with that inner and spiritual circumcision of which the great law-givers and teachers and prophets wrote and spoke. What then are the signs of that real circumcision? Paul sets out **three** signs.

(i) We worship in the Spirit of God; or, we worship God in the Spirit. Christian worship is not a thing of ritual and of the observation of details and regulations of the Law; Christian worship is a thing of the Spirit and of the heart. It is perfectly possible for a man to go through an elaborate and ancient and imposing liturgy, and yet to have a heart that is far away from God. It is perfectly possible for a man meticulously to observe all the outward observances of religion, and yet to have hatred and bitterness and pride and the unforgiving spirit in his heart. The true Christian, the truly circumcised man, the man who is really in the true relationship to God, worships God, not with outward forms and observances, but with the true devotion and the real sincerity of his heart. His worship is love of God, service of men, and the deep humility which knows its own sin, and whose delight is to serve.

(ii) Our only boast is in Jesus Christ. The only boast of the Christian is in, not what he has done for himself, but in what Christ has done for him. The only pride of the Christian is that he is a man for whom Christ died. He is the man whose sinful self is his only shame and whose only glory is the Cross.

> In the Cross of Christ I glory,
> Towering o'er the wrecks of time;
> All the light of sacred story
> Gathers round its head sublime.

(iii) The Christian is the man who has no confidence in the flesh, the man who places no confidence in merely human things. The Jew placed his confidence in the physical and fleshly badge of circumcision, and in the human performances of the ordinances and the duties of the Law. The Christian is the man who places his confidence only in the mercy and the grace of God, and in the love of Jesus Christ. The Jew in essence trusted himself; the Christian in essence trusts God.

The real circumcision is not a mark in the flesh of the body; it is that true worship; that true glory; and that true confidence in the grace of God in Jesus Christ, our Lord.

THE PRIVILEGES OF PAUL

Philippians 3: 4-7

> And yet it remains true that I have every ground of confidence from the human point of view. If anyone has reason to think that he has grounds for confidence in his human heritage and attainments, I have more. I was circumcised when I was eight days old: I am of the race of Israel, of the tribe of Benjamin: I am a Hebrew, born of Hebrew parents. As far as the Law goes, I was a Pharisee: as for zeal, I was a persecutor of the Churches: as for the righteousness which is in the Law, I was beyond blame. But such things as I could humanly reckon as profits, I came to the conclusion were all loss for the sake of Jesus Christ.

PAUL has just attacked the Jewish teachers, and has insisted that it is the Christians, not the Jews, who are the truly circumcised and who are truly the covenant people, and who are truly in a special and unique relationship with God. If his opponents were going to try to argue, they might have attempted to say, " But you are a Christian; therefore, you do not know what you are talking about; you do not what it is to be a Jew." And so Paul sets out his credentials. He does not do so to boast, or to bring credit to himself. He does so to show that he had enjoyed every privilege which a Jew could enjoy, and had risen to every attainment to which a Jew could rise. He knew what it was to be a Jew, and to be a Jew in the highest sense of the term, and he had deliberately and knowingly and willingly abandoned it all for the sake of Jesus Christ. Every phrase in this catalogue of Paul's privileges has its special meaning; therefore, let us look at them one by one.

(i) He had been *circumcised when he was eight days old.*

It had been the commandment of God to Abraham: " He that is eight days old shall be circumcised among you " (*Genesis* 17: 12); and that commandment had been repeated as a permanent law of Israel (*Leviticus* 12: 3). By this claim Paul makes it clear that he is not an Ishmaelite, for the Ishmaelites were circumcised in their thirteenth year (*Genesis* 17: 25); nor was he a proselyte who had come late into the Jewish faith, and who had been circumcised in manhood. Here he stresses the fact that he had been born into the Jewish faith, and had known its privileges and had observed its ceremonies since his birth.

(ii) He was of *the race of Israel*. When the Jews wished to stress their special relationship to God in its most unique sense it was the word *Israelite* that they used. *Israel* was the name which had been specially given to Jacob by God after his wrestling with God (*Genesis* 32: 28). It was to Israel that they in the most special sense traced their heritage. In point of fact the Ishmaelites could trace their descent to Abraham, for Ishmael was also Abraham's son by Hagar. The Edomites could trace their descent to Isaac, for Esau, the founder of the Edomite nation, was also Isaac's son; but it was the Israelites alone who could trace their descent to Jacob, whom God had called by the name of Israel. By calling himself an Israelite, Paul stressed the absolute purity of his race and his descent.

(iii) He was *of the tribe of Benjamin*. That is to say, Paul was not only an Israelite; he belonged to the élite of Israel. The tribe of Benjamin had a special place in the aristocracy of Israel. Benjamin was the child of Rachel, the well-loved wife of Jacob, and of all the twelve patriarchs Benjamin alone had been born in the Promised Land (*Genesis* 35: 17, 18). It was from the tribe of Benjamin that the first king of Israel had come, for it was from that tribe that Saul came (I *Samuel* 9: 1, 2). And it was no doubt from that very king that Paul had been given his original name Saul. When, under Rehoboam, the kingdom had been disrupted and split up, ten of the tribes went off with

Jeroboam, and the tribe of Benjamin was the only tribe which had remained faithful with Judah (I *Kings* 12: 21). When the nation returned from the exile, it was from the tribes of Benjamin and Judah that the nucleus of the reborn nation was formed (*Ezra* 4: 1). The tribe of Benjamin had the place of honour in Israel's battle-line, so that the battle-cry of Israel was : " After thee, O Benjamin! " (*Judges* 5: 14; *Hosea* 5: 8). The great feast of Purim, which was observed every year with such rejoicing, commemorated the deliverance of which the Book of Esther tells, and the central figure of that story is Mordecai, and Mordecai was a Benjamite. When Paul stated that he was of the tribe of Benjamin, it was a claim that he was not simply an Israelite, but that he also belonged to the highest aristocracy of Israel. It would be the equivalent in England of saying that he came over with the Normans or in America of saying that he traced his descent to the Pilgrim fathers.

So, then, Paul claims that from his birth he was a God-fearing, Law-observing Jew; that his lineage was as pure as Jewish lineage could be; and that he belonged to the most aristocratic tribe of the Jews. These were his advantages of birth, the privileges into which he had been born and bred.

THE ATTAINMENTS OF PAUL

Philippians 3: 4-7 (*continued*)

So far, Paul has been stating the privileges which came to him by birth; now he goes on to state the attainments which he had achieved by choice in the Jewish faith.

(i) He was a *Hebrew born of Hebrew parents*. This is not the same as to say that he was a true Israelite. The point is this. The history of the Jews had dispersed them all over the world. In every town and in every city and in every country there were Jews. There were tens of thousands of them in Rome; and in Alexandria there were more than a million of them. Now these Jews stubbornly refused to be assimilated to the nations amongst whom they lived; they retained faithfully their own religion, and their own customs and their own laws. But one thing frequently happened—they forgot their own language. They became Greek-speaking, because they had to be, because they lived and moved in a Greek environment. Now a Hebrew was a Jew who was not only of pure racial descent, but who had deliberately, and often laboriously and with great effort, retained the Hebrew tongue. Such a Jew would speak the language of the country in which he lived, but he also carefully learned, and refused ever to forget, the Hebrew which was his ancestral tongue. So Paul claims, not only to be a pure-blooded Jew, but to be a Jew who still spoke the Hebrew tongue. He had been born in the Gentile city of Tarsus, but he had come to Jerusalem to be educated at the feet of Gamaliel (*Acts* 22: 3). He could speak to the mob in Jerusalem in their own Hebrew tongue (*Acts* 21: 40). So Paul adds to his claims the fact that he was so loyal a Jew that he had learned, and had never forgotten, the Hebrew tongue.

(ii) As far as the Law went, he was *a trained Pharisee*. This is a claim that Paul makes more than once (*Acts* 22: 3; 23: 6; 26: 5). There were not very many Pharisees; there were never more than six thousand of them; but the Pharisees were the spiritual athletes of Judaism. Their very name means *The Separated Ones*. They had separated themselves off from all common life and from all common tasks in order to make it the one aim and duty of their lives to keep every smallest detail of the Law. It is Paul's claim that not only was he a Jew who had retained his ancestral religion, but he had also devoted his whole life to the most rigorous and unbending observance of it. No man knew better from personal experience what Jewish religion was at its highest and most demanding peak.

(iii) As far as zeal went, he had been *a persecutor of the Church.* To a Jew zeal was the greatest quality in the religious life. Phinehas had saved the people from the wrath of God, and had been given an everlasting priesthood, because he was zealous for his God (*Numbers* 25: 11-13). It is the cry of the Psalmist: " The zeal of Thine house hath eaten me up " (*Psalm* 69: 9). A burning zeal for God was the badge of honour and the hall-mark of Jewish religion. Paul had been so zealous a Jew that he had tried to wipe out the opponents of Judaism. That was a thing which Paul never forgot. Again and again he speaks of it (*Acts* 22: 2-21; 26: 4-23; I *Corinthians* 15: 8-10; *Galatians* 1: 13). Paul was never ashamed to confess his shame, and to tell men that once he had hated the Christ whom now he loved, and once he had sought to obliterate the Church which now he served. It is Paul's claim that he knew Judaism at its most intense and even fanatical heat.

(iv) As far as the righteousness which the Law could produce went, *he was blameless.* The word is *amemptos*, and J. B. Lightfoot remarks that the verb *memphesthai*, from which it comes, means *to blame for sins of omission.* So Paul claims that there was no demand of the Law which he did not fulfil. As far as the Law went, he was beyond criticism.

So Paul states his attainments. He was so loyal a Jew that he had never lost the Hebrew speech; he was not only a religious Jew, he was a member of the strictest and the most self-disciplined sect of the Jews; he had had in his heart a burning zeal for what he had thought was the cause of God; and he had a record in Judaism in which no man could mark a fault.

All these things Paul might have claimed to set down on the credit side of the balance; but when he met Christ, he wrote them all off as nothing more than bad and useless debts. The things that he had believed to be his glories were in fact quite useless. All human achievement had to be laid aside, in order that he might accept the free grace of Christ. He had to divest himself of every human claim of honour that he might accept in complete naked-ness and humility the mercy of God in Jesus Christ.

So Paul proves to these Jews that he has the right to speak. He is not condemning Judaism from the outside, as one who had no personal knowledge and experience of it. He had experienced it at its highest point; and he knew that it was nothing compared with the peace and joy which Christ had given. He knew that the only way to peace was once and for all to abandon the way of human achievement and to accept the way of grace.

THE WORTHLESSNESS OF THE LAW AND THE VALUE OF CHRIST

Philippians 3: 8, 9

> Yes, and I still count all things loss, because of the all-surpassing value of what it means to know Jesus Christ, my Lord. For His sake I have had to undergo a total abandonment of all things, and I count them as nothing better than filth fit for the refuse heap, that I may make Christ my own, and that it may be clear to all that I am in Him, not because of any right-eousness of my own, that righteousness whose source is the Law, but because of the righteousness which comes through Jesus Christ, the righteousness whose source is God and whose basis is faith.

PAUL has just said that he came to the conclusion that all his Jewish privileges and attainments were nothing but a total loss. But, it might be argued, that was a snap decision, a decision taken in some impulsive and unguarded moment, a decision to be regretted and to be reversed. So here Paul says, " I came to that conclusion—and I still think so. It was not a decision made in a moment of impulse. It is a decision by which I still stand fast."

In this passage there is one key-word, and that word is *righteousness*. *Dikaiosunē* is always a difficult word to translate in Paul's letters. The trouble is not to see its meaning; the trouble is to find one English word which covers all that it includes. Let us try to see what Paul thinks about when he speaks about righteousness. The great basic problem of life is to find fellowship with God, to be in a right relationship with God, not to disregard God nor to forget Him, not to fear God nor to seek to escape Him, but to be at peace and in friendship and in real fellowship with God. The way to that fellowship is through righteousness, through the kind of life and conduct and spirit and heart and attitude to Himself, which God desires. Just because of that, righteousness nearly always in Paul has the meaning of *a right relationship with God*, and to be righteous is to be in a right relationship with God. Remembering that, let us try to paraphrase this passage and to set down, not so much what Paul says, as what was in his inmost mind and heart.

Paul says this, " All my life I have been trying to get into a right relationship with God. I tried to find it by strict adherence to the Jewish Law; I tried to find it by keeping every smallest detail of the Law; I tried to please and to satisfy God in that way, and thus to get into the right relationship for which my heart and soul were longing. I found the Law and all its ways worse than useless to achieve that. I found it no better than *skubala*." This word *skubala* has two meanings. In common language it was popularly derived from *kusi ballomena*, which means *that which is thrown to the dogs*; and in medical language it means *excrement, dung*, as the Authorized Version translates it. So, then, Paul says, " I found the Law and all its ways of no more use than the refuse thrown on the garbage heap to help me to get into a right relationship with God. So I gave up trying to build up a goodness of my own; I gave up trying to achieve this relationship; and I came to God in humble faith, as Jesus told me to do, and I found that fellowship I had sought so long and had never found."

Paul had discovered that a right relationship with God

is not based on Law, but on faith in Jesus Christ; **it is** not *achieved* by any man, it is *given* by God; it is not *won* by *works*, it is accepted in *trust*.

So Paul says, " Out of my experience I tell you that the Jewish way is wrong and futile. You will never get into a right relationship with God by your own efforts and by your own achievements in keeping the Law. You can only get into a right relationship with God by taking Jesus Christ at His word, and by accepting what God Himself offers to you. The way to peace with God is not the way of works, it is the way of grace."

So the basic thought of this passage is the uselessness of Law and the all sufficiency of knowing Christ and accepting the offer of God's grace to be at peace with God, and the very language which Paul uses to describe the Law— excrement, refuse, off-scourings—shows the utter disgust for the Law with which his own frustrated and unavailing efforts to live by it had brought him; and the joy that shines through the passage shows how triumphantly adequate he found the grace of God in Jesus Christ.

WHAT IT MEANS TO KNOW CHRIST

Philippians 3: 10, 11

My object is to know Him, and I mean by that, to know the power of His Resurrection, and the fellowship of His sufferings, while I continue to be made like Him in His death, if by any chance I may attain to the resurrection of the dead.

PAUL has already spoken of the excellency of the knowledge of Christ, the surpassing value of the knowledge of Christ. To that thought he now returns, and he defines more closely what he means. It is important to note the verb which Paul uses for *to know*. It is part of the verb *ginōskein*, and *ginōskein* almost always indicates personal knowledge. It is not simply intellectual knowledge; it is not the knowledge of certain facts or theories or even principles.

78

It is the personal experience of another person. We may see the depth of this word *to know* from a fact of Old Testament usage. The Old Testament uses the verb *to know* of sexual intercourse. " Adam *knew* Eve his wife; and she conceived and bare Cain " (*Genesis* 4: 1). In Hebrew the verb is *yada,* and in Greek it is translated by this verb *ginōskein.* This verb indicates the closest and the most intimate and the most personal knowledge of another person. So, then, it is not Paul's aim *to know about Christ;* it is Paul's aim personally *to know Christ.* The knowledge in question is not knowledge of any fact or any theory or any theology; it is knowledge of a person. To know Christ means for Paul certain things.

(i) It means to know *the power of His Resurrection.* For Paul the Resurrection was not a past event in history, however amazing. It was not simply something which happened to Jesus, however important it was for Him. It was a living dynamic power which operated on the life of the individual Christian. We cannot know everything that Paul meant by this phrase; but the Resurrection of Christ is the great dynamic in at least three different directions. (*a*) It is the guarantee of the importance of this life and of this body in which we live. It was in the body that Christ rose, and it is this body which He sanctifies (I *Corinthians* 6: 13 ff). The fact of the bodily resurrection of Jesus Christ is the guarantee of the importance of the human body, and of the present life which we live. (*b*) It is the guarantee of immortality and of the life to come (*Romans* 8: 11; I *Corinthians* 15: 14 ff). Because He lives, we shall live also. His conquest is our conquest, and His victory is our victory. (*c*) It is the guarantee that in life and in death and beyond death the presence of the Risen Lord is always with us. It is the proof that His promise to be with us always even unto the end of the world is true. The Resurrection of Christ is the guarantee that this life is worth living, and that the physical body is sacred to God. It is the guarantee that death is not the end of life, but that there is a world beyond. It is the guarantee that nothing in life or in death can separate us from Him.

(ii) It means to know *the fellowship of His sufferings.* Again and again Paul returns to the thought that when the Christian has to suffer, he is in some strange way sharing the very suffering of Christ, and is even filling up the suffering of Christ (*2 Corinthians* 1: 5; 4: 10, 11; *Galatians* 6: 17; *Colossians* 1: 24). Whenever a Christian suffers, whenever he has to bear a cross, he is sharing in the suffering of Christ, and helping to carry the Cross of Christ. To suffer for the faith is not a penalty, it is a privilege, for thereby we share the very work and task of Christ.

(iii) It means to *be so united with Christ that day by day we come more to share in His death, so that finally we share in His Resurrection.* To know Christ is to become so one with Him that we share His every experience. It means that we share the way He walked; that we share the Cross He bore; that we share the death He died; and that finally we share the life He lives for evermore.

To know Christ is not to be skilled in any theoretical or theological knowledge. It is so to experience Him, and so to know Him with such intimacy that in the end we are as united with Him as we are with those whom we love on earth; and that, just as we share their experiences, so we also share His.

PRESSING ON

Philippians 3: 12-16

> Not that I have already obtained this, or that I am already all complete but I press on to try to grasp that for which I have been grasped by Jesus Christ. Brothers, I do not count myself to have obtained; but this one thing I do—forgetting the things which are behind, and reaching out for the things which are in front, I press on towards the goal, in order that I may win the prize which God's upward calling in Christ Jesus is offering to me.

> Let all of you who have graduated in the school of
> Christ have the same attitude of mind to life. And if
> anyone is otherwise minded in any way, this too
> God will reveal to him. Only we must always walk
> according to that standard which we have already
> reached.

THIS passage is punctuated by a word and an idea, whose
meaning it is not so difficult to understand in the Greek
original, but which it is difficult to transfer into English.
It is the word *perfect*. First of all, as the Authorized Version
has it, in verse 12 Paul says that he is not speaking as
though he were already *perfect*; and then again in verse 15
he speaks of those who are *perfect*.

The word is *teleios* and in Greek it has a variety of inter-
related meanings. In by far the most of these meanings
it does not signify what we might call philosophical and
abstract perfection; it signifies a kind of functional perfection. It signifies adequacy for some given purpose.
Let us then list some of its relevant meanings. It means
full-grown in contradistinction to undeveloped; for example,
it is used of a full-grown man as opposed to an undeveloped
youth. It is used to mean *mature in mind*, as opposed to
one who is a beginner in a subject; it therefore means
one who is qualified in a subject as opposed to a mere learner.
When it is used of offerings, it means *without blemish*
and fit to offer God. When it is used of Christians, it often
means *baptized persons who are full members of the Church,*
as opposed to those who are still under instruction and who
are still not qualified to be members of the Church. In
the days of the early Church it is quite often used to describe *martyrs*. A martyr is said to be *perfected by the sword,*
and the day of his death is said to be the day of his
perfecting. The idea is that a man's Christian witness and
maturity cannot go beyond martyrdom.

So when Paul uses it in verse 12, he is saying that he is
not by any means a complete Christian, but he is for
ever pressing on. Then he uses two vivid pictures.

(i) He says that he is trying to grasp that for which he has been grasped by Jesus Christ. That is a wonderful thought. Paul felt that when Jesus Christ stopped him on the Damascus Road, Jesus Christ had a dream and a vision and a purpose for which he grasped Paul; and Paul felt that all his life he was bound to press on, lest he disappoint Jesus and fail Jesus and frustrate the dream and the purpose for which Jesus had grasped him. Every man is grasped by Christ for some purpose; every man is a dream of Jesus. And, therefore, every man must all his life press on so that he may grasp and realize that dream and that purpose for which Christ grasped him.

(ii) To that end Paul says two things. He is forgetting the things which are behind. That is to say, he will never glory in any of his achievements; he will never use any task that he has achieved or any deed that he has done as an excuse for relaxation in the future. In effect Paul is saying that the Christian must forget all that he has done and remember only that which he has still to do. In the Christian life there is no room for a person or a Church which desires to rest upon its laurels. Then he says that he is *reaching out* for the things which are in front. The word he uses is very vivid (*epekteinomenos*). That is the word which is used of a racer going hard for the tape. It describes him with eyes for nothing but the goal. It describes him with arms almost clawing the air, with head forward, and with the body bent and angled to the goal. It describes the man who is going, as we might put it, *flat out* for the finish. So Paul says that in the Christian life we must forget every past achievement and we must remember only the goal which for ever lies ahead.

There is no doubt that Paul is here speaking to the antinomians. The antinomians were those who denied that there was any law at all in the Christian life. They declared that they were within the grace of God, and that, therefore, it did not matter what they did; God would forgive; they were quite safe; no further discipline and no further effort were necessary. Paul is insisting that to the end of the day the Christian life is the life of an athlete pressing onwards to a goal which is always in front.

Then in verse 15 again he used the word *teleios*. This must be the attitude of those who are *teleios*, *perfect* the Authorized Version calls them. What Paul means is: "Anyone who has graduated in Christianity, anyone who has come to be mature in the faith, and who knows what Christianity is, must feel the same, and must recognize the discipline and the effort and the agony of the Christian life." He may perhaps think differently, but, if he is an honest man, God will make it plain to him, that he must never relax his effort or lower his standards, but must press towards the goal, until the end.

As Paul saw it, the Christian is nothing less than the athlete of Christ.

DWELLER ON EARTH BUT CITIZEN OF HEAVEN

Philippians 3: 17-21

> Brothers, unite in imitating me, and keep your gaze on those who live, as you have seen us as an example. For there are many who behave in such a way—I have often spoken to you about them, and I do so now with tears—that they are enemies of the Cross of Christ. Their end is destruction: their god is their belly; that in which they glory is their shame. Men whose whole minds are earthbound! But our citizenship is in heaven, from which we also eagerly await the Lord Jesus Christ as Saviour, for he will refashion the body which we have in this state of our humiliation and make it like his own glorious body, by the working of that power of His whereby He is able to subject all things to Himself.

THERE are few preachers who would dare to make the appeal with which Paul begins this section. J. B. Lightfoot translates it: "Vie with each other in imitating me." Most preachers begin with the serious handicap that they have to say, not, "Do as I do," but, "Do as I say."

Paul could not only say, " Listen to my words," he could also say, " Follow my example." It is worth noting in the passing that Bengel, one of the greatest interpreters of scripture who ever lived, translates this in a different way: " Become fellow-imitators with me in imitating Jesus Christ." Bengel thinks that Paul is inviting the Philippians to join him in imitating Jesus Christ; but it is far more likely—as nearly all other interpreters are agreed—that Paul was able to invite his friends, not simply to listen to him, but also to imitate him.

There were in the Church at Philippi men whose conduct was an open scandal, and who, by their lives, showed themselves to be the enemies of the Cross of Christ. Who they were is not quite certain. But it is quite certain that they lived gluttonous and immoral lives, and used their so-called Christianity to justify themselves. We can only guess who they may have been.

They may have been Gnostics. The Gnostics were heretics who tried to intellectualize Christianity and to make a kind of philosophy out of it. They began with the principle that from the beginning of time there have always been two realities—spirit and matter. Spirit, they said, is altogether good; and matter is altogether evil. It is because the world was created out of this essential evil and flawed matter that sin and evil are in it. Now these Gnostics argued this way. If matter is essentially evil, then the body is essentially evil; and because it is matter, it will remain evil whatever you do with it. Therefore, do what you like with it. Glut and sate its appetites. Since the body is evil anyhow it makes no difference what you do with it. So these Gnostics taught that gluttony and adultery and homosexuality and drunkenness are of no importance, because they only affect the body, and the body does not matter.

There was another party of these Gnostics who held a different kind of doctrine. They argued that a man could not be called a complete man, until he had experienced everything that life had to offer, both good and bad. Therefore, they said, it is a man's duty to plumb the depths of sin just as much as it is to scale the heights of virtue. To such men to sin became nothing less than a duty so that experience might be complete.

Within the Church there were two sets of people to whom these accusations might apply. There were those who distorted the principle of Christian liberty. They said that in Christianity all law was gone, that the Christian had perfect liberty to do what he liked. In other words, they turned Christian liberty into unchristian licence, and gloried in giving their lusts and passions full play. There were those who distorted the Christian doctrine of grace. They said that grace was wide enough to cover every sin and stain; that the love of God was great enough to forgive any sin; therefore, let a man sin as he liked and not worry; it would make no difference to the all-forgiving grace of God.

So the people whom Paul attacks may have been the clever Gnostics who produced specious arguments to justify their sinning; or, they may have been misguided Christians who twisted the loveliest things into justifications for the ugliest sins.

Whoever they were, Paul reminds them of one great truth: " Your citizenship," he says, " is in heaven." Here was a picture the Philippians could understand. Philippi was a Roman colony. These Roman colonies were amazing places. Here and there at strategic military centres the Romans set down their colonies. They were not like modern colonies out in the unexplored wilds; they commanded great road centres, and passes across the hills, and routes by which the armies must march. In such places the Romans set down colonies, whose citizens were mostly soldiers who had served their time—twenty-one years—and who had been rewarded with full citizenship. Now the great characteristic of these Roman colonies was that, wherever they were, they remained fragments of Rome. No matter where they were, Roman dress was worn; Roman magistrates governed them; the Latin tongue was spoken; Roman justice was administered; Roman morals were observed. Even in the ends of the earth these colonies remained unshakably and unalterably Roman. So Paul says to the Philippians, " Just as the Roman colonists never forget that they belong to Rome, you must never forget that you are citizens of heaven; and your conduct must match your citizenship." Wherever the Christian is, his conduct must prove that he is a citizen of the Kingdom of Heaven.

So Paul finishes with the Christian hope. The Christian awaits the coming of Christ, at whose coming everything will be changed. Here the Authorized Version is dangerously misleading. In verse 21 it speaks about our *vile body*. In modern speech that would mean that the body is an utterly evil and horrible thing; but *vile* in 16th Century English still retained the meaning of its derivation from the Latin word *vilis* which in fact means nothing worse than *cheap*, *valueless*. The meaning is that, as we are just now, our bodies are subject to change and decay, weakness, illness and death; they are the bodies of mortal men; the bodies of a state of humiliation compared with the glorious state of the Risen Christ. And, says Paul, the day comes when we will lay aside this mortal body which we now possess and will become like Jesus Christ himself. The hope of the Christian is that the day will come when his humanity will be changed into nothing less than the divinity of Christ himself, and when the necessary lowliness of mortality will be changed into the essential splendour of deathless and eternal life.

GREAT THINGS IN THE LORD

Philippians 4: 1

> So, then, my brothers, whom I love and yearn for, my joy and crown, so stand fast in the Lord, beloved.

HERE is a passage through which there breathes the warmth of Paul's affection for his Philippian friends. He loves them, and he yearns for them. They are his joy and his crown. Those whom he had brought to Christ are his greatest joy, when the shadows are closing about him. Any teacher and any preacher knows what a thrill it is to point at some person who has done well, and to be able to say: " That was one of my boys."

There are vivid pictures behind the word when Paul says that the Philippians are his crown. There are two words for *crown* in Greek, and they have different backgrounds. There is *diadēma*, which means *the royal crown*, the crown of kingship. And there is *stephanos*, which is the word which is used here. *Stephanos* has two backgrounds. (i) It was the crown of the victorious athlete at the Greek games. It was made of wild olive leaves, interwoven with green parsley, and bay leaves. To win that crown was the summit and the peak of the athlete's ambition. (ii) It was the crown with which guests were crowned when they sat at a banquet or feast, at some time of great festive joy. It is as if Paul said that the Philippians are the crown of all his labour and his toil and his efforts; he was the athlete of Christ and they were his crown. It is as if Paul said that at the final banquet of God the Philippians were his festal crown. There is no joy in the world like bringing another soul to Jesus Christ.

Three times in the first three verses of this fourth chapter the words *in the Lord* occur. There are three great commands which Paul gives *in the Lord*, and which can only be fulfilled *in the Lord*.

(i) The Philippians are *to stand fast* in the Lord. Only with Jesus Christ can a man resist the seductions of temptation, and the weakness of cowardice. The word which Paul uses for *stand fast* (*stēkete*) is the word which would be used for a soldier standing fast in the shock of battle, with the enemy surging down upon him. We know very well that there are some people in whose company it is easy to do the wrong thing, and there are some people in whose company it is easy to resist the wrong thing. Sometimes when we look back and remember some time when we made a mistake or took the wrong turning or fell to temptation or shamed ourselves, we say wistfully, when we think of someone whom we love: " If only he or she had been there, it would never have happened." Our only safety against temptation is to be *in the Lord*, always to remember Him, always to walk with Him, always to feel His presence around us and about us.

> In vain the surge's angry shock,
>   In vain the drifting sands:
> Unharmed upon the eternal Rock
>   The eternal City stands.

The Church and the individual Christian can only stand fast when they stand in Christ.

(ii) Paul bids Euodia and Syntyche to be *of one mind* in the Lord. There can be no unity, unless that unity is in Christ. People will never love each other, unless they love Christ. In ordinary human affairs it repeatedly happens that the most diverse people are held together in a common fellowship because they all give allegiance to a great leader. Their loyalty to each other depends entirely on their loyalty to the leader. Take the leader away, and the whole group would disintegrate into isolated and often warring units. Men can never love each other, until they love Jesus Christ. The brotherhood of man is impossible without the lordship of Jesus Christ.

(iii) Paul bids the Philippians *to rejoice* in the Lord. The one thing that all men need to learn about joy is that joy has nothing to do with material things, or with a man's outward circumstances. It is the simple fact of human experience that a man living in the lap of luxury can be wretched, and a man in the depths of poverty can overflow with joy. A man upon whom life has apparently inflicted no blows at all can be gloomily or peevishly discontented, and a man upon whom life has inflicted every possible blow can be serene in his indestructible joy. In his rectorial address to the students of St. Andrews University, J. M. Barrie quoted the immortal letter which Captain Scott of the Antarctic wrote to him, when the chill breath of death was already on his expedition: " We are in a very comfortless spot. . . . We are in a desperate state—feet frozen, etc., no fuel, and a long way from food, but it would do your heart good to be in our tent, to hear our songs and our cheery conversation." The secret is this—it is one of the basic laws of life that happiness depends not on things or on places, but always on persons. If we are with the right person, nothing else matters; and if we are not with the right person, nothing else can make up for that absence. In the presence of Jesus Christ, in the Lord, the greatest of all friends and lovers is with us; nothing can separate us from that presence, and in Him nothing can take away our joy.

HEALING THE BREACHES

Philippians 4: 2, 3

I urge Euodia and I urge Syntyche to agree in the Lord. Yes, and I ask you too, true comrade in my work, help these women, because they toiled with me in the gospel, together with Clement, and my other fellow-labourers, whose names are in the book of life.

THIS is one of these passages about which we would very much like to know more. There is obvious drama behind it; there is heartbreak and there are great deeds behind it; but of the *dramatis personae* we know nothing, and can only guess. First of all, there are certain problems to be settled in regard to the names in the passage. The Authorized Version speaks of *Euodias* and Syntyche. Syntyche is a woman's name, and *Euodias* would be a man's name. There was an ancient conjecture that Euodias and Syntyche were the Philippian gaoler and his wife

(*Acts* 16: 25-34): that they had become leading figures in the Church at Philippi, and that they had quarrelled. But it is certain that the name is not *Euodias* but *Euodia*, as indeed the Revised Version, Moffatt, and the American Revised Standard Version all print it; and *Euodia* is a woman's name. Therefore, Euodia and Syntyche were two women who had quarrelled.

It may well have been that Euodia and Syntyche were two women in whose homes two of the house congregations of Philippi met. It is very interesting to see women playing so leading a part in the affairs of one of the early congregations. In Greece women remained very much in the background. It was the aim of the Greeks that a respectable woman should "see as little, hear as little and ask as little as possible." A respectable woman never appeared on the street alone; she had her own apartments in the house, and never joined the male members of the family even for meals. Least of all had she any part in public life. But Philippi was in Macedonia, and in Macedonia things were very different. In Macedonia women had a freedom and a place in life which they had nowhere in the rest of Greece.

We can see that emerging even in the narrative of *Acts* which relates Paul's work in Macedonia. In Philippi, Paul's first contact was with the meeting for prayer by a riverside, and he spoke to the women who resorted there (*Acts* 16: 13). Lydia was obviously a leading figure in Philippi (*Acts* 16: 14). In Thessalonica many of the chief women were won for Christianity, and the same happened in Berea (*Acts* 17: 4, 12). The evidence of inscriptions points the same way. A wife erects a tomb for herself and for her husband out of their joint earnings, so she must have been in business. We even find monuments erected to women by public bodies. We know that in many of the Pauline Churches, as, for example, in Corinth, women had to be content with a very subordinate place. But it is well worth remembering, when we are thinking of Paul's attitude to women in the Church, and of the place of women in the early Church, that in the Macedonian Churches women clearly had a leading place.

There is another matter of doubt here. In this passage someone is addressed who is called in the Authorized Version *true yokefellow*. It is just barely possible that *yokefellow* is in fact a proper name—*Sunzugos*. The word for true is *gnēsios*, which means genuine. And there may just possibly be a pun here. Paul may be saying: " I ask you, Sunzugos—and you are rightly named—to help." He may be saying: "You are *Sunzugos*—yokefellow—by name, and *sunzugos*—yokefellow—by nature." If *sunzugos* is not a proper name, no one knows who the person is, who is being addressed. All kinds of suggestions and guesses have been made. It has been suggested that the yoke-fellow is Paul's wife, that he is the husband of Euodia or Syntyche who is called on to help his wife to mend the quarrel, that it is Lydia who is meant, that it is Timothy, or Silas, or the minister of the Philippian Church. Maybe the best suggestion is that the reference is to Epaproditus, the bearer of the letter, and that Paul is not only entrusting him with the letter, but also with the task of making peace at Philippi. Of the person who bears the one other name, Clement, we know nothing. There was later a famous Clement who was bishop of Rome, and who may have known Paul, but the name is a common name, and of its bearer we know nothing.

There are two things to be noted here.

(i) It is significant to see that when there was a quarrel in the Church at Philippi, Paul mobilized the whole re-sources of the Church to mend it. Paul thought no effort too great to maintain the peace of the Church. A quarrelling Church is not a Church at all, for a quarrelling Church is a Church from which Christ has been shut out, and to which He cannot gain access. No man can be at peace with God and at variance with his fellow-men.

(ii) It is a grim thought that all we know about Euodia and Syntyche is that they were two women who had quarrelled! It makes us think. Suppose our life was to be summed up in one sentence, what would that sentence be? Suppose we were to go down to history with one thing known about us, what would that one thing be? Clement goes down to history as the peacemaker; Euodia and Syntyche go down to history as the breakers of the peace. What would be the one sentence verdict on our life in the world and in the Church?

THE MARKS OF THE CHRISTIAN LIFE

Philippians 4: 4, 5

> Rejoice in the Lord at all times. I will say it again—Rejoice! Let your gracious gentleness be known to all men. The Lord is near.

HERE Paul sets before the Philippians two great qualities of the Christian life.

(i) The first is the quality of joy. " Rejoice," says Paul. " I will say it again—Rejoice! " It is as if he said, " Rejoice! " And suddenly there flashed into his mind a picture of all that was to come. He himself was lying in prison with almost certain death awaiting him; the Philippians were setting out on the Christian way, and dark days, and dangers, and persecutions inevitably lay ahead. So Paul says, " I know what I'm saying. I've thought of everything that can possibly happen. And still I say it—Rejoice! " The Christian joy is independent of all things on earth, because the Christian joy has its source in the continual presence of Christ. Two lovers are always happy when they are together, no matter where they are. That is why the Christian can never lose his joy, because he can never lose Jesus Christ.

(ii) Paul goes on, as the Authorized Version has it: " Let your moderation be known to all men." The word that the Authorized Version translates *moderation* is one of the most untranslatable of all Greek words. The noun is *epieikeia* and the adjective is *epieikēs*. The difficulty of translating this word can be seen in the number of translations of it. To go back first of all to the old translations —Wicliffe translates it *patience*; Tyndale, *softness*; Cranmer, *softness*; The Geneva Bible, *the patient mind*; the Rheims Bible, *modesty*. Of the modern versions, the Revised Version translates it *forbearance*, but in the margin suggests *gentleness*. Moffatt translates it *forbearance*, and Weymouth, the *forbearing spirit*. C. Kingsley Williams has: "Let all the world know that you will *meet a man halfway*."

Let us see how the Greeks themselves explained this word. The Greeks said that this quality of *epieikeia* was "justice and something better than justice." They said that *epieikeia* ought to come in in those cases when strict justice becomes unjust because of its generality. A law or a regulation or a condition may be in itself perfectly just; but there may be cases in individual instances, where a perfectly just law becomes unjust, or where, to use modern terms, justice is not the same thing as equity. A man has the quality of *epieikeia* if he knows when *not* to apply the strict letter of the law, if he knows when to relax justice and to introduce mercy. Let us take a simple example of this, an example which meets every teacher almost every day. Here are two students. We correct their examination papers. We apply justice, and we find that the one has eighty per cent and the other has fifty per cent. From the point of view of justice there is nothing to be said against these marks. But we go a little further; we find that the man who got eighty per cent has been able to do his work in ideal conditions; he has books, he has leisure, he has peace to study, a room where he can have quiet, he has no worries and no distractions, everything has been in his favour. We find that the man who got fifty per cent comes from a poor home, where his equipment is the bare minimum, or he may have been ill and in pain, or he may have recently come through some time of sorrow or of stress or strain, that, in fact, all the conditions were against him. In justice this man deserves fifty per cent and no more; but *epieikeia* will value his paper far higher than that; when we go beyond justice he in equity deserves far more. *Epieikeia* is the quality of the man who knows that rules and regulations are not the last word; it is the quality of the man who knows when not to apply the letter of the law. A kirk session may sit with the book of practice and procedure on the table in front of it, and every one of its decisions may be taken in strict accordance with the law of the Church; but anyone knows that there are times when the welfare of some individual, and indeed the welfare of the whole Church, and the Christian treatment of some situation, demands that that book of practice and procedure should remain shut, and should not be regarded as the last word. The Christian, as Paul sees it, is the man who knows that for him there is something beyond justice. When the woman taken in adultery was brought before Him, Jesus could have applied the letter of the Law, and she should, according to it, have been stoned; but He went beyond justice. As far as justice goes, there is not one of us who deserves anything but the condemnation of God, but God goes far beyond justice. Paul lays it down that the mark of a Christian in his personal relationships with his fellow-men must be that he knows when, and when not, to insist on justice, and that he always remembers that there is something which is beyond justice, and which makes a man like God.

And why should a man be like this? Why should he have this joy and this gracious gentleness in his life? Because, says Paul, the Lord is at hand. If we remember the coming triumph of Christ, then we can never lose our hope and our joy. If we remember that life is short, and that the end comes, then we will not wish to enforce the stern justice which so often divides men; we will wish to deal with men in love, as we hope that God will deal with us. Justice is human, but *epieikeia* is divine.

THE LETTER TO THE PHILIPPIANS

THE PEACE OF BELIEVING PRAYER

Philippians 4: 6, 7

> Do not worry about anything; but in everything with
> prayer and supplication, with thanksgiving, let your
> requests be made known to God. And the peace of
> God, which surpasses all human thought, will stand
> sentinel over your hearts and minds in Christ Jesus.

FOR the Philippians life was bound to be a worrying thing.
Even to be a human being, to be involved in the human
situation, to be vulnerable to all the chances and the
changes of this mortal life, is in itself a worrying thing;
and in the early Church, to the normal worry of the human
situation, there was added the worry of being a Christian,
in a situation in which the man who was a Christian took
his life in his hands. Paul's solution for worry is prayer.
As M. R. Vincent puts it: " Peace is the fruit of believing
prayer." In this passage there is in brief compass a whole
philosophy of prayer.

(i) Paul stresses that we can take everything to God in
prayer. It is in *everything* that we are to make prayer and
supplication with thanksgiving. As it has been beautifully
put: " There is nothing too great for God's power; and
nothing too small for His fatherly care." A child can take
anything great or small, to a parent; so we can take
anything to God. A little child is quite sure that whatever
happens to him is of interest to his father and mother.
His little triumphs and his little disappointments, his
passing cuts and bruises, the many things that he would
like—he tells them all, never doubting that his parents
will be ready and willing to listen to him. We should be
exactly so with God.

(ii) We can bring our prayers, our supplications and our
requests to God. We can pray for *ourselves*. We can pray
for forgiveness for the *past*, for the things we need in the
present, and for help and guidance for the *future*. We can
take our own past and present and future, with all our shame
with all our needs, with all our fears, into the presence of

God. We can pray for *others*. We can commend to God's care those near and far who are for ever within our memories and within our hearts.

(iii) Paul lays it down that " thanksgiving must be the universal accompaniment of prayer." It was his conviction that every prayer must include thanksgiving. The Christian must feel, as it has been put, that all his life he is, " as it were, suspended between past and present blessings." Every prayer must surely include thanks for the great privilege of prayer. Surely we can never forget to be grateful for this privilege of being able to take everything to God in prayer. Paul insists that we must give thanks *in everything*, in laughter and in tears, in sorrows and in joys alike. That implies two things. It implies *gratitude*, but it also implies *perfect submission* to the will of God. It is only when we are fully convinced that God is working all things together for good that we can really feel to Him the perfect gratitude which believing prayer demands.

When we pray, we must always remember three things. We must remember *the love of God*, which ever seeks and desires only what is best for us. We must remember *the wisdom of God*, which alone knows what is best for us. We must remember *the power of God*, which alone can bring to pass that which is best for us. He who prays with a perfect belief and trust in the love, the wisdom and the power of God will find God's peace.

The result of believing prayer is that the peace of God will stand like a sentinel on guard upon our hearts. The word that Paul uses (*phrourein*) is the military word for *standing on guard*. That peace of God, says Paul, as the Authorized Version has it, *passes understanding*. That does not mean that the peace of God is such a mystery that man's mind cannot understand it, although that also is true. It means that the peace of God is so precious that man's mind, with all its skill and all its knowledge and all its understanding, can never contrive it or find it or produce it. It is utterly and entirely beyond man's ability to obtain by himself. This peace can never be of man's contriving; it is only of God's giving. The way to peace is to take ourselves and all whom we hold dear, to take all life, and to place them and ourselves and it trustingly in prayer in the hands of God.

TRUE COUNTRIES OF THE MIND

Philippians 4: 8, 9

Finally, brothers, whatever things are true, whatever things have the dignity of holiness on them, whatever things are just, whatever things are pure, whatever things are winsome, whatever things are fair-spoken, if there are any things which men count excellence, and if there are any things which bring men praise, think of the value of these things. Practise these things which you have learned and received, and heard and seen in me, and the God of peace will be with you.

THE human mind will always set itself on something, and Paul wished to be quite sure that the Philippians would set their minds on the right things. This is something of the utmost importance, because it is a law of life that, if a man thinks of something often enough and long enough, he will come to the stage when he cannot stop thinking about it. His thoughts will be quite literally in a groove out of which he cannot jerk them. It is, therefore, of the first importance that a man should set his thoughts upon the fine things. So here Paul makes a list of the fine things on which men's thoughts should be set.

There are the things which are *true*. There are many thing in this world which are deceptive and illusory; they promise that which they can never perform. They offer a man a specious peace and happiness which, in fact, they can never supply. A man should always set his thoughts on the things on which he can rely, the things which will not fail him, or let him down.

There are the things which are, as the Authorized Version has it, *honest*. This is an archaic use of the word *honest* in the sense of *honourable*, as the American Revised Standard Version translates it. The Authorized Version suggests in the margin *venerable*. The Revised Version has *honourable* and suggests in the margin *reverend*. Moffatt has *worthy*. It can be seen from all this that this is a difficult word to translate. It is the word *semnos*. It is the word which is characteristically used of the gods; it is the word which is used of the temples of the gods. When it is used to describe a man, it describes a person, who, as it has been said, moves throughout the world as if the whole world were the temple of God. Matthew Arnold suggested the translation *nobly serious*. But the word really describes *that which has the dignity of holiness upon it*. There are things in this world which are flippant and cheap, things which are attractive to the light-minded; but it is on the things which are grave and serious and dignified that the Christian will set his mind.

There are things which are *just*. The word is *dikaios*, and the Greeks defined the man who is *dikaios*, the righteous man, as the man who gives to gods and men that which is their due. In other words, we may put it this way— *dikaios* is the word of *duty faced and duty done*. There are those who set their minds and thoughts on pleasure, comfort, easy things and easy ways. The Christian's thoughts are on duty to man and duty to God.

There are the things which are *pure*. The word is *hagnos* and it describes that which is morally pure, that which is undefiled. When it is used ceremonially, it describes that which has been so cleansed that it is fit to be brought into the presence of God, and used in the service of God. This world is full of things which are sordid and shabby and soiled and smutty. Many a man gets his mind into such a state that it soils everything of which it thinks. The Christian's mind is set on the things which are pure; his thoughts are so clean that they can stand even the scrutiny of God.

There are the things which the Authorized Version calls *lovely*. Moffatt translates *attractive*. *Winsome* is the best translation of all. The word in Greek is *prosphilēs*, and it might be paraphrased as *that which calls forth love*. There are those whose minds are so set on vengeance and punishment that they call forth bitterness and fear in others. There are those whose minds are so set on criticism and rebuke that they call forth resentment in others. The mind of the Christian is set on the lovely things—kindness, sympathy, forbearance, love—so that the Christian is a winsome person, whom to see is to love.

There are the things which are, as the Authorized Version has it, *of good report*. In the margin the Revised Version suggests *gracious*. Moffatt has *high-toned*. The American Revised Standard Version has *gracious*. C. Kingsley Williams has *whatever has a good name*. It is not easy to get at the meaning of this word. It literally means *fair-speaking*; but it has one special connection; it is connected with the holy silence at the beginning of a sacrifice in the presence of the gods. It might not be going too far to say that it describes *the things which are fit for God to hear*. There are ugly words, and false words, and impure words, and far too many of them, in this world. On the lips of the Christian, and in the mind of the Christian there will be only words which are fit for God to hear.

Paul goes on, *if there be any virtue*. Both Moffatt and the American Revised Standard Version use the word *excellence* instead of *virtue*. The word is *aretē*. The odd fact is that *aretē* was one of the great classical words, and yet Paul usually seems deliberately to avoid it, and this is the only time it occurs in his writings. In classical thought it described every kind of excellence. It could describe the excellence of the ground in a field, the excellence of a tool for its purpose, the physical excellence of an animal, the excellence of the courage of a soldier, and the virtue of a man. Lightfoot suggests that with this word Paul calls in as an ally all that was excellent in the pagan background of his friends. It is as if he said, " If the old pagan idea of excellence, in which you were brought up, has any influence over you—think of that." It is as if he said, " Think of your past life at its very highest, to spur you on to the new heights of the Christian way." The world has its impurities and its degradations, but the world has also its nobilities and its chivalries, and it is of the high things that the Christian must think.

Finally, in the list Paul says, *if there be any praise.* In a sense it is true that the Christian never thinks of the praise of men, but in another sense it is true that every good man is moved and uplifted by the praise of good men. So Paul says that the Christian will live in such a way that he will neither conceitedly desire nor foolishly despise the praise of men whose praise is a thing to be desired.

THE TRUE TEACHING AND THE TRUE GOD

Philippians 4: 8, 9 (*continued*)

In this passage Paul lays down the way of true teaching.

He speaks of the things which the Philippians have *learned.* These are the things in which he personally instructed them. This stands for the personal interpretation of the gospel and of its truth which Paul brought to them. He speaks of the things which the Philippians have *received.* The word is *paralambanein,* and that word characteristically means to accept and to receive a fixed tradition. This then stands for the accepted doctrine and teaching of the Church which Paul had handed on to them. From these two words we learn that teaching consists of two things; it consists of handing on to men the accepted body of truth and doctrine which the whole Church holds; and it consists of illuminating that body of doctrine by the personal interpretation and the personal instruction of the teacher. If we would teach or preach we must know the accepted body of the Church's doctrine; and then we must pass it through our own minds, and hand it on to others, both in its own

simplicity and in the significances which our own experiences and our own thinking have given to it.

But Paul goes further than that. He tells the Philippians
to copy that which they have heard and seen in himself.
There are tragically few teachers and preachers who can
speak like that. And yet it remains true that personal
example is an essential part of teaching. The teacher must
practise the doctrine which he professes, and must demonstrate in action the truth which he expresses in words.

Finally, in this section, Paul tells his Philippian friends
that, if they faithfully do all this, the God of peace will
be with them. It is of great interest to study Paul's titles
for God.

(i) To Paul, God is *the God of peace*. This, in fact, is his
favourite title for God (*Romans* 16: 20; I *Corinthians*
14: 33; I *Thessalonians* 5: 23). To a Jew peace was never
merely a negative thing; it was never merely the absence
of trouble; peace was everything which makes for a man's
highest good. Only in the friendship of God can a man find
life as life was meant to be. But also to a Jew this peace
issued specially in *right relationships*. It is only by the
grace of God that we can enter into a right relationship
with God and with our fellow men. The God of peace is
the God who is able to make life what it was meant to be
by enabling us to enter into fellowship with Himself and
fellowship with our fellow men.

(ii) To Paul God is the *God of hope* (*Romans* 15: 13).
Belief in God is the only thing which can keep a man from
the ultimate despair. Only the sense of the grace of God
can keep a man from despairing about himself; and only
the sense of the over-ruling providence of God can keep
a man from despairing about the world. The Psalmist
sang: "Why are thou cast down, O my soul? . . . Hope
thou in God: for I shall yet praise Him, who is the health
of my countenance and my God" (*Psalm* 42: 11; 43: 5).
F. W. Faber wrote:

> For right is right, since God is God,
>   And right the day must win;
> To doubt would be disloyalty,
>   To falter would be sin.

The hope of the Christian is an indestructible hope because it is founded on the eternal God.

(iii) To Paul God is *the God of patience, of comfort, and of consolation* (*Romans* 15: 5; *2 Corinthians* 1: 3; *consolation* and *comfort* both translate the same Greek word *paraklēsis*). Here we have two great words. Patience is in Greek *hupomonē*, which never means simply the ability to sit down and bear things; it means to rise up and conquer things. It does not mean simply to accept things; it means to accept them, and to change them into glory. God is the God who gives us the power to use any experience and any situation in life to lend greatness and glory to life. God is the God in whom we learn to use joy and sorrow, success and failure, achievement and disappointment alike, to enrich and to ennoble life, to make us more useful to others, and to bring us nearer to Himself. *Consolation* and *comfort* are the Greek word *paraklēsis*. *Paraklēsis* is far more than soothing sympathy; it is encouragement. *Paraklēsis* is the help which not only puts an arm of comfort round a man, but which sends him out to face the world; it not only wipes the tears from his eyes, it enables him to face the world with steady eyes. *Paraklēsis* is comfort and strength combined. God is the God in whom any situation becomes our glory, and in whom a man finds strength to go on gallantly when life has fallen in.

(iv) God is *the God of love and peace* (*2 Corinthians* 13: 11). Here we are at the heart of the matter. Behind everything is the love of God, that love which will never let us go, that love which bears with all our sinning, that love which will never cast us off, that love which never sentimentally weakens, but always manfully strengthens a man for the battle and the struggle of this life.

Peace, hope, patience, comfort, love—these were the things which Paul found in God. Indeed, " our sufficiency is of God " (2 *Corinthians* 3: 5).

THE SECRET OF TRUE CONTENT

Philippians 4: 10-13

I rejoiced greatly in the Lord that now at length you have made your thoughtfulness for me to blossom again. That was a matter indeed about which you were always thoughtful, but you had no opportunity. Not that I speak as if I were in a state of want, for I have learned to be content in whatever situation I am. I know both how to live in the humblest circumstances, and how to have far more than enough. In everything and in all things I have learned the secret of being well fed and of being hungry, of having more than enough and of having less than enough. I can do all things through Him who infuses strength into me.

As the letter draws to an end Paul generously expresses his gratitude for the gift which the Philippians had sent to him. He knew that he had always been much in the minds and hearts and thoughts, but circumstances had up till now given them no opportunity to show their mindfulness of him.

It was not that he was dissatisfied with his own state, for he had learned the gift of *content*. It is here that Paul uses one of the great words of pagan ethics. He says that he had learned to be *autarkēs*, which means *entirely self-sufficient*. This *autarkeia*, this self-sufficiency was the highest aim of Stoic ethics. By *autarkeia* the Stoics meant a state of mind in which a man was absolutely and entirely independent of all things and of all people, a state in which a man had taught himself to need nothing and to need no one. The Stoic proposed to reach that state by a certain pathway of the mind. (i) He proposed to eliminate all desire. The Stoic rightly believed that contentment did not consist in possessing much but in wanting little

" If you want to make a man happy," they said, "add not to his possessions, but take away from his desires." Socrates was once asked who was the wealthiest man. He answered: " He who is content with least, for *autarkeia*, *self-sufficiency*, is nature's wealth." The Stoic believed that the only way to content was to abolish all desire until a man had come to a stage when nothing and no one were essential to him. (ii) The Stoic proposed to eliminate all emotion, all feeling, until he had come to a stage when he did not care what happened either to himself or to anyone else. Epictetus says, "Begin with a cup or a household utensil; if it breaks, say, ' I don't care.' Go on to a horse or pet dog; if anything happens to it, say, ' I don't care.' Go on to yourself, and if you are hurt or injured in any way, say, ' I don't care.' If you go on long enough, and if you try hard enough, you will come to a stage when you can watch your nearest and dearest suffer and die, and say, ' I don't care.' " The Stoic aim was to abolish every feeling and emotion of the human heart. (iii) How was this to be done? It was to be done by a deliberate act of will which saw in everything the will of God. The Stoic believed that literally nothing could happen to him or to anyone else which was not the will of God. However painful it might be, however disastrous it might seem, it was God's will. It was, therefore, useless to struggle against it; a man must will himself, and steel himself into accepting everything.

In order to achieve content the Stoic abolished all desires and eliminated all emotions. Love was rooted out of life, and caring was forbidden. As T. R. Glover said, " The Stoics made of the heart a desert, and called it a peace."

We see at once the difference between the Stoics and Paul. The Stoic said, " I will learn content by a deliberate act of my own will." Paul said, " I can do all things through Christ who infuses His strength into me." For the Stoic contentment was a human achievement; for Paul it was a divine gift. The Stoic was *self-sufficient*; but Paul was

God-sufficient. Stoicism failed because it was inhuman; Christianity succeeded because it was rooted in the divine. Paul could face anything; he could have nothing and he could have all things; it made no difference, because, in any situation he had Jesus Christ. The man who walks with Christ and lives in Christ can cope with anything·

THE VALUE OF THE GIFT

Philippians 4: 14-20

All the same, I am most grateful to you for your readiness to share the burden of my troubles. You too, know, Philippians, that in the beginning of the gospel, when I left Macedonia, no Church entered into partnership with me in the matter of giving and receiving except you alone, for in Thessalonica not merely once but twice you sent to help my need. It is not that I am looking for the gift; but I am looking for the fruit which increases to your credit. I have enough and more than enough of everything. I am fully supplied, now that I have received from Epaphroditus the gifts which came from you, the odour of a sweet savour, an acceptable sacrifice, well-pleasing to God. And my God will gloriously supply every need of yours according to His wealth in Jesus Christ. Glory be to our God and Father for ever and ever. Amen.

THE generosity of the Philippian Church to Paul went back a long way. In *Acts* 16 and 17 we read how Paul preached the gospel in Philippi, and then moved on to Thessalonica and Berea. As far back as that the Philippian Church had given practical proof of its love for Paul. Paul was in a position in regard to the Philippians that he was not with any other Church. From no other Church had he ever accepted any gift or any help. It was in fact that very circumstance which irritated and annoyed the Corinthians (2 *Corinthians* 11: 7-12). There was a bond between him and them which existed between him and no other Church.

Then Paul says a fine thing. He says, " It is not that I desire a gift and a present from you for my own sake, although your gift touches my heart and makes me very glad. I don't need anything, for I have more than enough. But I am glad that you gave me a gift for your own sake, for your kindness and your thoughtfulness and your generosity will stand greatly to your credit in the sight of God." Their generosity made him glad, not for his own sake, but for their sake. Then he uses words which turn the gift of the Philippians, not into a gift to Paul, but into a sacrifice to God. " The odour of a sweet savour," he calls it. That was a regular Old Testament phrase for a sacrifice which was welcome and acceptable to God. It is as if the smell of the sacrifice was sweet in the nostrils of God (*Genesis* 8: 21; *Leviticus* 1: 9, 13, 17). Paul's joy in the gift is not in what it did for him, but in what it did for them. It was not that he did not value the gift for its own sake; it was not that he did not appreciate it for what it did for him; but his greatest joy was that the gift of the Philippian Church, and the love which prompted it, were dear to God.

And in a last sentence, Paul lays it down that no gift ever made any man the poorer. The wealth of God is open to those who love God and who love their fellow men. The giver of a gift does not make himself poorer; he makes himself richer, for his own gift opens to him the gifts and the riches of God.

GREETINGS

Philippians 4: 21-23

> Greet in Christ Jesus every one of God's dedicated people. The brothers who are with me send you their greetings, especially those of Caesar's household. The grace of the Lord Jesus Christ be with your spirit.

So the letter comes to the end with greetings. In this final section there is one intensely interesting phrase.

Paul sends special greetings from the Christian brothers who are of *Caesar's household*. It is important to understand this phrase rightly. It does not mean those who are of the personal family of Caesar, those who are of Caesar's kith and kin. Caesar's household was the regular phrase for what we would call the Imperial Civil Service. All over the world there were members of Caesar's household. The palace officials, the secretaries, the people who had charge of the imperial revenues, those who were responsible for the day to day administration of the empire, all that vast staff and entourage which we would call the civil service were Caesar's household. It is of the greatest interest to note that even as early as this Christianity had penetrated right into the very centre of the Roman government. Even amongst those who ruled and administered the empire of Rome there were Christians. There is hardly any sentence which shows more how Christianity had infiltrated even into the highest positions in the empire. It was to be another three hundred years before Christianity became the religion of the empire, but already the first signs of the ultimate triumph of Christ were to be seen. The crucified Galilaean carpenter had already begun to rule those who ruled the greatest empire in the world.

And so the letter ends: " The grace of the Lord Jesus Christ be with your spirit." The Philippians had sent their gifts to Paul. Paul had only one gift to send to them— his blessing. But what greater gift can we give to any man than to remember him in our prayers?

THE LETTER TO THE COLOSSIANS

THE LETTER TO THE COLOSSIANS

INTRODUCTION

The Towns of the Lycus Valley

About one hundred miles from Ephesus, in the valley of the River Lycus, near where it joins the Maeander, there once stood three important cities—Laodicaea, Hierapolis and Colosse. Originally they had been Phrygian cities, but now they were part of the Roman province of Asia. They stood almost within sight of each other. Hierapolis and Laodicaea stood one on either side of the valley with the River Lycus flowing between; they were only six miles apart, and they were in full view of each other. The third city, Colosse, straddled the river, twelve miles further up.

The Lycus Valley had two remarkable characteristics.

(i) It was notorious for earthquakes. Strabo describes it by the curious adjective *euseistos*, which in English means *good for earthquakes*. More than once Laodicaea had been destroyed by an earthquake, but she was a city so rich and so independent that she had risen from the ruins without the financial help which the Roman government had offered. As the John who wrote the *Revelation* was to say of her, in her own eyes she was rich and had need of nothing (*Revelation* 3: 17).

(ii) The waters of the River Lycus and of its tributaries were impregnated with chalk. This chalk gathered, and all over the countryside built up the most amazing natural formations. Lightfoot writes in description of that area: " Ancient monuments are buried; fertile land is overlaid; rivers beds choked up and streams diverted; fantastic grottoes and cascades and archways of stone are formed, by this strange, capricious power, at once destructive and creative, working silently throughout the ages. Fatal to vegetation, these incrustations spread like a stony shroud over the ground. Gleaming like glaciers on the hillside, they attract the eye of the traveller at a distance of twenty miles, and form a singularly striking feature in scenery of more than common beauty and impressiveness."

A Wealthy Area

In spite of these things this was a wealthy area. It was famous for two closely allied trades. Volcanic ground is always fertile ground; and the part of the ground which was not covered by the chalky incrustations was magnificent pasture land. On these pastures there were great flocks of sheep, and the whole area was perhaps the greatest centre of the woollen industry in the world. Laodicaea was specially famous for the production of garments of the finest quality. The allied trade was the dyeing trade. There was some quality in those chalky waters which made them specially suitable for dyeing cloth, and Colosse was so famous for this trade that a certain dye was called by its name.

So, then, these three cities stood in a district of considerable geographical interest and of great commercial prosperity.

The Unimportant City

Originally the three cities had been of equal importance, but as the years went on their ways parted. Laodicaea became the political centre of the district and the financial headquarters of the whole area, a city of splendid prosperity. Hierapolis had become a great trade-centre, and a notable spa. In that volcanic area there were many chasms in the ground from which there came hot vapours and springs, which were famous for their medicinal quality; and people came in their thousands to Hierapolis to bathe in them and to drink the waters.

Colosse had at one time been as great as the other two. Behind her rose the Cadmus range of mountains and she commanded the roads to the mountain passes. Both Xerxes and Cyrus had halted there with their invading armies, and Herodotus had called her " a great city of Phrygia." But for some reason or other the glory had departed. How great that departure was can be seen from the fact that Hierapolis and Laodicaea are both to this day clearly discernible because of the ruins of the great buildings which still stand; but there is not a stone to show where Colosse stood, and her site can only be guessed at. Even when Paul wrote Colosse was a small town; and Lightfoot says of her that she was the most unimportant town to which Paul ever wrote a letter.

But the fact remains that in this town of Colosse there had arisen a heresy, which, if it had been allowed to develop unchecked, might well have been the ruination of the Christian faith.

The Jews in Phrygia

There is one other fact which must be added to complete the picture of the situation. These three cities stood in an area in which there were many Jews amongst the population. Many years before Antiochus the Great had transported two thousand Jewish families from Babylon and Mesopotamia into the regions of Lydia and Phrygia. These Jews had settled there and had prospered, and, as always happens in such a case, more of their fellow countrymen had come into the area to share their prosperity. So many Jews came to the area that the stricter Jews of Palestine lamented the number of Jews who left the rigours of their ancestral Palestine for " the wines and baths of Phrygia."

The number of Jews who resided there can be seen from the following historical incident. Laodicaea, as we have seen, was the administrative centre of the district. In the year 62 B.C., Flaccus was the Roman governor resident there. He sought to put a stop to the practice of the Jews of sending money out of the province to pay the Temple tax. He did so by placing an embargo on the export of currency from the province. And in his own part of the province alone he seized as contraband no less than twenty pounds of gold, destined to be sent to the Temple at Jerusalem. That amount of gold would represent the Temple tax of no fewer than 11,000 people. And since women and children were exempt from the tax, and since many Jews would successfully evade the capture of their money, we may well put the Jewish population as high as almost 50,000 people.

The Church at Colosse

The Christian Church at Colosse was a Church which Paul had not himself founded and which he had never visited. He classes the Colossians and the Laodicaeans with those who had never seen his face in the flesh (2: 1). But no doubt the founding of the Church sprang from Paul's directing. During Paul's three years stay in Ephesus the whole province of Asia was evangelized, so that all its inhabitants, both Jews and Greeks, heard the word of the Lord (*Acts* 19: 10). As we have already seen, Colosse was about one hundred miles from Ephesus, and it was, no doubt, in that campaign of expansion that the Colossian Church was founded. We do not know who the founder of the Church at Colosse was; but it may well have been Epaphras, who is described as Paul's fellow-servant and the faithful minister of the Colossian Church, and who is later connected also with Hierapolis and Laodicaea (1: 7; 4: 12, 13). If Epaphras was not the founder of the Christian Church there, he was certainly the minister in charge of the area.

A Gentile Church

It is clear that the Colossian Church was mainly a Gentile Church. The phrase *aliens and enemies in your mind* (1: 21) is the kind of phrase which Paul regularly uses of those who had once been strangers to the covenant of promise. In 1: 27 he speaks of making known the mystery of Christ among the Gentiles, when the reference is clearly to the Colossians themselves. In 3: 5-7 he gives a list of their sins before they became Christians, and the sins are characteristically Gentile sins. We may conclude that the membership of the Church at Colosse was largely composed of Gentiles.

The Threat to the Church

It must have been Epaphras who brought to Paul, in prison in Rome, news of the situation which was developing in Colosse. Much of the news that Epaphras brought was good. Paul is grateful for news of their faith in Christ and their love of the saints (I: 4). He rejoices at the Christian fruit which they are producing (I: 6). Epaphras had brought him news of their love in the Spirit (I: 8). He is glad when he hears of their order and steadfastness in the faith (2: 5). There was trouble at Colosse certainly; but that trouble had not yet become an epidemic. There was something there which was as yet only a threat, but which, if it was allowed to develop, might well become a ruination. Paul believed that prevention is better than cure. And in this letter he is grasping this evil before it has time to spread, to flourish and to grow.

The Heresy at Colosse

What the heresy which was threatening the life of the Church at Colosse was no one can tell for sure. " The Colossian Heresy " is one of the great problems of New Testament scholarship. All we can do is to go to the letter itself, and search there for indication of what it was We shall list these characteristics which we find in the letter itself, and then we shall see if there was any general heretical tendency which fits the list.

(i) It was clearly a heresy which attacked the total adequacy and the unique supremacy of Christ. No Pauline letter has such a lofty view of Jesus Christ, and such an insistence on His completeness and His finality. Jesus Christ is the image of the invisible God; in Him all fulness dwells (I: 15, 19). In Him are hid all the treasures of wisdom and of knowledge (2: 2). In Him dwells the fulness of the Godhead in bodily form (2: 9). No greater claims were ever made for Christ, and no greater claims can ever be made.

(ii) We must also note that Paul goes out of his way to

stress the part that Jesus Christ played in creation, the creating work of the Son. By Him all things were created (1: 16); in Him all things cohere (1: 17). The Son was the Father's instrument in the creation of the universe.

(iii) Yet at the same time Paul goes out of his way to stress the real humanity of Jesus Christ, His flesh and blood manhood. It was in the body of His flesh that He did His redeeming work (1: 22). The fulness of the Godhead dwells in Him *sōmatikōs*, in bodily form (2: 9). For all His deity Jesus Christ was really and truly human flesh and blood.

(iv) There seems to have been an astrological element in this heresy. In 2: 8, as the Authorized Version has it, he says that they were walking after the *rudiments* of this world; and in 2: 20 he says that they ought to be dead to the *rudiments* of this world. The word for *rudiments* is *stoicheia*. Now this word has two meanings. (a) Its basic meaning is *a row of things*; it can, for instance, be used for a file of soldiers. But one of its commonest meanings is the A B C, the letters of the alphabet, set out, as it were, in a row. From that it develops the meaning of *the elements of any subject*, the rudiments, the first steps, the A B C of it. It is in that sense that the Authorized Version takes it; and, if that is the sense, Paul means that the Colossians are slipping back to an elementary kind of Christianity when they ought to be going on to maturity. (b) But we think that the second meaning is more likely. *Stoicheia* can mean *the elemental spirits of the world*, and especially the spirits of the stars and planets. The ancient world was dominated by the thought of the influence of the stars. Even the greatest and the wisest men would not act without consulting the stars. The ancient world believed that all things and all men were in the grip of an iron fatalism settled by the influence of the stars; and the science of astrology professed to provide men with the passwords and the secret knowledge which would rid them of their slavery to the elemental spirits of the world. It is most likely that the Colossian false teachers were teaching that it needed something more than Jesus Christ to rid men of their subjection to the elemental spirits of the world and to the stars.

(v) This heresy made much of the powers of demonic spirits. There are frequent references to *principalities* and *powers*, which are Paul's names for these spirits (1: 16; 2: 10; 2: 15). The ancient world believed implicitly in these demonic powers. The air was full of them. Every natural force, the wind, the thunder, the lightning, the rain, had its demonic superintendent. Every place, every tree, every river, every lake had its spirit. The atmosphere was filled with them. And they were in one sense intermediaries to God, and in another sense barriers to God, for the vast majority of them were hostile to men. The ancient world lived in a demon-haunted universe. The Colossian false teachers were clearly saying that something more than Jesus Christ was needed to defeat the power of the demons, that Jesus Christ was not adequate to deal with them by Himself, but needed the ally of some other knowledge and power.

(vi) There was clearly what we might call a philosophical element in this heresy. The heretics are out to spoil men with philosophy and vain deceit (2: 8). Clearly the Colossian heretics were saying that the simplicities of the gospel needed a far more elaborate and recondite knowledge added to them.

(vii) There was a tendency in this heresy to insist on the observance of special days and rituals—festivals, new moons and sabbaths (2: 16). Ritualism and the special observance of times and seasons was a feature of the false teaching.

(viii) Clearly there was a would-be ascetic element in this heresy. It laid down laws about food and drink (2: 16). Its slogans were: " Touch not; taste no; handle not " (2: 21). It was a heresy which was out to limit Christian freedom by all kinds of insistence on legalistic ordinances and rules and regulations.

(ix) Equally this heresy had at least sometimes an antinomian streak in it. It tended to make men careless of the purity and the chastity which the Christian should have, and to make him think lightly of the physical and the bodily sins (3: 5-8).

(x) Apparently this heresy gave at least some place to the worship of angels (2: 18). Beside the demons it introduced angelic intermediaries between man and God.

(xi) Lastly, there seems to have been in this heresy something which can only be called spiritual and intellectual snobbery. In 1: 28 Paul lays down his aim; it is to warn *every man*; to teach *every man* in *all* wisdom; and to present *every man perfect* in Jesus Christ. We see how the phrase *every man is* stressed and reiterated, and how the aim is to make a man *perfect* in *all* wisdom. The clear implication is that the heretics limited the universality of, the gospel to some chosen few. They introduced a spiritual and intellectual aristocracy into the wide welcome of the Christian faith.

The Gnostic Heresy
Is there then any general heretical tendency of thought which would explain and include all this? There was a kind of thought which was called by the name of *Gnosticism*. Gnosticism began with two basic assumptions about matter. First, it believed that spirit alone is good, and that matter is essentially flawed and evil. Matter is basically an evil thing. Second, it believed that matter is eternal; and that the universe was not created out of nothing—which is orthodox belief—but that this flawed matter is the stuff and material out of which this world was made. Now this basic belief has certain inevitable and logical consequences.

(i) It has an effect on the doctrine of creation. If God is spirit, then God is altogether good, and, therefore, God cannot possibly touch or work with this flawed and evil matter. Therefore God is *not* the creator of the world. What then happened? God, said the Gnostics, put out a whole series of emanations. Each emanation was a little more distant from God, until at the end of the series there is an emanation so distant that it can touch and handle matter; and it was this emanation which created the world. But the Gnostics went further. As each emanation was more distant from God, so each emanation was still more ignorant of God. Gradually as the series went on that ignorance turned to more than ignorance; it turned to hostility. So the emanations most distant from God are at once ignorant of Him and hostile to Him. It follows that the God who created the world is at once completely ignorant of, and utterly hostile to, the true God. It is to meet that Gnostic doctrine of creation that Paul insists that the agent of God in creation is not some ignorant and hostile power, but the Son, who perfectly knows and perfectly loves the Father.

(ii) It has its effect on the doctrine of the person of Jesus Christ. If matter is altogether evil, and if Jesus is the Son of God, then Jesus cannot have had a flesh and blood body—so the Gnostic argued. Jesus must have been a kind of spiritual phantom. He must have looked as if He had a body, and yet not have had one. So the Gnostic romances say that when Jesus walked, He left no footprints on the ground, because He had no body to leave them. This, of course, completely removes Jesus from humanity, and makes it completely impossible for Him to be the Saviour of men. It is to meet this Gnostic doctrine that Paul insists on the flesh and blood body of Jesus, and insists that Jesus saved men in the body of His flesh.

(iii) It has its effect on the ethical approach to life. If matter is evil, then it follows that our bodies are evil. If our bodies are evil, one of two consequences follows. (a) We must starve and beat and deny the body; we must practise a rigid asceticism in which the body is kept under, and in which its every need and desire are refused. If the body is evil, then the body must continually be held down. (b) But if the body is evil, it is possible to take precisely the opposite point of view. If the body is evil, it does not matter what a man does with it. Spirit is all that matters; the body is quite unimportant. Therefore a man can glut and sate its appetites and its desires—and it will make no difference, because what we do with the body does not matter.

Gnosticism can, therefore, issue in asceticism, with all kinds of food laws and restrictions; or, it can issue in antinomianism, in which any immorality is justified. And we can see precisely both these tendencies at work in the teaching of the false teachers at Colosse.

(iv) One thing follows from all this—Gnosticism is a highly intellectual way of life and thought. There is this long series of emanations between a man and God; man must fight his way up that long ladder to get to God. In order to do that he will need all kinds of secret knowledge, and esoteric learning, and hidden passwords. He will need an elaborate system of secret and recondite knowledge in order to reach God. If he is to practise a rigid asceticism, he will need to know the rules; and so rigid will his asceticism be, that it will be impossible for him to embark on the ordinary activities of life. The Gnostics were, therefore, quite clear that the higher reaches of religion were open only to the chosen few, and that the vast majority of ordinary men could never attain to them. This conviction of the necessity of belonging to an intellectual and religious aristocracy precisely suits the situation at Colosse.

(v) There remains one thing to fit into this picture. It is quite obvious that there was a Jewish element in the false teaching which was threatening the Church at Colosse. The festivals and the new moons and the sabbaths are characteristically Jewish. The laws about food and drink are essentially Jewish levitical laws. Where then do the Jews come into this system? It is a strange thing that many Jews were sympathetic to Gnosticism. They knew all about angels and demons and spirits. But above all they took up this position. They said, " We know quite well that it takes special knowledge to reach God. We know quite well that Jesus and His gospel are far too simple—and that special knowledge is to be found nowhere else than in the Jewish law. It is our ritual and ceremonial law which is indeed the special knowledge which enables a man to reach God.'' The result of this was that there was not infrequently a strange alliance between Gnosticism and Judaism; and it is just that alliance that we find in Colosse, where, as we have seen, there were so many Jews.

It is then clear that the false teachers of Colosse were tinged with Gnostic heresy. They were trying to turn Christianity into a philosophy and a theosophy, and, if they had been successful, the Christian faith would have been destroyed.

The Authorship of the Letter
One question remains. There are many scholars who do not believe that Paul wrote this letter at all. They have three reasons.

(i) They say that in *Colossians* there are many words and phrases which do not appear in any other of Paul's letters. That is perfectly true. But it does not prove anything. We cannot demand that a man should always write in the same way and with the same vocabulary. In *Colossians* we may well believe that Paul had new things to say and found new ways to say them.

(ii) They say that the development of Gnostic thought was, in fact, much later than the time of Paul, and, if the Colossian heresy was connected with Gnosticism, then the letter is necessarily later than Paul. It is true that the great written Gnostic systems are later. But the idea of two worlds, the idea of the evil of matter, the idea that the body is a tomb, and that the flesh is evil, are ideas which are deeply woven into both Jewish and Greek thought. There is nothing in Colossians which cannot be explained by long-standing Gnostic tendencies in ancient thought, although it is true that the systematization of Gnosticism came later.

(iii) They say that the view of Christ in *Colossians* is far in advance of the view in any of the letters certainly written by Paul. They say that the idea of Christ as creator and as the fulness of God is something for which we have to go to the Fourth Gospel, forty years later. There are two answers to that.

First, Paul speaks of the unsearchable riches of Christ. In Colosse a new situation met Paul, and out of these unsearchable riches Paul drew new answers to meet it. It is true to say that the Christology of *Colossians* is an advance on anything in the earlier letters of Paul; but that is far from saying that Paul did not write it, unless we are willing to argue that Paul's thought remained for ever static, and never developed to meet a new situation. It is true to say that a man thinks out the implications of his faith only as circumstances compel him to do so. And in face of a new set of circumstances Paul thought out new implications of Christ.

Second, the germ of all Paul's thought about Christ in *Colossians* does, in fact, exist in one of his earlier letters. In I *Corinthians* 8: 6 he writes of *one Lord Jesus Christ by whom are all things and we by him.* In that phrase is the essence of all that Paul says in *Colossians.* The seed was there in Paul's mind, ready to blossom when a new climate and new circumstances called it into growth.

We need not hesitate to accept *Colossians* as a letter written by Paul.

The Great Letter

It remains a strange and a wonderful fact that Paul wrote the letter which contains the highest reach of his thought to so unimportant a town as Colosse then was. But in doing so he checked a tendency, which, if it had been allowed to develop, would have wrecked Asian Christianity, and which might well have done irreparable damage to the faith of the whole Church.

THE LETTER TO THE COLOSSIANS

CHRISTIAN GREETINGS

Colossians 1: 1

> This is a letter from Paul, an apostle of Jesus Christ
> by the will of God, and from Timothy, the brother,
> to the dedicated people of God and faithful brothers
> in Christ who are in Colosse.

A MAN who is a dedicated Christian cannot write a single
sentence without making clear the great beliefs which under-
lie all his thought. Paul had never actually been in Colosse;
therefore, he has to begin by making clear what right he
has to send a letter to the Colossians. He does that in one
word; he is an *apostle*, a chosen ambassador of God. The
word *apostolos* literally means *one who is sent out*. Paul's
right to speak was that he had been sent out by God to be
God's ambassador to the Gentiles. But Paul adds something—he is an apostle *by the will of God*. The office of
apostle is not something which he has earned or achieved;
it is something which has been given to him by God. It
is not something which he has taken; it is something which
has been conferred upon him. " Ye have not chosen me,"
said Jesus, " but I have chosen you " (*John* 15 : 16).
Here, right at the outset of the letter, is the whole doctrine
of grace. A man is not what he has made himself, but what
God has made him. There is no such thing as a self-made
man; there are only men whom God has made, and men
who have refused to allow God to make them.

With himself Paul associates Timothy; and he gives
Timothy a lovely title. He calls him Timothy, *the brother*.
That is a title which is given to Quartus (*Romans* 16:
23); to Sosthenes (I *Corinthians* 1: 1); to Apollos (I *Corinthians* 16: 12). The fundamental necessity for Christian
service and for Christian office is nothing other than
brotherliness. Premanand, the highborn Indian who
became a Christian, tells in his autobiography of Father
E. F. Brown of the Oxford Mission in Calcutta. E. F. Brown
was every man's friend; but he was specially the friend of
the hackney carriage drivers, the carters, the tram con-

ductors, the menial servants, and the hundreds of poor street boys. Later in his life, when he was travelling about India, Premanand would often meet people who had stayed in Calcutta, and they would always ask for E. F. Brown, saying, " Is that friend of the Calcutta street boys still alive, who used to walk arm-in-arm with the poor? " It was his brotherliness which brought men to his Master. Sir Henry Lunn tells of how his father used to describe his grandfather: " He was a friend of the poor without patronage, and of the rich without subservience." To use our modern idiom, the first necessity for Christian service is the ability to "get alongside" all kinds of people. Timothy is not described as the preacher, the teacher, the theologian, the administrator, but as the *brother*. He who walks in aloofness can never be a real servant of Jesus Christ.

There is another interesting and significant fact in this opening address. It is addressed to God's dedicated people and to the faithful brothers in Colosse. Now in the matter of opening addresses Paul's custom changed. In his earlier letters he always addressed the letter to the *Church*. *1 and 2 Thessalonians*, *1 and 2 Corinthians* and *Galatians* are all addressed to the *Church* of the district to which they are sent. But beginning with *Romans* all Paul's letters are addressed to God's dedicated people in such and such a place. It is so in *Romans*, *Colossians*, *Philippians* and *Ephesians*. As Paul grew older, he came more and more to see that what matters is individual people. The Church is people. The Church is not a kind of vague, abstract entity; it is individual men and women and children. And, as the years went on, Paul began to think less and less of the Church as a whole, and more and more of the Church as individual men and women. And so, in the end, he sends his greetings, not to a kind of abstract society called the Church, but rather to the individual men and women of whom the Church must always be composed.

The opening greeting closes with a most significant

placing of two things side by side. He writes to the Christians who are *in Colosse* and who are *in Christ*. A Christian always moves in two spheres. He is in the town, the place, the society where he happens to stay in this world; but he is also in Christ. The Christian lives in two dimensions. He lives in this world, and he does not take the duties and relationships of this world lightly; he fulfils his every obligation to the world in which he lives. But above and beyond that he lives in Christ. In this world he may move from place to place, so that now he is in one place and now in another; but wherever he is, he is in Christ. That is why outward circumstances will make very little difference to the Christian; his happiness and his peace and his joy are not dependent on them; these things can change, but the fact that he is in Christ can never change. That is why the Christian will do any job and any task with all his heart. It may be menial, it may be unpleasant, it may be painful, it may be far less distinguished than he might expect to have; its rewards may be small, and its praise may be non-existent; nevertheless the Christian does it diligently, uncomplainingly and cheerfully, for he is in Christ and does all things as to the Lord. We are all in our own Colosse, wherever that Colosse may be, but we are all in Christ, and it is Christ who sets the tone of our life and our living.

THE DOUBLE COMMITMENT

Colossians I: 2-8

> Grace be to you and peace from God our Father. We always thank God, the Father of our Lord Jesus Christ, for you in our prayers; for we have heard of your faith in Christ Jesus, and of the love you have to all God's dedicated people, because of the hope which is laid up for you in heaven. Of that hope you have already heard in the true word of the gospel, which has come to you, just as in all the world it is bearing fruit and increasing, just as it did among

you too, from that day on which you heard and knew
the grace of God as it truly is, as you learned it from
Epaphras, my beloved fellow-bondman, who is a faithful servant of Christ on our behalf, and who has made
known to us your love in the Spirit.

HERE in this passage we are presented with the essence of
the Christian life. The fact which delights Paul's heart,
and the fact for which he gives God thanks, is the fact
that he has been told that the Colossians are showing two
great qualities in their lives. They are showing *faith in
Christ* and *love for their fellow-men*.

These are the two sides of the Christian life. The
Christian life must show loyalty to Christ and love to men,
The Christian must have faith; he must know what he
believes. But he must also have love for men; he must
turn that belief into action. It is not enough simply to
have faith, for there can be an orthodoxy which knows no
charity, and there can be such a thing as a loveless goodness.
It is not enough only to have love for men, for without the
basis of real belief that love can become a mere
sentimentality. The Christian has a double loyalty—
a loyalty to Christ and a loyalty to men. The Christian
has a double commitment—he is committed to Jesus
Christ and he is committed to his fellow-men. The
Christian faith is not only a conviction of the mind; it is
also an outflow of the heart. It is not only correct thought;
it is loving conduct. Faith in Christ and love to men are
the twin pillars of the Christian life.

That faith and that love depend on the hope that is laid
up in heaven. What exactly does Paul mean by that?
Is he asking the Colossians to show faith in Christ and love
for men only for the hope of some reward that is going to
come to them some day? Is he asking them to be good in
order that they may get something out of being good?
Is this, in the modern slang phrase, " pie in the sky "?
There is something much deeper than that here.

Think of it this way. Loyalty to Christ may involve a

man in all kinds of loss and pain and suffering and unpopularity. In order to be loyal to Christ there may be many things to which he has to say goodbye. The way of love may seem to many to be the way of a fool. Why seek to serve others? Why forgive others? Why spend life in selfless service? Why not use life " to get on " as the world counts getting on? Why not push the weaker brother out of the way? Why not take part in the competition and the race in which the strongest and the fittest survive? The answer is—*because of the hope that is set before us.*

As C. F. D. Moule puts it, the hope is the certainty that in spite of the world's ways and the world's standards God's way of love has the last word. As James Russell Lowell put it in *The Present Crisis*, the hope is that:

> Though the cause of Evil prosper, yet 'tis truth alone is strong . . . .
> Truth for ever on the scaffold, wrong for ever on the throne,—
> Yet that scaffold sways the future, and, behind the dim unknown,
> Standeth God within the shadow, keeping watch above His own.

The Christian hope is that God's way is the best way, that the only happiness, the only peace, the only joy, the only true and lasting reward are to be found in the way of God. Loyalty to Christ may bring trouble here—but that is not the last word. The world may laugh contemptuously at the folly of the way of love—but the foolishness of God is wiser than the wisdom of man. The Christian hope is the certainty that it is better to stake one's life on God than to believe the world.

THE ESSENCE OF THE GOSPEL

Colossians I: 2-8 *(continued)*

IN this passage there is, in verses 6-8, a kind of summary of what the gospel is and does. In that section Paul has much to say of the hope which had already come to the Colossians, to which they had already listened and which they had already accepted.

(i) The gospel is a *gospel*; that is to say, it is good news. By far the best definition of the gospel is that it is *good news of God*. The message of the gospel is the message of a God who is a Friend and Lover of the souls of men, First and foremost, the gospel sets us in a right relationship with God.

(ii) The gospel is *truth*. All previous religions could be entitled " guesses about God." The Christian gospel gives a man, not guesses, but certainties about God.

(iii) The gospel is *universal*. It is for all the world. It is not confined to any one race or nation, not to any one class or condition. There are very few things in this world which are open to all men. A man's mental calibre decides the studies which he can undertake. A man's social class decides the circle amidst which he will move. A man's material wealth determines the material possessions which he can amass. A man's particular gifts and talents decide the things which he can do. But the message of the gospel, and the joy and the peace of the gospel, are open without exception to all men.

(iv) The gospel is *productive*. It bears fruit and increases. It is the plain fact of history and experience that the gospel has power to change the individual lives of men, and the society in which men live. The power of the gospel can change the sinner into a good man, and the power of the gospel can slowly take the selfishness and the cruelty out of society, and give to all men the chance that God would wish them to have.

(v) The gospel tells of *grace*. The gospel is not just another of these many things to set before men, another hopeless and daunting task. The gospel is not the message of what God demands, but of what God offers. It does not tell of God's demand from men, but of God's gift to men.

(vi) The gospel is *humanly transmitted*. It was Epaphras who brought the gospel to the Colossians. There must be a human channel through which the gospel can come to men. And this is where we come in. The possession of the good news of the gospel involves the obligation to share it. That which is divinely given must be humanly passed on. Jesus Christ needs us that we may be the hands and feet and lips which will bring His gospel to those who have never heard it. We who have received the privilege of the gospel have also received the responsibility of passing it on.

THE ESSENCE OF PRAYER'S REQUEST

Colossians 1: 9-11

That, in fact, is why, from the day we heard about it, we do not cease to pray for you, asking that you may be filled with an ever-growing knowledge of His will, in all spiritual wisdom and understanding, so that you may conduct yourselves worthily of the Lord, and in such a way as to be altogether pleasing to Him, bearing fruit in every good work, and increasing in the fuller knowledge of God. May you continue to be strengthened with all strength according to His glorious power, so that you may possess all fortitude and patience with joy.

IT is a very precious thing to hear the prayers of a saint for his friends; and that is what we hear in this passage. It may well be said that this passage teaches us more about the essence of prayer's request than almost any other passage in the New Testament. From it we learn, as C. F. D. Moule has said, that prayer makes two great requests. It asks for the discernment of God's will, and then for the power to perform that will.

(i) Prayer begins by asking that we may be filled with an ever-growing knowledge of the will of God. The great object of prayer is to know the will of God. In prayer we are not so much trying to make God listen to us, as we are trying to make ourselves listen to God; in prayer we are not trying to persuade God to do what we want Him to do, we are trying to find out what He wants us to do. It so often happens that in prayer we are really saying, " Thy will be changed," when we ought to be saying, " Thy will be done." The first object of prayer is not so much to speak to God, as it is to listen to God.

(ii) This knowledge of God must be translated into terms of our own human situation. We pray for spiritual wisdom and understanding. *Spiritual wisdom* is *sophia*, and we could describe *sophia* as *knowledge of first principles*. *Understanding* is *sunesis*, and *sunesis* is what the Greeks sometimes described as *critical knowledge*; by that they meant *the ability to apply first principles to any given situation which may arise in life*. So when Paul prays that his friends may have *wisdom* and *understanding*, he is praying that they may understand the great truths of Christianity, and that they may be able to apply these truths to the tasks and decisions which meet them in everyday living. A man can quite easily be a master of theology and a failure in living. He may be able to write and talk about the great eternal truths, and yet be quite helpless to apply these truths to the things which meet him every day. The Christian must know what Christianity means, not, as it were, in a vacuum, but in the business of living from day to day.

(iii) This knowledge of God's will, and this wisdom and understanding, must issue in right conduct. Paul prays that his friends may conduct themselves in such a way as to please God. There is nothing in this world so practical as prayer. Prayer is not escape from reality. Prayer is not a secluded meditation on, and communion with, God. Prayer and action go hand in hand. We pray, not in order to escape life, but in order to be better able to meet life. We pray, not in order to withdraw ourselves from life, but in order to live life in the world of men as it ought to be lived.

(iv) To do this we need power. Therefore, Paul prays that his friends may be strengthened with the power of

God. The great problem in life is not to know what to do, but to do it. For the most part, we are well aware in any given situation what we ought to do ; our problem is to put that knowledge into action. What we need is power; and what we receive in prayer is power. If God only told us what His will for us was, that might well be a frustrating and torturing situation; but God not only tells us His will, He also enables us to perform it.

> Knowledge we ask not, knowledge Thou hast lent,
> But Lord—the will, there lies our deepest need.
> Grant us to build above the high intent—
>   The deed—the deed.

Through prayer we reach the greatest gift in all the world—knowledge plus power.

THE THREE GREAT GIFTS

Colossians I: 9-11 (*continued*)

WHAT we might call the *asking* part of Paul's prayer ends with a prayer for three great qualities. He prays that his Colossian friends may possess all *fortitude*, *patience* and *joy*.

The two words *fortitude* and *patience* are two great Greek words which often keep company. *Fortitude* is *hupomonē*, and *patience* is *makrothumia*. There is a distinction between these two words. It would not be true to say that Greek always rigidly observes this distinction, but when the words occur together, the distinction is there.

Hupomonē is usually translated *patience* in the Authorized Version. But *hupomonē* does not mean patience in the sense of sitting down and bearing things, and of simply bowing the head and letting the tide of events flow over one. *Hupomonē* means not only the ability to bear things, but the ability, in bearing them, to turn them into glory. It is a conquering patience. *Hupomonē* is the spirit which no circumstance in life can ever defeat, and which no event can ever vanquish. *Hupomonē* is the ability to deal triumphantly with anything that life can do to us.

Makrothumia is usually translated *long-suffering* in the Authorized Version. Its basic meaning is *patience with people*. It is the quality of mind and heart which enables a man so to bear with people that their unpleasantness and maliciousness and cruelty will never drive him to bitterness, that their unteachableness and foolishness will never drive him to despair, that their folly will never drive him to irritation, and that their unloveliness will never alter his love. *Makrothumia* is the spirit which never loses patience with, belief in, and hope for men.

So Paul prays for these two great qualities—the *hupomonē*, the *fortitude*, which no situation can defeat, the *makrothumia*, the *patience*, which no person can defeat. He prays that the Christian may be such that no circumstances can defeat his strength, and no human being defeat his love. He prays for that spirit which will never despair about any situation or person, which will refuse to grow hopeless either about things or people. The Christian's fortitude in events and patience with people must be indestructible.

And added to all this there is *joy*. All this is not a grim struggle with events and with people; it is a radiant and sunny-hearted attitude to life. The Christian joy is joy in any circumstances. As C. F. D. Moule puts it: " If joy is not rooted in the soil of suffering, it is shallow." It is easy to be joyful when things go well, but the Christian radiance is something which not all the shadows of life can quench.

So the Christian prayer is: " Make me, O Lord, victorious over every circumstance; make me patient with every person; and withal give me the joy which no circumstance and no man will ever take from me."

PRAYER'S GREAT THANKSGIVING

Colossians 1:12-14

May you give thanks to the Father, who enabled us to obtain our share of the inheritance of God's dedicated people in the Kingdom of light; for He rescued us from the power of darkness, and brought us over into the kingdom of His beloved Son, in whom we have redemption and the forgiveness of sins.

Now Paul turns to grateful thanksgiving for the benefits which the Christian has received in Christ. There are two key ideas here.

(i) God has given to the Colossians a share in the inheritance of God's dedicated people. There is in this whole passage a very close correspondence with the passage in Paul's speech before Agrippa, when Paul told Agrippa of the work that God had given to him. That task was: " To open their eyes, and to turn them from darkness to light, and from the power of Satan unto God, that they may receive forgiveness of sins, and inheritance among them which are sanctified by faith that is in God " (*Acts* 26: 18). The first privilege is that there has been given to the Gentiles a share in the inheritance of the chosen people of God. The Jews had always been God's chosen people, the peculiar and special and unique possession of God; but now the door has been opened to the Gentiles and to all men; not only the Jews, but all men of all nations have entered into the inheritance of the people of God.

(ii) The second key idea lies in the phrase which, as the Authorized Version has it, says that God has *translated us into the kingdom of His dear Son*, or, as we have translated it, that God has *brought us over* into the kingdom of His beloved son. The word which Paul uses for *to translate* or *to bring over* is the Greek verb *methistēmi*. This is a word with a special use. In the ancient world, when one empire won a victory over another, it was the custom to take the population of the defeated country and to transfer them lock, stock and barrel to some other land. So the people of the Northern Kingdom were taken away to Assyria, and so the people of Jerusalem and the people of the Southern Kingdom were taken away to Babylon. This transference of whole populations was a characteristic of the ancient world. So Paul says that God has transferred the Christian into His own realm and His own kingdom; He has taken them right out of the sphere in which they used to live into His own kingdom and into His own power. That transference carried out by God was not only a transference, it was also a rescue. It meant four great things.

(a) It means a transference *from darkness to light.* Without God men grope and stumble like men walking in the dark. They know not what to do; they know not where they are going. Life is lived in the shadows of doubt, and in the darkness of ignorance. When Bilney the martyr read that Jesus Christ came into the world to save sinners, he said that it was like the dawn breaking on a dark night. In Jesus Christ, God has given us a light to live by and to die by.

(b) It meant a transference *from slavery to freedom.* It is *redemption,* and that is the word which is used for the emancipation of a slave, and for the buying back of something which was in the power of someone else. Without God men are slaves to their fears, slaves to their sins, slaves to their own helplessness and their own faults. In Jesus Christ there comes a liberation, in which fear and frustration are taken away.

(c) It means a transference from *condemnation to forgiveness.* Man in his sin deserves nothing but the condemnation of God; but through the work of Jesus Christ he discovers the love of God and the forgiveness of God; and he knows that he is no longer a condemned criminal at God's judgment seat, but a lost son for whom the way home is always open.

(a) It means a transference from *the power of Satan to the power of God.* Through Jesus Christ man is liberated from the grip of Satan and is able to become a citizen of the Kingdom of God. Just as an earthly conqueror transferred the citizens of the land he had conquered into a new kingdom and a new land, so God in His triumphant love transfers men from the realm of sin and darkness into the realm of holiness and light and love.

THE TOTAL ADEQUACY OF JESUS CHRIST

Colossians I: 15-23

> He is the image of the invisible God, begotten before all creation, because by Him all things were created, in heaven and upon earth, the things which are visible and the things which are invisible, whether thrones or lordships or powers or authorities. All things were created through Him and for Him. He is before all things, and in Him all things cohere. He is the head of the body, that is, of the Church. He is the beginning, the firstborn from the dead, that He might be supreme in all things. For in Him God in all His fulness was pleased to take up His abode, and through Him to reconcile all things to Himself, when He had made peace through the blood of His Cross. This was done for all things, whether on the earth or in the heavens. And you, who were once estranged and hostile in your minds, in the midst of evil deeds, He has now reconciled in the body of His flesh, through His death, in order to present you before Him consecrated, unblemished, irreproachable, if only you remain grounded and stablished in the faith, not shifting from the hope of the gospel which you have heard, which has been proclaimed to every creature under heaven, of which I, Paul, have been made a servant.

THIS is a passage of such difficulty and of such importance that we shall have to spend some considerable time on it. We shall divide what we must say about it into certain sections. We must begin with the situation which, as it were, gave birth to this passage, and to the whole view of Christ which Paul sets out in this letter.

I. THE MISTAKEN THINKERS

It is one of the facts of the human mind that a man only thinks as much as he has to. For the most part men need something to make them think. It is not until a man finds his faith opposed and attacked that he really begins to think out the implications of that faith. It is not until the Church is confronted with some dangerous heresy that she begins to realize the riches and the wonder of orthodoxy. It is characteristic of Christianity that it has an inexhaustible riches, and that it can always produce new riches to meet any new situation.

When Paul wrote *Colossians*, he was not writing in a vacuum. He was writing, as we have already seen in the introduction, to meet a very definite situation. There was a tendency of thought in the early Church which goes by the name of Gnosticism. Its devotees were called *Gnostics*, which more or less means *the intellectual ones*. These men were dissatisfied with what they considered the rude simplicity of Christianity, and they wished to turn Christianity into a philosophy and to align it with the other philosophies which held the field at that time.

These Gnostics began with one basic assumption, the assumption that matter is altogether evil and that spirit is altogether good. They further held that matter is eternal, that matter has always existed, and that it is out of this flawed and evil matter that the world was created. The Christian, to use the technical phrase, believes in creation out of nothing; the Gnostic believed in creation out of this essentially evil matter.

Now God is spirit, and if spirit is altogether good and matter is essentially evil, it follows, as the Gnostic saw it, that the true God cannot touch matter. Since God is altogether good and matter is basically evil, God cannot Himself be the agent of creation. So the Gnostics believed that God put forth a series of powers, or aeons, or emanations. Each of these emanations was a little further away from God. There was an infinite series of these emanations, until at last there was an emanation which was so distant from God, that it could touch and handle and shape matter, and create the world out of matter. So, then, it was not God, but this distant emanation who created the world.

But the Gnostic went further than that. As the emanations were further and further from God, they became more and more ignorant of God. And in the very distant emanations, there was not only ignorance of God, there was also hostility to God. And so the Gnostic came to the conclusion that the emanation who created the world was both ignorant of and hostile to the true God. Sometimes the Gnostics identified that ignorant and hostile and distant emanation with the God of the Old Testament, while the true God was the God of the New Testament.

All this has certain logical consequence.

(i) As the Gnostics saw it, the creating God is not the true God. The creating God is ignorant of, and hostile to, the true God. The world is essentially evil; the world is not God's world; it is the world of a power hostile to God. That is why Paul insists that God did create the world, and that God's agent in creation was no ignorant and hostile emanation, but Jesus Christ, His Son (*Colossians* I: 16). The Christian doctrine of the creating agency of Jesus Christ was thought out to combat the Gnostic doctrine of an ignorant and a hostile creating God.

(ii) As the Gnostics saw it, Jesus Christ was by no means unique. We have seen how the Gnostics postulated a whole series of emanations between the world and God. They insisted that Jesus was merely one of these emanations. He was merely one of the intermediaries between God and man. He might stand high in the series; He might even stand highest in the series; but none the less He was not unique, because He was only one in a series, one of many. Paul meets this by insisting that in Jesus Christ all fulness dwells (*Colossians* I: 19); that in Him there is the fulness of the godhead in bodily form (*Colossians* 2: 9). One of the supreme objects of *Colossians* is to insist that Jesus is not one in a series, one among many, that He is not the partial revelation of God, but that He is utterly unique, and that in Him there is the whole of God, the fulness of God.

(iii) As the Gnostics saw it, this had another consequence, when they were thinking about Jesus. If matter is altogether evil, then it follows that the body is altogether evil. If the body is evil, then it follows that He who was the revelation of God, cannot have had a real body; He cannot have been real flesh and blood, as we are flesh and blood; He cannot have had real manhood. He was nothing more than a spiritual phantom in a bodily form. The Gnostics completely denied the true and real manhood of Jesus. To them Jesus was a spirit who took a bodily form. In their own writings they, for instance, set it down that when Jesus walked, He left no footprints on the ground, because He had no real body of flesh and blood to leave such footprints. That is why Paul uses such startling phraseology in *Colossians*. He speaks of Jesus reconciling man to God *in the body of His flesh* (*Colossians* 1: 22); he says that the fulness of the godhead dwelt in Him *bodily*. In opposition to the Gnostics, with their idea of a kind of phantom Jesus, Paul insisted on the flesh and blood manhood of the Son of God.

(iv) The task of man is to find his way to God. As the Gnostics saw it, that way to God is barred. Between this world and God there is this vast series of emanations. Before the soul can rise to God, it has to get past each one of these emanations. It has, as it were, to climb up this endless ladder; and at each step in the ladder there is an opposing power, a barrier in the way. To pass each barrier special knowledge and special passwords were needed. The soul needed an elaborate equipment of knowledge and a whole host of passwords in its climb to the Eternal. It was these passwords and that knowledge that the Gnostics claimed to give. This meant two things, (*a*) It meant that salvation is *intellectual knowledge*. To meet that Paul insists that salvation is not knowledge; it is *redemption* and the *forgiveness of sins*. The Gnostic teachers held that the so-called simple truths of the gospel are not nearly enough. To find its way to God the soul needs far more than that; it needs the elaborate knowledge and the secret passwords which Gnosticism alone can give. So Paul insists that Christianity is not knowledge; it is redemption; and that nothing more is needed than the saving truths of the gospel of Jesus Christ. (b) It must be clear that, if salvation depends on this elaborate knowledge, then salvation is not for every man. It can only be for the intellectual; it is far beyond the mental grasp of simple people. So the Gnostics divided mankind into the spiritual and the earthly, and only the spiritual could be truly saved. Full salvation was utterly beyond the scope of the ordinary man. Gnosticism was founded on an intellectual aristocracy from which the common man was shut out. It is with that in mind that Paul wrote the great verse *Colossians* I: 28. It was Paul's aim to warn *every man*, and to teach *every man*, and so to present *every man* perfect in Christ Jesus. In face of a salvation possible only for a limited intellectual minority, Paul presents a gospel which is for every man, however simple and unlettered, or however wise and learned he may be. The Gnostics preached salvation for a limited caste; Paul preached salvation for every man.

These, then, were the great Gnostic doctrines; and all the time we are studying this passage, and indeed all the time we are studying the whole letter, we must have them in our mind, for only against them does Paul's language become intelligible and relevant.

II. WHAT JESUS CHRIST IS IN HIMSELF

Colossians I: 15-23 (*continued*)

IN this passage Paul says two great things about Jesus. They are both in answer to the Gnostics. The Gnostics had said that Jesus was merely one among many intermediaries, and that, however great He might be, He was only a partial revelation of God.

(i) Paul says that Jesus Christ is *the image* of the invisible
God (*Colossians* 1: 15). Here Paul uses a word and a
picture which would waken all kinds of memories in the
minds of those who heard it. The word is *eikōn*, and it is
correctly translated *image*. Now, as Lightfoot points out,
an image can be two things which merge into each other.
An image can be a *representation*; but a representation,
if it is perfect enough, can become a *manifestation*. When
Paul uses this word, He lays it down that Jesus is the
perfect manifestation of God. To see what God is like, we
must look at Jesus. Jesus perfectly represents, perfectly
manifests God to men, in a form which men can see and
know and understand. But it is what is behind this word
which is of entrancing interest.

(a) The Old Testament and the inter-testamental books
have a great deal to say about *Wisdom*. In *Proverbs* the
great passages on Wisdom are in chapters 2 and 8. There
Wisdom is said to be co-eternal with God, and to have
been with God when He created the world. Now in the
Wisdom of Solomon 7: 26, this very word is used of Wisdom.
Wisdom is the *image* of the goodness of God. It is as if
Paul turned to the Jews and said, " All your lives you
have been thinking and dreaming and writing about this
Wisdom, this divine Wisdom, this Wisdom which is as
old as God, this Wisdom which made the world, and this
Wisdom which gives wisdom to men. In Jesus Christ this
Wisdom has come to men in bodily form for all to see."
Jesus is the fulfilment of the dreams of Jewish thought.

(b) The Greeks were haunted by the thought of the
Logos, the word, the reason of God. It was that Logos
which created the world. It was that Logos which put
sense into the universe, which kept the stars in their
courses, which made the universe, which made the seasons
return in their appointed order, which made this a reliable
and dependable world, which put a thinking mind into man.
Now this very word *eikōn* is used again and again by Philo,
of the Logos of God. " He calls the invisible and divine

Logos, which only the mind can perceive, the *image (eikōn)* of God " (Philo: *Concerning the Creator of the World: 8*). It is as if Paul said to the Greeks: " For the last six hundred years you have dreamed and thought and written about the reason, the mind, the word, the Logos of God; you called it God's *eikōn*; in Jesus Christ that Logos has come plain for all to see. Your dreams and philosophies, your speculations and your adventures of thought are all come true in Him."

(c) In these connections of the word *eikōn* we have been moving in the highest realms of thought, where only the philosophers can move familiarly. But there are two much simpler connections which would immediately flash across the minds of those who heard or read this for the first time. Their minds would at once go back to the creation story. There the old story tells of the culminating act of creation. " God said, Let us make man in our *image*." " So God created man in His own *image*, in the *image* of God created He him " (*Genesis* 1: 26, 27). Here indeed is illumination. Man was made that he might be nothing less than the *eikōn*, the image of God, for the word in the *Genesis* story is the same word. That is what man was meant to be, but sin came in, and man never achieved his destiny, and things went tragically wrong. So by using this word of Jesus, Paul in effect says, " Look at this Jesus. He shows you not only what God is; He also shows you *what man was meant to be*. Here is manhood as God designed it. Jesus is the perfect manifestation of God, and the perfect manifestation of man." There is what we can only call a double revelation in Jesus Christ, the revelation of godhead and the revelation of manhood.

(d) But we come at last to something much simpler than any of these things. And there is no doubt that many of the simpler of Paul's readers would think of this. Even if they knew nothing of the Wisdom Literature, and nothing of Philo, and nothing of the *Genesis* story they would know this. The word *eikōn*—sometimes in its diminutive form *eikonion*—was the word which was used for a *portrait* in Greek. There is a papyrus letter from a soldier lad called Apion to his father Epimachus. Near the very end he writes: " I send you a little portrait (*eikonion*) of myself painted by Euctemon." It is the nearest equivalent in ancient Greek to our modern word *photograph*. But this word had still another use. When a legal document was drawn up, such as a receipt or an IOU, it always included a description of the chief characteristics and distinguishing marks of the contracting parties, so that there could be no evasion and no mistake. The Greek word for such a description is *eikōn*. The *eikōn* was a kind of brief summary of the personal characteristics and the distinguishing marks of the contracting parties. So, then, to the very simplest Paul is saying, " You know how if you enter into a legal agreement, there is included an *eikōn*, a description by which you may be recognized. Jesus is the portrait of God. In Jesus Christ you see nothing less than the personal characteristics and the distinguishing marks of God. If you want to see what God is like, look at Jesus."

In truth there is a word of meaning in this word *eikōn*, to tell us who and what Jesus Christ is.

(ii) The other word Paul uses is in verse 19. He says that Jesus is the *plērōma* of God. *Plērōma* means *fullness, completeness*. This is the word which is needed to complete the picture. Jesus is not simply a sketch of God; He is not a summary of God; He is more than a lifeless portrait of God. In Him there is nothing left out; He is the full and the final revelation of God, and nothing more is necessary.

III. WHAT JESUS CHRIST IS TO CREATION

Colossians 1:15-23 (continued)

WE will remember that according to the Gnostics the work of creation was carried out by an inferior god, ignorant of, and hostile to, the true God. It is Paul's teaching that God's agent in creation is the Son. In this passage Paul has four things to say of the Son in regard to creation.

(i) He is the firstborn of all creation (*Colossians* 1: 15). We must be very careful to attach the right meaning to this phrase. As it stands in English it might well mean that the Son was part of creation, that He was, in fact, the first person to be created, that He was the first production in God's creation. But in Hebrew and Greek thought the word *firstborn* (*prōtotokos*) has only very indirectly a time significance at all. There are two things to note. *Firstborn* is very commonly a title of *honour*. Israel, for instance, as a nation is the firstborn son of God (*Exodus* 4: 22). The meaning of that phrase is that the nation of Israel is the chosen, the most honoured, and the most favoured child of God. Second, we must note that *firstborn* is a title of the *Messiah*. In *Psalm* 89: 27, as the Jews themselves interpreted it, the promise regarding the Messiah is " I will make him my firstborn, higher than the kings of the earth." Clearly the word *firstborn* is not used in a time sense at all, but in the sense of special honour. So when Paul says of the Son that he is the *firstborn* of all creation, the means that the highest honour which creation hold belongs to the Son; to Him God has given a place and an honour that are completely unique. If we wish to keep the time sense and the honour sense combined, we may translate the phrase: " He was begotten before all creation."

(ii) It was by the Son that all things were created (verse 16). This is true of things in heaven and things in earth, of things seen and unseen. The Jews themselves, and even more the Gnostics, had a highly-developed and elaborate system of angels. With the Gnostics that would be only to be expected with their long series of intermediaries between man and God. Thrones, lordships, powers and authorities were different grades of angels having their places in different spheres of the seven heavens. Paul dismisses them all with complete indifference. He is in effect saying to these Gnostics, "You give a great place in your thinking to angels. You rate Jesus Christ merely as one of these angels and one of these heavenly powers. So far from being one of them, He created them. He is as far above them as the creator is above the creature." So Paul lays it down that the agent of God in creation is no inferior, ignorant and hostile secondary god, but the Son Himself.

(iii) It was for the Son that all things were created (verse 17). The Son is not only the agent of creation, He is also the goal and the end of creation. That is to say, creation was created to be His, and to give Him glory. Creation was created by the Son, and it was created that finally it might be His, and that in its worship and its love He might find His honour and His joy. The world was created in order that it might ultimately belong to Jesus Christ.

(iv) Paul uses the strange phrase : " In Him all things cohere." This means that the Son is the agent of creation in the beginning, and the goal of creation in the end, and between the beginning and the end, during time as we know it, it is the Son who, as it were, holds the world together. That is to say, all the laws by which this world is an order and not a chaos are an expression of the mind of the Son. The law of gravity and all the so-called scientific laws are not only scientific laws; they are divine laws. They are the laws which make sense of the universe. They are the laws which make this a reliable and a dependable world. Every law of science and of nature is, in fact, an expression of the thought of God. It is by these laws, and therefore by the mind of God, that the universe hangs together, and does not disintegrate in chaos.

So, then, the Son is the beginning of creation, and the end of creation, and the power who holds creation together. He is the Creator, the Sustainer, and the Final Goal of the world.

IV. WHAT JESUS CHRIST IS TO THE CHURCH

Colossians I: 15-23 (*continued*)

PAUL sets out now, in verse 18, what Jesus Christ is to the Church; and in that verse Paul distinguishes four great facts in Jesus relationship to the Church.

(i) He is *the head of the body*, that is, of the Church. The Church is the body of Christ; that is, the Church is the organism through which Christ acts, and which shares all the experiences of Christ. But, humanly speaking, the body is the servant of the head and of the mind and of the brain. The body moves at the head's bidding; the body itself is powerless and dead without the head. So Jesus Christ is the guiding, directing, dominating spirit of the Church. Every word and action of the Church must be governed and directed by Him; it is at His bidding that the Church must live and move. Without Him the Church cannot think the truth; without Him the Church cannot act correctly; without Him cannot decide its direction. The thought and the action of the Church must be governed, guided and directed by Jesus Christ. There are two things combined here. There is the idea of *privilege*. It is the privilege of the Church to be the instrument through which Christ works. There is the idea of *warning*. If a man neglects or abuses his body, he can make it unfit to be the servant of the great schemes and purposes of his mind and brain; so by indisciplined and by careless living the Church can unfit herself to be the instrument of Christ, who is her head.

(ii) He is *the beginning of the Church*. The Greek word for beginning is *archē*. The word *archē* means *beginning* in a double sense. It means not only first in the sense of time, as, for instance, A is the beginning of the alphabet, and I is the beginning of the series of numbers. It means first in the sense of originating power; it means the source from which something came; the moving power which set something in operation. We will see more clearly what

Paul is getting at, if we remember what he has just said. *The world* is the *creation* of Christ; and *the Church* is the *new creation* of Christ.

> She is His new creation
> By water and the word.

So, then, Jesus Christ is the source of the Church's life and being, and the director of the Church's continued activity.

(iii) He is *the firstborn from among the dead.* Here Paul comes back to the event which was at the centre of all the thinking and all the belief and all the experience of the early Church—the event of the Resurrection. This Christ is not someone who lived and died and of whom we read and learn. He is someone who, because of the Resurrection, is alive for evermore, and whom we meet and experience. Christ is not a dead hero, not a past founder, but a living presence.

(iv) The result of all this is that *He has the supremacy in all things.* The Resurrection of Jesus Christ is His title to supreme lordship. By His resurrection He has shown that He has conquered every enemy and every opposing power, and that there is nothing in life and in death which can bind or hold Him. The final triumph of His Resurrection has given Him the right to be Lord of all.

So there are four great facts about Jesus Christ in His relationship to the Church, which now we can put in order. He is the living Lord; He is the source and origin of the Church; He is the constant director of the Church; and He is the Lord of all, by virtue of His victory over death.

V. WHAT JESUS CHRIST IS TO ALL THINGS

Colossians I: 15-23 (*continued*)

IN verses 19 and 20 Paul sets down certain great truths about the work of Christ for the whole universe.

(i) The object of His coming was *reconciliation.* He came

to heal the breach and to bridge the chasm between God and man. We must note one thing quite clearly, and we must always retain it in our memories. The initiative in reconciliation was with God. The New Testament never talks of God being reconciled to men, but always of men being reconciled to God. God's attitude to men was love, and it was never anything else but love. Sometimes a theology is preached in which it is implied that something that Jesus did changed the attitude of God, that God would have condemned men had it not been for the action of Jesus, that Jesus changed the wrath of God into the love of God. There is no justification in the New Testament for any such view. It was God who began the whole process of salvation and reconciliation. It was because God so *loved* the world that He sent His Son. His one object in sending His Son into this world was to woo men back to Himself, and, as Paul puts it, to reconcile all things to Himself.

(ii) The medium of reconciliation was *the blood of the Cross*. The dynamic of reconciliation is the death of Jesus Christ. What does Paul mean by that? He means exactly what he said in *Romans* 8: 32 : " He that spared not His own Son, but delivered Him up for us all, how shall He not with Him also freely give us all things? " In the death of Jesus, God is saying to us, " I love you like that. I love you enough to see my Son suffer and die for you. I love you enough to bear the Cross on my heart, if only it will win you to myself." The Cross is the proof that there is no length to which the love of God will refuse to go, in order to win men's hearts. The Cross is the medium of reconciliation because the Cross is the final proof of the love of God; and a love like that demands an answering love. If the Cross will not waken love and wonder in men's hearts, nothing will.

(iii) We must note one point in the way that Paul defines the scope of reconciliation. He say that in Christ God was reconciling *all things* to Himself. The Greek is

a neuter (*panta*). Now the point of this is that the reconciliation of God extends not only to all persons, but to
all creation, animate and inanimate. The vision of Paul
was a redeemed universe, a universe in which not only
the people but the very things were redeemed. This is
an amazing thought. It must mean that God's love does
something for every part and particle of the created
universe. There is no doubt that Paul was thinking of
the Gnostics here. We will remember that the Gnostics
regarded matter as essentially and incurably evil; therefore
the world is evil; but, as Paul sees it, the world is not
evil. The world is God's world and shares in the universal
reconciliation. There is a lesson and a warning here. Too
often in Christianity there has been a suspicion of the
world. " Earth is a desert drear." Too often Christians have
regarded the world as evil. We remember the story of the
Puritan. Someone said to him, as they walked along the
road, " That's a lovely flower". And the Puritan answered,
" I have learned to call nothing lovely in this lost and sinful world." So far from being the Christian attitude that
is in fact heresy, for that was the very attitude of the
Gnostic heretics, who threatened to destroy the faith.
This is God's world, and it is a redeemed world, for in some
amazing way God in Christ was reconciling the whole
universe of men and living creatures and even inanimate
things to Himself.

(iv) The passage ends with a curious little phrase. Paul
says that this reconciliation extended not only to things
on earth, but also to things in heaven. How was it that any
reconciliation was necessary for heavenly things and
heavenly beings? This is a passage which has exercised the
thought and the ingenuity of many commentators. Let
us look at some of the explanations.

(a) It has been suggested that even the heavenly places
and even the angels there were under sin, and needed to be

redeemed and reconciled to God. In *Job* we read: " His angels He charged with folly " (*Job* 4: 18). ' The heavens are not clean in His sight " (*Job* 15: 15). So it is suggested that even the angelic beings needed the reconciliation of the Cross.

(*b*) Origen, the great universalist, thought that the phrase refers to nothing other than the devil and his angels Origen—and he was one of the greatest and most adventurous thinkers the Church ever had—believed that in the end even the devil and all his angels would be reconciled to God through the work of Jesus Christ.

(*c*) It has been suggested that when Paul said that the reconciling work of Christ extended to all things in earth and in heaven, he did not mean anything definite and precise, but that it is simply a magnificent and sonorous phrase in which the complete adequacy of the reconciling work of Christ is set out. On this view it is a mistake to try to attach a precise meaning to the words, and they are to be taken simply as a resounding phrase.

(*d*) The most interesting suggestion was made by Theodoret and followed by Erasmus. He suggested that the point of this is, not that the heavenly angels were reconciled to God, but that they were reconciled to *men*. The suggestion is that the angels were angry with men for what men had done to God, that the angels resented the rebellion and the disobedience of men, and wished to destroy men, and the work of Christ took away the wrath of the angels when they saw how much God still loved men.

However these things may be, this much is certain, God's only aim was to reconcile men to Himself in Jesus Christ, the medium by which He did so was the death of Christ which proved that there were no limits to His love, and that reconciliation extends to all the universe, in earth and in heaven alike.

VI. THE AIM AND OBLIGATION OF RECONCILIATION

Colossians I: 15-23 *(continued)*

IN verses 21 to 23 are set out the aim and the obligation of reconciliation.

(i) The aim of reconciliation is *holiness*. Christ carried out his sacrificial work of reconciliation in order to present us to God consecrated, unblemished and irreproachable. It is easy to twist and to distort the idea of the love of God. It is easy to say, " Well, if God loves me like this, and if God wishes nothing but this reconciliation, then sin does not matter. I can do what I like and God will still love me." The very reverse is true. The fact that a man is loved does not give him *carte blanche* to do as he likes; it lays upon him the greatest obligation in the world, the obligation of being worthy of that love. In one sense the love of God makes things easy, for it takes away the fear of God, and we are no longer criminals at the bar of judgment, certain of nothing but condemnation. But in another sense it makes things almost agonizingly and impossibly difficult, for it lays upon us this ultimate obligation of seeking to be worthy of the love of God.

(ii) Reconciliation has another kind of obligation. It lays upon us the obligation to stand fast in the faith, and never to lose or abandon the hope of the gospel. Reconciliation demands loyalty; and reconciliation demands that through sunshine and through shadow we should never lose confidence in the love of God. Out of the wonder of reconciliation are born the strength of unshakable loyalty and the radiance of unconquerable hope.

THE PRIVILEGE AND THE TASK

Colossians I: 24-29

Now I rejoice in my sufferings for you, and in my flesh, for the sake of His body, I fill up what is lacking in the afflictions of Christ. By His body, I mean the Church, of which I was made a servant, according to the office which God gave me to exercise for your sakes. That office is to make the word of God fully known, that secret which has remained hidden throughout all the ages and the generations, but which has now been made manifest to God's dedicated people; for God desired to make known to them how great was the glorious wealth among the Gentiles of this secret now revealed, and that secret is, Christ in you, your glorious hope. It is that Christ whom we proclaim, warning every man, and teaching every man in all wisdom, that we may present every man complete in Christ. That is the end for which I toil, striving with His energy, which works mightily within me.

PAUL begins this passage with a daring thought. He thinks of the sufferings and the imprisonment through which he is passing as filling up and completing the sufferings of Jesus Christ Himself. Jesus died to save His Church; but the Church must be upbuilt, and extended; it must be kept strong and pure and true; therefore, anyone who serves the Church by widening her borders, establishing her faith, saving her from errors, is doing the work of Christ. And if such service involves suffering and pain and sacrifice, that affliction is filling up and sharing the very suffering of Christ Himself. To suffer in the service of Christ is not a penalty, it is a privilege and an honour, for it is sharing in the work of Christ.

Here Paul sets out the very essence of the task which has been given to him by God. That task was to bring to men a new discovery, a secret kept throughout the ages and the generations and now revealed. That discovery and that secret were that the glory of the hope of the gospel was not only for the Jews, but was for all men everywhere. This was Paul's great contribution to the Christian faith; he took Christ to the Gentiles. He destroyed for ever the idea that God and the love and the mercy of God were the property of any one people and of any one nation. He confronted men with the conviction that Christ is for

Gentile and Jew alike. That is why Paul is in a special sense our saint and our apostle, because, had it not been for him, Christianity might have become nothing wider than a new Judaism, and we and all other Gentiles might never have received it.

So Paul sets down his great aim. It is to warn *every man*, and to teach *every man*, and to present *every man* complete in Christ. Here is the very dream of God—and it was a new dream.

The *Jew* would never have agreed that God had any use for every man; the Jew would have refused to accept the idea that God was the God of the Gentiles. That God wanted every man, that every man could be presented to God, would have seemed incredible and even blasphemous to a Jew. The *Gnostic* would never have agreed that every man could be warned and taught and presented complete to God. As we have seen, he believed that the knowledge necessary for salvation was so involved and elaborate and difficult that it must be the possession of the spiritual aristocracy and of the chosen few. E. J. Goodspeed quotes a passage from Walter Lipman's *Preface to Morals*: " As yet no teacher has ever appeared who was wise enough to know how to teach his wisdom to all mankind. In fact, the great teachers have attempted nothing so utopian. They were quite well aware how difficult for most men is wisdom, and they have confessed frankly that the perfect life was for the select few. It is arguable, in fact, that the very idea of teaching the highest wisdom to all men is the recent notion of a humanitarian and romantically democratic age, and that it is quite foreign to the thought of all great teachers." It has always been the case that men have openly or tacitly agreed that wisdom is not for every one.

The fact is that the only thing in this world which is for every man is Christ. It is not every man who can be a thinker. There are gifts which are not granted to every man. Not every man can master every craft, or even every game. There are those who are colour-blind and to whom the loveliness of art means nothing. There are those who are tone-deaf and to whom the glory of music does not exist. Not every man can be a writer, or a student, or a preacher, or a singer or a speaker. Even human love at its highest is not granted to all men. The one thing which is for every man is Jesus Christ. There are gifts a man will never possess; there are privileges a man will never enjoy; there are heights of this world's attainment which a man will never scale; but to every man there is open the good news of the gospel, and the love of God in Christ Jesus our Lord, and the transforming power which can bring holiness into life.

LOVE'S STRUGGLE

Colossians 2: 1

> I want you to know how great a struggle I am going through for you, and for the people of Laodicaea, and for all those who have never seen me face to face.

HERE is a brief lifting of the curtain, and a poignant glimpse into the heart of Paul. Paul is going though a struggle for these Christians whom he had never seen, but whom he loved.

He associates the Laodicaeans with the Colossians, and speaks of all those who had never seen his face. He is thinking of that group of three towns in the Lycus valley, Laodicaea, Hierapolis and Colosse stood close together. Laodicaea and Hierapolis stood in full view of each other, on either side of the valley, with the river Lycus flowing between them, six miles apart; and Colosse was twelve miles further up the river. It is the groups of Christians in that area of three towns of which Paul is thinking, and which he is picturing in his mind's eye.

The word he uses for *struggle* is a vivid word; it is the word *agōn*, from which there comes our own word *agony*. Paul is fighting a hard battle for his friends. We must remember where Paul was when he wrote this letter; he was in prison in Rome, awaiting judgment, and almost certain condemnation. What then was his struggle?

(i) It was a struggle in prayer. Paul must have longed to go to Colosse himself. He must have longed to face himself the false teachers, and himself to deal with their arguments, and himself to recall those who were straying away from the truth. But Paul was in prison. There had come to Paul a time when there was nothing left to do but to pray. What he could not do himself, he must leave to God. So Paul wrestled in prayer for those whom he could not see. When time and distance and circumstance separate us from those whom we long to help, there is always one way left to help them, and that is to wrestle in prayer for them.

(ii) But it may well be that there was another struggle going on in Paul's mind. Paul was a human being with all a man's natural problems. He was in prison and he was awaiting trial before Nero. And the issue was almost certainly death. It would have been easy to play the coward, it would have been so easy to abandon the truth for the sake of safety. It would have been so easy to fail Jesus Christ, and to desert from the cause. Paul well knew that such a desertion and such a failure would be disastrous in their consequences. If the young Churches knew that Paul had failed and given in and denied Christ, the heart would have been taken from them, their resistance power would have been destroyed, and it would have been the end of Christianity for many. Paul's struggle was not for the sake of himself alone; it was also for the sake of those whose eyes were fixed upon him, and who regarded him as their leader and father in the faith. We will do well to remember in any situation in life that there are those who are watching us; and our action will either confirm or destroy their faith. Our struggle in life is never for ourselves alone; always the honour of Christ is in our hands, and the faith of others is in our keeping.

THE LETTER TO THE COLOSSIANS

THE MARKS OF THE FAITHFUL CHURCH (1)

Colossians 2: 2-7

My struggle is that their hearts may be encouraged, that they may be united together in love, that they may come to all the wealth of the assured ability to take the right decision in any situation, to the knowledge of that truth which only God's own may know, I mean of Christ, in whom are hidden all the treasures of wisdom and of knowledge.

I say this so that no one may lead you into error by false reasoning with persuasive arguments. For, even if I am absent from you in the body, I am with you in spirit, happy when I see you maintaining your ranks and the solid bulwark of your faith in Christ.

So, then, as you have received Christ, Jesus the Lord, live your life in Him. Continue to remain firmly rooted, and go on being built up in Him. Continue to be established more and more firmly in the faith, as you were taught it, and to overflow with thanksgiving.

HERE is Paul's prayer for the Church, and in it we can distinguish the great marks which should distinguish a living and a faithful Church.

(i) It should be a Church of *courageous hearts*. Paul prays that their hearts may be *encouraged*. The word which he uses for to encourage is *parakalein*. Sometimes that word means to *comfort*, sometimes it means to *exhort*, but always at the back of it there is the idea of enabling a person to meet some difficult situation with confidence and with gallantry. One of the Greek historians uses this word in a most interesting and suggestive way. There was a Greek regiment which had lost heart, lost courage, and which was utterly dejected. The general sent a leader to talk to that regiment, and he talked to it to such purpose that courage was reborn, and a body of dispirited men became a body of men fit again for heroic action. That is what *parakalein* means here. It is Paul's prayer that the Church may be filled with that courage which can cope heroically with any situation.

(ii) It should be a Church in which the members are *knit together in love*. Without love there can be no such thing as a Church. The method of Church government is of no importance; the ritual of a Church is of no importance. These things are things which may change from time to time and from place to place. The one mark which should distinguish a true Church is love for God and love for the brethren. When love dies, the Church dies. When love is there, the Church is strong, because when love is there Jesus Christ, the Lord of love, is also there.

(iii) It should be a Church *equipped with every kind of wisdom*. Paul here uses three words for wisdom.

(a) In verse 2 he uses the word *sunesis*, which the Authorized Version translates *understanding*. We have already seen that *sunesis* is what we might call *critical knowledge*. It is the ability to apply first principles to any given situation; it is the assured ability to assess any situation and to decide what practical course of action is necessary within it. A real Church will have the practical knowledge of what to do whenever action is called for.

(b) He says that in Jesus are hid all the treasures of *wisdom* and *knowledge*. Wisdom is *sophia* and knowledge is *gnōsis*. These two words do not simply repeat each other; there is a difference between them. *Gnōsis* is the power to apprehend the truth; it is almost intuitive and instinctive; it is the power to grasp the truth when we see it and hear it, and when, as it were, it flashes on us. But *sophia* is the power to support and to confirm and to commend the truth with wise and intelligent argument and presentation, once it has been intuitively grasped. *Gnōsis* is that by which a man grasps the truth; *sophia* is that by which a man is enabled to give a reason for the hope that is in him.

So, then, the real Church will have the wisdom which can act for the best in any given situation, the wisdom which is clear and far-sighted, the wisdom which is not blinded by prejudice or ignorance. It will have the wisdom which can instinctively recognize and grasp the truth when it sees and hears the truth. And it will have the wisdom which can make the truth intelligible to the thinking mind, and which can wisely and persuasively command the truth to others.

All this wisdom, says Paul, is *hidden* in Christ. The word that Paul uses for hidden is the word *apokruphos*. His very use of that word is a blow aimed at the Gnostics. The word *apokruphos* means *hidden from the common gaze*, and therefore *secret*. We have seen that the Gnostics believed that a great mass of elaborate and involved knowledge was necessary for salvation. That knowledge they set down in their books, and they called these books *apokruphos* because they were hidden and barred to the ordinary and to the simple man. By using this one word Paul is saying, " You Gnostics have your wisdom, shut off, hidden, barred from ordinary people; you call it *apokruphos*. We too have our knowledge; but that knowledge of ours is not hidden in unintelligible books; it is hidden in Christ; and therefore it is open to all men everywhere." The truth of Christianity is not a secret which is hidden; it is a secret which is revealed.

THE MARKS OF THE FAITHFUL CHURCH (2)
Colossians 2: 2-7 (continued)

(iv) The true Church must have *the power to resist seductive teaching*. It must be such that men cannot beguile it with *enticing words*. *Enticing words* translates the Greek word *pithanologia*. This was a word of the law-courts; it was the word for the persuasive power of a lawyer's arguments, the kind of persuasive power which could make the worse appear the better reason, and which could enable the criminal to escape the just punishment he should have suffered, the power which could sway an assembly—and sometimes sway it into mistaken ways. The true Church should have such a grip of the truth that it cannot listen to specious and seductive arguments.

(v) The true Church should have in it *a soldier's discipline*. As the Authorized Version has it, Paul is glad to hear of the *order* and of the *steadfastness* of the faith of the Colossians. These two words present a vivid picture, for they are both military words. The word which is translated *order* is *taxis*, which means a *rank* or an ordered arrangement. The Church should be like an ordered army, rank upon rank, with every man in his appointed place, ready and willing to obey the word of command. The word which is translated *steadfastness* is *stereōma*, which means a solid *bulwark*, an immovable *phalanx*. It describes an army set out in an unbreakable square, solidly immovable against the shock of the charge of the enemy. Within the Church there should be a disciplined order and a strong steadiness, like the order and the steadiness of a trained and disciplined body of troops.

(vi) In the true Church *life must be in Christ*. Its members must walk in Christ; their whole lives must be lived in the conscious presence of Christ. They must be *rooted* and *built* in Him. There are two pictures here. The word which is used for *rooted* is the word which would be used of a tree, with its roots deep in the soil. The word which is used for *built* is the word which would be used of a house erected on a strong and firm foundation. Just as the great tree is deep-rooted in the soil, and draws its nourishment from it, so the Christian is rooted in Christ, and Christ is the source of his life and his strength. Just as the house stands fast because it is built on strong foundations, so the Christian life is strong against any storm because it is founded, not on any man's strength, but on the strength of Christ. Christ is alike the source of the Christian's life, and the foundation of the Christian's stability.

(vii) The true Church *holds fast to the faith which it has received*. It never forgets the teaching about Christ which it has received and the faith which it has been taught. It is to be noted that this does not mean a frozen orthodoxy in which all change and all adventure of thought is heresy. We have only to remember how, in *Colossians*, Paul strikes out quite new lines in his thinking about Jesus Christ to see how far that was from his intention. But it does mean this—that there are certain beliefs which remain the foundation of all belief, and that they do not change. Paul might travel down new pathways and avenues of thought, but he always began and ended with the unchanging and unchangeable truth that Jesus Christ is Lord.

(viii) The distinguishing mark of the true Church is *an abounding and overflowing gratitude*. Thanksgiving is the constant and characteristic note of the Christian life. As J. B. Lightfoot put it: " Thanksgiving is the end of all human conduct, whether observed in words or works." The one concern of the Christian is to tell in words and to show in life his gratitude to God for all that God has done for him in nature and in grace. Epictetus was not a Christian, but that little, old, lame slave who became one of the great moral teachers of paganism, wrote: " What else can I, a lame old man, do but sing hymns to God? If, indeed, I were a nightingale, I would be singing as a nightingale; if a swan, as a swan. But, as it is, I am a rational being, therefore I must be singing hymns of praise to God. This is my task; I do it, and will not desert this post, as long as it may be given me to fill it; and I exhort you to join with me in this same song." (Epictetus, *Discourses* I.16.21). The Christian will always praise God from whom all blessings flow.

ADDITIONS TO CHRIST

Colossians 2: 8-23

> Beware lest there will be anyone who will carry you off as his spoil, by insisting on the necessity of a so-called philosophy, which is, in fact, an empty delusion, a philosophy which has been handed down by human tradition, and which is concerned with the elements

of this world, and not with Christ; for in Him there dwells the fulness of the divine nature; and you have found this fulness in Him who is the head of every power and authority. In Him you have been circumcised with a circumcision not made by man's hands, a circumcision which consists in putting off the whole of that part of you which is dominated by sinful human nature, which you were able to do by the circumcision which belongs to Christ. You were buried with Him in the act of baptism, and in that act you were raised with Him through your faith in the effective working of God, who raised Him from the dead. God made you alive with Him, when you were dead in your sins, and when you were still uncircumcised Gentiles. He forgave you all your sins, and wiped out the charge-list, which set out all your self-admitted debts, a charge-list which was based on the ordinances of the law, and which was in direct opposition to you. He nailed it to His Cross, and put it right out of sight. He stripped the powers and authorities of all their power, and publicly put them to shame, and, through the Cross, lead them captive in His triumphal train.

Let no one take you to task in matters of food or drink, or with regard to yearly festivals, and monthly new moons, and weekly sabbaths. These are only the shadow of things to come; the real substance belongs to Christ. Let no one rob you of your prize, by walking in ostentatious humility in the worship of angels, making a parade of the things he has seen, vainly inflated with pride because he is dominated by his sinful human nature, and not holding fast to the head, from whom the whole body, supplied and held together by the joints and muscles, increases with the increase which only God can give.

If you died with Christ to the elements of this world, why do you continue to submit yourselves to their rules and regulations, as if you were still living in a world without God? " Handle not! Taste not! Touch not! " are their slogans. These are rules which are humanly taught and humanly imposed, and they are rules which deal with things which are destined for decay as soon as they are used. These things have a reputation for wisdom, with their self-imposed devotion, and their flaunting humility, and their stern treatment of the body, but they have no kind of value in remedying the indulgence of sinful human nature.

THERE can be no doubt that for us this is one of the most difficult passages that Paul ever wrote. For those who heard it or read it for the first time it would be crystal clear. The trouble about it is that it is packed from beginning to end with allusions to the false teaching which was threatening to wreck the Colossian Church. We do not know precisely and in detail what that teaching was. Therefore to us the allusions are obscure, and we can only guess and grope. But every sentence and every phrase would go straight home to the minds and the hearts of the Colossians.

It is so difficult that we propose to treat it in a slightly different way from our usual practice. We have set it out as a whole, in what is more of a paraphrase than a translation. We will take out of it its leading ideas, for in it is possible to see the main lines of the false teaching which was troubling Colosse; and then, after we have looked at it as a whole, we shall examine it in more detail in shorter sections.

The one thing that is clear is that the false teachers wished the Colossians to accept what can only be called *additions to Christ*. They were teaching that Jesus Christ Himself is not sufficient; that He was not unique; that He was one among many manifestations of God; and that it was necessary to worship and to serve and to know other so-called divine and angelic powers in addition to Him. We can distinguish five additions to Christ which these false teachers wished to make.

(i) They wished to teach men an additional *philosophy* (verse 8). As they saw it, the simple truth preached by Jesus, and written down in the gospel, was not enough. It had to be filled out and assisted and completed by an elaborate system of pseudo-philosophical thought, which was far too difficult for the simple, and which only the intellectual could understand.

(ii) They wished men to accept a system of *astrology* (verse 8). As we shall see, there is a doubt about the meaning of the matter, but we think that it is most likely that *the elements of the world* are the elemental spirits of the universe, and especially of the stars and the planets It was the teaching of these false teachers that men were still under these influences and under these powers, and they needed a special knowledge, beyond that which Jesus could give, to be liberated from these powers.

(iii) They wished to impose *circumcision* on Christians (verse 11). Faith was not enough; to faith circumcision had to be added. A badge in the flesh was to take the place of, or at least to be an addition to, an attitude of the heart.

(iv) They wished to lay down *ascetic rules and regulations* (verses 16, 20-23). They wished to introduce all kinds of rules and regulations about what a man might eat and drink, and about what days he must observe as festivals and fasts. All the old Jewish food laws, and all the old Jewish regulations—and more—were to be brought back.

(v) They wished to introduce *the worship of angels* (verse 17). They were teaching that Jesus was only one of many intermediaries between God and man, and that all these intermediaries must receive their worship and their service.

It can be seen that here there is a mixture of Gnoticism and Judaism. The intellectual knowledge and the astrology come direct from Gnosticism; the asceticism and the rules and regulations come direct from Judaism. What happened was this. We have seen that the Gnostics believed that all kinds of special knowledge and special teaching, beyond the gospel, were needed for salvation. There were Jews who joined forces with the Gnostics, and who declared that the special knowledge required was none other than the knowledge which Judaism could give. This explains why the teaching of the Colossians false teachers combined the beliefs of Gnosticism with the practices of Judaism.

The one thing that is certain is that the false teachers

taught that Jesus Christ, and the teaching of Jesus Christ, and the work of Jesus Christ, were not in themselves enough, and were not sufficient for salvation. Let us now take the passage section by section.

TRADITIONS AND THE STARS

Colossians 2: 8-10

> Beware lest there will be anyone who will carry you off as his spoil, by insisting on the necessity of a so-called philosophy, which is, in fact, an empty delusion, a philosophy which has been handed down by human tradition, and which is concerned with the elements of this world and not with Christ; for in Him there dwells the fulness of the divine nature; and you have found this fulness in Him who is the head of every power and authority.

PAUL begins by drawing a vivid picture of the false teachers. He speaks of anyone who will *carry you off as his spoil*. The word is *sulagōgein*, and it could be used of a slave dealer carrying away the people of a conquered nation into slavery. To Paul it was an amazing and a tragic thing that men who had been ransomed and redeemed and liberated (*Colossians* 1: 12-14). could contemplate submitting themselves to a new and disastrous slavery.

These men offer a philosophy, which they declare is necessary in addition to the teaching of Christ and the words of the gospel.

(i) It is a philosophy which has been *handed down by human tradition*. The Gnostics were in the habit of claiming that their special teaching was, in fact, teaching which had been told by word of mouth by Jesus, sometimes to Mary, sometimes to Matthew, and sometimes to Peter. They did, in fact, say that there were things which Jesus never told the crowd and which He communicated only to the chosen few. The charge which Paul makes against these teachers is that their teaching is a human thing; it has no guarantee and basis in Scripture. It was a product of the human mind; and not a message of the Word of God. To speak like this is not to drift into fundamentalism or to submit to a tyranny of the written word, but it is to hold that no teaching can be Christian teaching which is at variance with the basic truths of Scripture, and with the Word of God.

(ii) It is a philosophy which has to do with the *elements of this world*. This is a much-discussed phrase of which the meaning is still in doubt. The word for elements is *stoicheia*, and *stoicheia* has two meanings.

(a) *Stoicheia* means literally *things which are set out in a row*. It is, for instance, the word for a file of soldiers. But one of its commonest meanings is the A B C, the letters of the alphabet, no doubt because they form a series which can be set out in a row. Now because *stoicheia* can mean the letters of the alphabet, it can also very commonly mean *elementary instruction in any subject*. We still speak of learning the A B C of a subject, when we mean taking the first steps in it. It is possible that that is the meaning here. Paul may be saying, " These false teachers claim that they are giving you knowledge which is very advanced and very profound. In point of fact it is knowledge which is uninstructed and rudimentary, because at the best it is knowledge of the human mind. The real knowledge, the real fulness of God, is in Jesus Christ. And, if you listen to these false teachers, so far from receiving deep and profound spiritual knowledge, you are simply slipping back into rudimentary and mistaken introduction, which you should have left behind long ago." It may well be that Paul is saying that to listen to the so-called philosophy of these false teachers is a retrograde and not a forward step.

(b) But *stoicheia* has a second meaning. It means the *elemental spirits of the world*, and especially the spirits of the stars and planets. There are still people today who take astrology seriously. They wear signs of the zodiac badges and charms, and they read newspaper columns which tell what is forecast for them in the stars. But it is almost impossible for us to realize how dominated the ancient world was by the idea of the influence of the elemental spirits and of the stars. Astrology was then, as someone has said, the queen of the sciences. Even men so great as Julius Caesar and Augustus, even men so cynical as Tiberius, and even men so level-headed as Vespasian would take no step without consulting the stars. Alexander the Great believed implicitly in the influence of the stars. Men and women believed that their whole lives were fixed and settled by the stars. If a man was born under a fortunate star all was well. If he was born under an unlucky star, he could not look for happiness. If any undertaking was to have any chance of success, the stars must be observed. Men felt themselves to be in the grip of a rigid determinism which was settled by the influence of the stars and of the elemental spirits of the world: men were the slaves of the stars.

Now, there was one possibility of escape. If men only knew the right pass-words and the right formulae, they might escape from this fatalistic influence of the stars; and a great part of the secret knowledge and the secret teaching of Gnosticism and of kindred faiths and philosophies was knowledge which claimed to give the devotee power to escape from the power of the stars; and in all probability that was what the false teachers of Colosse were offering. They said, " Jesus Christ is all very well, He can do much for you; but He cannot enable you to escape from your subjection to the stars. We alone have the secret knowledge which can enable you to do that." Paul was sufficiently the child of his age to believe in these elemental spirits, the principalities, the powers and the authorities. His answer is: " You need nothing but Christ to overcome any power in the universe; for in Him is nothing less than the fulness of God; and He is the head of every power and authority, for He created them."

The Gnostic teachers offered an additional philosophy

and an additional astrology; Paul insisted on the triumphant adequacy of Christ to overcome any power in any part of the universe. You cannot at one and the same time believe in the power of Christ and the influence of the stars.

THE REAL AND THE UNREAL CIRCUMCISION

Colossians 2: 11, 12

> In Him you have been circumcised with a circumcision not made by man's hands, a circumcision which consists in putting off the whole of that part of you which is dominated by sinful human nature, which you were able to do by the circumcision which belongs to Christ. You were buried with Him in the act of baptism, and in that act you were raised with Him through you faith in the effective working of God, who raised Him from the dead.

THE false teachers were demanding that Gentile Christians should be circumcised. Circumcision was the badge of God's chosen people. God, they argued, had said to Abraham, " This is my covenant, which ye shall keep, between me and you, and thy seed after thee; Every man child among you shall be circumcised " (*Genesis* 17: 10).

All through the history of Israel there had been two views of circumcision. There was the view of those who said that circumcision in itself was enough to put a man right with God, that the physical act of circumcision was all that was required. They argued that it did not matter whether an Israelite was a good man or a bad man; all that mattered was that he was an Israelite, and that he had been circumcised. But the great thinkers, and the great spiritual leaders of Israel, and the great prophets took a very different view of things. They insisted that circumcision was only the outward mark of a man who was inwardly dedicated to God. They used the very word *circumcision* in an adventurous sense. They talked of

166

uncircumcised *lips* (*Exodus* 6: 12), of a *heart* which was circumcised or uncircumcised (*Leviticus* 26: 41; *Ezekiel* 44: 7, 9; *Deuteronomy* 30: 6); of the *uncircumcised* ear (*Jeremiah* 6: 10). To the great thinkers to be circumcised meant not to have a certain operation carried out on a man's flesh, but to have a change effected in his heart and in his whole life. Circumcision was the badge of a person dedicated to God; but the dedication lay not in the circumcision of the flesh, but in the excision from life of everything which was against the will of God.

That was the answer of the prophets centuries before; and that was still Paul's answer to the false teachers. He said to them, " You demand circumcision; but you must remember that circumcision does not mean the removal of the foreskin from a man's body; it means the putting off of that whole part of his human nature which sets him at variance with God." And Paul then went on: " And only Jesus Christ can do that. Any priest can circumcise a man's foreskin; only Christ can bring about that spiritual circumcision which means cutting away from a man's life and self everything which keeps him from being God's obedient child."

Paul goes still further. For him this was not theory, it was fact. " That very act," he said, " has already happened to you in baptism." When we think of Paul's claim for baptism and of Paul's view of baptism we must remember three things. In the early Church, as today in the mission field, and even in the Church extension areas, men were coming straight out of heathenism into Christianity. They were knowingly and deliberately leaving one way of life for another. They were making in the act of baptism a voluntary, conscious and deliberate act of decision. This is before the days of infant baptism. Infant baptism did not and could not come until the Christian family had become a reality. All this of which Paul is thinking happened in the days of the Christian individual, before the Christian family had become a reality at all. Baptism in the time of

Paul was three things. It was *adult* baptism; it was *instructed* baptism; and, wherever possible, it was baptism by *total immersion*.

Therefore, in the days of Paul the symbolism of baptism was manifest. As the waters closed over the man's head, it was as if he died. As he rose again from the cleansing water, it was as if he rose to life anew. His old life was dead; the new life stretched in front of him. Part of him was dead and gone for ever; he was a new man risen to a new life.

But, it must be noted, that that symbolism could only become a reality under one condition. It could only become real when a man believed intensely in the life and the death and the resurrection of Jesus Christ. It could only happen when a man believed in the effective working of God, that power of God which raised Jesus Christ from the dead. Only then could he be convinced that the power which had brought Jesus Christ through the Cross and which had raised Him in the Resurrection could do the same for him. Baptism for the Christian was in truth a dying and a rising again, because he believed that Christ had died and risen again, and that he was sharing the experience of his Lord.

" You speak about circumcision," said Paul. " The only true circumcision is when a man dies and rises with Christ in baptism, in such a way that it is not part of his body which is cut away, but his whole sinful self is destroyed, and he is filled with newness of life, and with the very holiness of God."

TRIUMPHANT FORGIVENESS

Colossians 2: 13-15

God made you alive with Christ, when you were dead in your sins, and when you were still uncircumcised Gentiles. He forgave you all your sins, and wiped out the charge-list, which set out all your self-admitted debts, a charge-list which was based on the ordinances of the law, and which was in direct opposition to you. He nailed it to His Cross and put it right out of sight. He stripped the powers and authorities of all their power, and publicly put them to shame, and, through the Cross, led them captive in His triumphal train.

ALMOST all great teachers and preachers have thought in pictures; and here Paul uses a series of vivid pictures to show what God in Christ has done for men. The intention behind it all is to show that Christ has done all that can be done, and all that need be done, and that there is no need to bring in any other intermediaries for the full salvation of men. There are three main pictures here.

(i) Men were dead in their sins; they were utterly defeated by sin; they were powerless to break the chains of sin; they were powerless to meet the condemnation of sin. They had no more power than dead men either to overcome sin or to atone for sin. Jesus Christ by His work has liberated men both from the power and from the consequences of sin. He has given them a life so new and so vital and so liberated and emancipated that it can only be said that He has raised them from the dead, and given them a new life. Further, it was the old belief that only the Jews were dear to God, that they were the chosen people, the special and the peculiar possession of God. But this saving and atoning power of Christ has come even to the uncircumcised Gentile, even to the man with whom God had no special covenant at all. The work of Christ is a work of power, because it put life into dead men; it is a work of grace, because it reached out to those who had no reason to expect the benefits of God.

(ii) But the picture becomes even more vivid. As the Authorized Version has it, Jesus Christ blotted out the handwriting of ordinances which was against us. As we have translated it, he wiped out the charge-list, which set out all our self-admitted debts, a charge-list which was based on the ordinances of the law. There are two Greek words here on which the whole picture depends.

(a) Paul speaks of the *handwriting which was against us, or, the charge-list which set out our self-admitted debts.* The word for *handwriting* or *charge-list* is *cheirographon.* It literally means an *autograph*; but its technical meaning— a meaning which everyone would understand—was a note of hand signed by a debtor acknowledging his indebtedness. It was almost exactly what we call an I O U. It was a signed admission of debt and default. Men's sins had piled up a vast list of debts to God. Further, it could be said that men quite definitely acknowledged that debt. More than once the Old Testament shows the children of Israel hearing and accepting the laws of God, and calling down curses on themselves, if they failed to keep them (*Exodus* 24: 3; *Deuteronomy* 27: 14-26). And in the New Testament we find the picture of the Gentiles as having, not the written law and the written revelation of God which the Jews had, but the unwritten law in their hearts, and the voice of conscience speaking within (*Romans* 2: 14, 15). Men were in debt to God because of their sins, and men knew it; they could not do other than admit it. There was a self-confessed indictment against them; there was a charge-list which, as it were, they themselves had signed and had admitted was accurate.

(b) Then comes the second great word. God *blotted out, or wiped out* that charge-list and indictment. The word for wiping out is the Greek verb *exaleiphein.* To understand that word is to understand the amazing mercy of God. The substance on which ancient documents were written was papyrus, a kind of paper made of the pith of the bulrush; or it was vellum, a substance made of the skins of animals. Both were fairly expensive and certainly could not be wasted. Now ancient ink had no acid in it; it lay on the surface of the paper and did not, as modern ink usually does, bite into it. Sometimes a scribe, to save paper, used papyrus or vellum that had already been written upon. When he did that, he took a sponge and wiped the writing out. And in the ancient times it could be wiped out. Ancient ink was indelible so long as it was left alone; but because it was only on the surface of the paper it could be wiped clean away. It was wiped out as if it had never been. It is as if God, in His amazing mercy, banished the record of our sins so completely that it was as if it had never been. It was gone in such a way that not a trace remained.

(c) But Paul still goes on. God took that indictment and He nailed it to the Cross of Christ. It used to be said that in the ancient world when a law or a decree or an ordinance was cancelled, it was fastened to a board and a nail was driven clean through it. But it is doubtful if that was the case and if that is the picture. Rather it is this—on the Cross of Christ the indictment that was against us was itself crucified. The very indictment was, as it were, executed. It was wiped out as if it had never been; it was executed on the Cross; and it was put clean out of the way, so that it might never be seen again. Paul seems to have searched human activity to find a series of pictures which would show how completely God in His mercy in Christ destroyed and banished and wiped out the condemnation that was against us.

Here indeed is grace. And that new era of grace is further underlined in another rather obscure phrase. The condemnation, the indictment, the charge-list had been *based on the ordinances of the law*. Before Christ came men were under law; they broke the law because no man can perfectly keep the law. The indictment took its force and power from the regulations and decrees of the law. But now law is banished and grace has come. Man is not longer a criminal who has broken the law and who is at the mercy of the judgment of God; man is a son who was lost and who can come home and who is wrapped around with grace of God.

(iii) Still one other great picture flashes on the screen of Paul's mind. Jesus has stripped the powers and authorities and made them his captives. As we have seen, the ancient world believed in all kinds of classes and grades of angels, and in all kinds of elemental spirits and demons. Many of these demons and spirits were out to ruin men. It was they who were responsible for demon-possession and the like. They were hostile, malicious, malignant to men. Jesus conquered them for ever. He *stripped* them; the word that is used is the word for stripping the weapons and the armour from a defeated foe. Once and for all Jesus broke their power. He put them to open shame and lead them captive in His triumphant train. The picture is the picture of the triumph of a Roman general. When a Roman general had won a really notable triumph, he was allowed to march his victorious armies through the streets of Rome, and behind him there followed the wretched company of the kings and the leaders and the peoples he had vanquished and conquered. They were openly branded as his victims and his spoils. Paul thinks of Jesus as a triumphant conqueror, enjoying a kind of cosmic triumph; and in His triumphal procession are the powers of evil, beaten for ever, for every one to see.

Here in these vivid pictures Paul sets out the total adequacy of the work of Christ. Sin is forgiven; evil is conquered; what more is necessary? There is nothing that the Gnostic knowledge and the Gnostic intermediaries can do for men—Christ has done it all already.

RETROGRESSION

Colossians 2: 16-23

> Let no one take you to task in matters of food or drink, or with regard to yearly festivals, and monthly new moons, and weekly sabbaths. These are only the shadow of things to come; the real substance belongs to Christ. Let no one rob you of your prize, by walking in ostentatious humility in the worship of angels, making a parade of the things which he has seen, vainly inflated with pride because he is dominated by his sinful human nature, and not holding fast to the head, from which the whole body, supplied

and held together by the joints and muscles, increases with the increase which God alone can give.

If you died with Christ to the elements of this world, why do you continue to submit yourselves to their rules and regulations, as if you were still living in a world without God? " Handle not! Taste not! Touch not! " are their slogans. These are rules which are humanly taught and humanly imposed, and they are rules which deal with things which are destined for decay as soon as they are used. These things have a reputation for wisdom, with their self-imposed devotion, and their flaunting humility, and their stern treatment of the body, but they have no kind of value in remedying the indulgencies of sinful human nature.

THIS passage has certain basic Gnostic ideas intertwined and intermingled all through it. In it Paul is warning the Colossians not to adopt certain Gnostic practices, on the grounds that to do so would not be progress but rather retrogression in the faith. Behind this there are four Gnostic practices.

(i) There is Gnostic *asceticism* (verses 16 and 21). There is the teaching which involves a whole host of regulations about what can and what can not be eaten and drunk. In other words there is a return to all the food laws of the Jews, with their lists of things clean and unclean. As we have seen, the Gnostics considered all matter to be essentially evil. If matter is evil, then the body is evil. If the body is evil, two opposite conclusions can be drawn. (*a*) If the body is essentially evil, then it does not matter what we do with it. It makes no difference, if we glut and sate its appetites and treat it with contempt. Being evil it can be used or abused in any way, and it makes no difference. (*b*) If the body is evil, then it must be kept down; it must be beaten and starved, and its every need must be refused and its every impulse chained down. That is to say Gnosticism could issue either in complete immorality or in rigid asceticism. It is the rigid asceticism with which Paul is dealing here. In effect he says, " Have nothing to do with people who identify religion with laws about what you may or may not eat or drink." Jesus Himself had said that it made no difference what a man ate or drank (*Matthew* 15: 10-20: *Mark* 7: 14-23). Peter himself had to learn to cease to talk about clean and unclean foods (*Acts* 10). Paul uses an almost crude phrase which repeats in different words what Jesus had already said. He said, " These things are to perish with the using " (verse 22). He meant exactly what Jesus said when He said that food and drink are eaten, and digested and then eliminated and excreted from the body, and are flushed away down the drain (*Matthew* 15: 17; *Mark* 7: 19). Food and drink are so unimportant that they are destined for decomposition and decay as soon as they are eaten. The Gnostics, then, wished to make religion a thing of rules and regulations about eating and drinking; and there are still those who are more concerned with rules about food than about the charity of the gospel.

(ii) There is the Gnostic and the Jewish *observation of days* (verse 16). They observed yearly feasts, and monthly new moons and weekly sabbaths. They drew out lists of days which specially belonged to God, days on which certain things must be done, and certain things must not be done. They identified religion with ritual and with Sabbath observance.

Paul's criticism of this asceticism and this stress on days is quite clear and logical. He says, " You have been delivered and rescued from all this tyranny of legal rules and regulations. Why then do you want to go and enslave yourself all over again? Why do you want to go back to Jewish legalism and abandon Christian freedom? " The spirit which makes Christianity a thing of rules and regulations is by no means dead yet.

(iii) There were the Gnostic *special visions*. The Authorized Version in verse 18 speaks of the false teacher " intruding into those things which he hath not seen." That is a mistranslation. The correct translation should be

" making a parade of the things which he has seen." The Gnostic prided himself upon special visions and special revelations of secret things, things which were not open to the eyes of ordinary men and women. No one will deny the visions of the mystics, but there is always a danger when a man begins to think that he has attained a height of holiness which enables him to see what common men— as he calls them—cannot see; and the danger is that men will so often see, not what God sends them, but what they want to see.

(iv) There is the *worship of angels* (verses 18 and 20). As we have seen, the Jews had a highly-developed doctrine of angels, and the Gnostics believed in all kinds of inter-mediaries. They worshipped these, while the Christian knows that worship must be kept for God and for Jesus Christ.

Paul makes four criticisms of all this.

(i) He says that all this kind of thing is only a shadow of truth; the real truth is in Christ (verse 17). That is to say, a religion which is founded on eating and drinking certain kinds of food and drink, and on abstaining from others, a religion which is founded on Sabbath observance and the like, is only a shadow of real religion; for real religion is fellowship with Christ.

(ii) He says that there is such a thing as a false humility (verses 18 and 23). When they talked of the worship of angels, both the Gnostics and the Jews would have justified it by saying that God is so great and high and holy that we can never have direct access to Him, and that we must be content to pray to the angels and not direct to God. But the great truth that Christianity preaches is, in fact, exactly the truth that the way to God is open to the humblest and the simplest person, because it was opened by Jesus Christ and no man can ever close it.

(iii) He says that this can lead to sinful pride (verses 18 and 23). The man who is meticulous in his observance of special days, who keeps all the food laws and the regulations, who practices ascetic abstinence, is in very grave danger of thinking himself specially good and of looking down on other people. And it is a basic truth of Christianity that no man who thinks himself good is good, least of all the man who thinks himself better than other people.

(iv) He says that all this is a return to unchristian slavery instead of Christian freedom (verse 20), and that in any event, it does not free a man from fleshly lusts, it only keeps them on the leash (verse 23). The Christian freedom come not from restraining desires by rules and regulations, but from the death of evil desires and the springing to life of good desires, because Christ is in the Christian and the Christian is in Christ.

THE RISEN LIFE

Colossians 3: 1-4

> If then you were raised with Christ, set your hearts on the things which are above where Christ is seated at the right hand of God. Have a mind all of whose thoughts are fixed on the things which are above, not upon the things on earth. For you died, and your life is hidden with Christ in God. Whenever Christ, your life, shall appear, then you too shall appear with Him in glory.

THE point that Paul is making here is this. In baptism the Christian dies and rises again. As the waters close over him, it is as if he was buried in death; as he emerges from the waters, it is like being resurrected into a new life. Now, if that is so, the Christian cannot rise from baptism the same man as he went down into baptism; there must be a difference. Wherein is the difference? The difference lies in the fact that now the thoughts of the Christian must be set on the things which are above. He can no longer be concerned with the trivial passing things of earth; he must be totally concerned with the eternal verities of heaven.

We must note carefully what Paul means by that. He is certainly not pleading for an other-worldliness in which the Christian has withdrawn himself from all the work and all the activities of this world, and in which he does nothing but, as it were, contemplate eternity. Immediately after this Paul goes on to lay down a series of ethical principles which make it quite clear that he expects the Christian to go on with the work of this world, and to maintain all the normal relationships of this world. But there will be this difference—from now on the Christian will see everything in the light and against the background of eternity. He will no longer live as if this world was all that mattered; he will see this world against the background of the larger world of eternity.

This will obviously give him a new set of values, a new way of judging things, a new sense of proportion. Things which the world thought important, he will no longer worry about. Ambitions which dominated the world, will be powerless to touch him. He will go on doing the work of the world, and using the things of the world, but he will use them in a new way. He will, for instance, set giving above getting, serving above ruling, forgiving above avenging. The Christian will see things, not as they appear to men, but as they appear to God. His standard of values will be God's standard, not the standard of men.

And how is this to happen, and to be accomplished? The life of the Christian is hid with Christ in God. There are at least two vivid pictures here.

(i) We remember how we have seen repeatedly that the early Christians regarded baptism as a dying and a rising again. When he entered the water, the Christian was buried with Christ, and when he emerged, he had risen to life anew. Now, when a man was dead and buried, the Greeks very commonly spoke of him as being *hidden in the earth*; when a man died in physical death he was *hidden in the earth*. But the Christian had died a spiritual death in baptism, and he is not hidden in the earth, but *hidden in Christ*. It was the

177

experience of these early Christians that the very act of baptism wrapped a man round with Christ.

(ii) There may well be a word play here which any Greek would recognise at once. We remember how the false teachers called their books of so-called wisdom *apokruphoi*, the books that were hidden from all except from those who were initiated into seeing them; these *apokruphoi*, these hidden books, for the Gnostic held the treasures of wisdom. Now the word which Paul uses to say that our lives are *hidden* with Christ in God, is part of the verb *apokruptein*, from which the adjective *apokruphos* comes. Undoubtedly the one word would suggest the other. It is as if Paul said, " For you the treasures of wisdom are hidden in your secret books; for us Christ is the treasury of wisdom; and we are hidden in Him."

There is still another thought here. The life of the Christian is *hidden* with Christ in God. That which is hidden is concealed and unseen. The world cannot recognize the Christian; the true greatness of the Christian is hidden from the world; but Paul goes on: " The day is coming when Christ will return in glory, and then the Christian, whom no one recognized, will share that glory—and it will be plain for all to see." In a sense Paul is saying—and saying truly—that some day the verdicts of eternity will reverse the verdicts of time, and the judgments of God will overturn the judgments of men.

CHRIST OUR LIFE

Colossians 3: 1-4 (*continued*)

In verse 4 Paul gives to Jesus Christ one of the great titles of devotion. He calls Him *Christ our life*. Here is a thought which was very dear to the heart of Paul. When he was writing to the Philippians, he said, " Christ means life to me " (*Philippians* 1: 21). Years before, when he was writing to the Galatians, he had said, " I live; yet not I, but

Christ liveth in me " (*Galatians* 2 : 20). As Paul saw it, to the Christian Jesus Christ is the most important thing in life; nay more, He *is* life itself.

This is the kind of peak of devotion which we can only dimly understand and which we can only haltingly and imperfectly express. Sometimes we say of a man, " Music is his life—Sport is his life—He lives for his work." Such a man finds life and all that life means in music, in sport, in work, as the case may be. For the Christian, Christ is his life. Jesus Christ dominates his thought and fills his life.

And here we come back to where this passage started— that is precisely why the Christian can and does set his mind and heart and affections on the things which are above, and not on the things of the world. He judges everything in this world by the light of the Cross. He assesses everything in the light of the love which loved him and gave itself for him. In the light of that Cross the world's wealth and the world's ambitions and the world's activities are seen in their true value. In the light of that Cross he sees that love is the only kingliness and service the only royalty; and, therefore, he is delivered from the earthly things and is enabled to set his whole heart and affections on the things which are above.

THE THINGS WHICH LIE BEHIND

Colossians 3: 5-9a

> So, then, put to death these parts of you which are earthly—fornication, uncleanness, passion, evil desire, the desire to get more than you ought—for this is idol worship ; and because of these things the wrath of God comes upon those who are disobedient. It was amongst these things that you once spent your lives, when you lived among them; but now you must divest your-selves of all these things—anger, temper, malice, slander, foul talk which issues from your mouth. Do not lie to one another.

HERE this letter makes the change that Paul's letters always make. After the theology there comes the ethical demand. Paul could think more deeply than any man who ever tried to work out and to express the Christian faith. He could, and did, travel along uncharted pathways of thought; he could, and did, scale the heights of the human mind, where even the best equipped theologian finds it hard to follow him; but always at the end of his letters he turns to the practical consequences of all his thinking. He always ends with an uncompromising and crystal clear statement of the ethical demands of Christianity in the situation in which his friends at the moment are. It is here that the ethical section of this letter definitely begins.

Paul begins with a vivid demand. The New Testament never hesitates to demand with a certain violence the complete elimination of everything in life which is against God. The Authorized Version translates the first part of this section: "Mortify your members which are upon earth." In seventeenth century English that was clear enough: but to some extent it has lost its force in modern languUage. Nowadays *to mortify the flesh* means rather to practise ascetic discipline and self-denial. And that is not enough. What Paul is saying is, "Put to death every part of your self and personality which is against God, and which keeps you from fulfilling the will of God." He uses the same line of thought in *Romans* 8: 13: "If you kill the deeds of sinful human nature, you will live." It is exactly the same line of thought as the thought of Jesus, when He demanded that a man should cut off a hand or a foot, or tear out an eye which was leading him into sin (*Matthew* 5: 29, 30).

We may put this in more modern language, as C. F. D. Moule expresses it. The Christian must kill self-centredness; he must regard as dead all private desires and ambitions. There must be in his life a radical transformation of the will, and a radical shift of the centre. Everything which would keep him from fully obeying God and fully surrendering to Christ must be surgically excised.

Then Paul goes on to list some of the things which the Colossians must cut right out of life.

Fornication and *uncleanness* must go. As we have again and again pointed out, chastity was the one completely new virtue which Christianity brought into the world. In the ancient world relationships before marriage, and outside marriage, brought no shame and were the normal and accepted practice. The ancient world regarded the sexual appetite as a thing to be gratified and not to be controlled. That is an attitude which is by no means gone, although nowadays it is supported by specious and distorted arguments. In his autobiography, *Memory to Memory*, Sir Arnold Lunn has a chapter on Cyril Joad, the well-known philosopher, whom he knew well. In his pre-christian days Joad could write: " Birth control (he meant more bluntly the use of contraceptives) increases the possibilities of human pleasure. In enabling the pleasures of sex to be tasted without its penalties it has removed the most formidable deterrent not only to regular but to irregular sexual intercourse . . . The average clergymen is shocked and outraged by the prospect of shameless, harmless and unlimited pleasure which birth control offers to the young, and, if he can stop it, he will." Towards the end of his life Joad came back to religion and returned to the family of the Church; but it was not without a struggle, and it was the insistence of the Christian Church on sexual purity which kept him so long from making the final decision. " It's a big step," he said, " and I can't persuade myself that the very severe attitude to sex which the Church thinks it necessary to adopt is really justified." The insistence of the Christian ethic is on purity and chastity. It insists that the relationship between the sexes is something so precious that indiscriminate use of it in the end destroys it.

There was *passion* and *desire*. There is a kind of person who is the slave of his passions, and who is driven by the desire for the wrong things, which is what *epithumia* means. There is the kind of person who has no idea of how to control anger, no intention of limiting his desire for the pleasures of the table, the kind of man who is ruled by his desires, and who never even attempts to rule them.

There is the sin which the Authorized Version calls *covetousness*. The Greek word is *pleonexia*. This sin of *pleonexia* is one of the ugliest of sins; it is quite clear what it means, but it is by no means so easy to find a single word to translate it. It comes from two Greek words; the first half of the word is from *pleon* which means more; the second half is from *echein* which means *to have*. *Pleonexia* is basically *the desire to have more*. The Greeks themselves defined it as insatiate desire, and said that you might as easily satisfy it as you might fill with water a bowl with a hole in it. They defined it as the sinful desire for that which belongs to others. They defined it as the passion of acquisitiveness. It has been described as ruthless self-seeking. Its basic idea is the desire for that which a man has no right to desire. It is, therefore, a sin with a very wide range. If it is the desire for money, it leads to theft. If it is the desire for honour and prestige, it leads to evil ambition. If it is the desire for power, it leads to sadistic tyranny. If it is the desire for a person, it leads to sexual sin. C. F. D. Moule well describes it as " the opposite of the desire to give." It is the desire to get—and always to get that which a man has no right to have.

Such a desire, says Paul, is idolatry. How can that be? The essence of idolatry is the desire to get. A man sets up an idol and worships it because he desires to get something out of God. To put it bluntly, he believes that by his sacrifices and his gifts and his worship, he can persuade, or even bribe, God into giving him what he desires. To quote C. F. D. Moule, " idolatry is an attempt to use God for man's purposes, rather than to give oneself to God's service." The essence of idolatry is, in fact, the desire to have more. Or to come at it another way, the man whose whole life is dominated by the desire to get things, has set up things in the place of God. In fact, he worships things and not God—and that precisely is idolatry.

Upon all such things the wrath of God must fall. The wrath of God is simply the rule of the universe that a man will sow what he reaps, and that no one ever escapes the consequences of his sin. The wrath of God and the moral order of the universe are one and the same thing.

THE THINGS WHICH MUST BE LEFT BEHIND

Colossians 3: 5-9a (*continued*)

IN verse 8 Paul says that there are certain things of which the Colossians must strip themselves. The word he uses is the word which is used for *putting off clothes*. There is here a picture from the life of the early Christian. When the Christian was baptized, he put off his old clothes when he went down into the water, and when he emerged, he was clothed in a new and pure white robe. He divested himself of one kind of life, and put on another. In this passage Paul speaks of the things of which the Christian must divest himself, and in verse 12 he will continue the picture and will speak of the things which the Christian must put on. Let us look at them one by one.

The Christian must put off *anger* and *temper*. The two words are *orgē* and *thumos*, and the difference between them is this. *Thumos* is a blaze of sudden anger, which is quickly kindled and which just as quickly dies. The Greeks likened it to a fire amongst straw, which quickly blazed and which just as quickly burned itself out and subsided. On the other hand, *orgē* is anger which has become inveterate; it is long-lasting, slow-burning, smouldering anger, which refuses to be pacified and which nurses its wrath to keep it warm. For the Christian, the burst of temper and the long-lasting anger are alike forbidden.

There is *malice.* The word we have so translated is *kakia*:

it is a difficult word to translate, for it really means that viciousness of mind from which all the individual vices spring. It is all-pervading evil.

The Christian must put off *slander*, *foul talk* and Christians must not *lie to one another*. The word for slander is *blasphēmia*, which the Authorized Version translates *blasphemy*. *Blasphēmia* is insulting and slanderous speaking in general. When that insulting speech is directed against God, then it becomes blasphemy. In this context it is much more likely that what is forbidden is slanderous talk against one's fellow-men. The word we have translated *foul talk* is *aischrologia*; it could well mean *obscene language*. These last three forbidden things have all to do with speech. And when we turn them into positive commands, instead of negative prohibitions, we find for ourselves three laws for Christian speech.

(i) Christian speech must be *kind*. All slanderous and malicious talking and gossip is forbidden. The old advice still stands, when it says that before we say anything about anyone we should ask three questions: " Is it true? Is it necessary? Is it kind? " The New Testament is unsparing in its condemnation of the gossiping tongues which poison truth.

(ii) Christian speech must be *pure*. There can never have been a time in history when so much filthy language is used as it is today. And the tragedy is that today there are many people who have become so habituated to unclean talk that they are unaware that they are using it. The Christian should never forget that he will give account for every idle word he speaks.

(iii) Christian speech must be *true*. Dr. Johnson believed that there are far more falsehoods told unaware than deliberately; and he believed that a child should be checked when he deviates in the very smallest detail from the truth. It is easy to distort the truth; an alteration in the tone of voice in which a story is told, an eloquent look will do it; and there are silences which can be as false and misleading as any words.

If the Christian is to observe the rules of Christian speech, his speech must be kind and pure and honest to all men and in all places.

THE UNIVERSALITY OF CHRISTIANITY

Colossians 3: 9b-13.

> Strip off the old self with all its activities. Put on the new self, which is ever freshly renewed until it reaches fulness of knowledge, in the likeness of its creator. In it there is neither Greek nor Jew, circumcision nor uncircumcision, barbarian, Scythian, slave nor free man, but Christ is all in all. So then, as the chosen of God, dedicated and beloved, clothe yourself with a heart of pity, kindness, humility, gentleness, patience. Bear with one another, and, if anyone has a ground of complaint against someone else, forgive each other; as the Lord has forgiven you, so you must forgive each other.

WHEN a man becomes a Christian, there ought to be a complete change in his personality. He puts off his old self, and puts on a new self, just as the candidate for baptism puts off his old clothes and puts on the new white robe. We very often evade the truth on which the New Testament insists, the truth that a Christianity which does not change a man is a most imperfect Christianity. Further, this change is a progressive change. This new creation is a continual renewal. It makes a man grow continually in grace and knowledge until he reaches that which he was meant to be—manhood in the image of God. Christianity is not really Christianity unless it recreates a man into what he was meant to be.

One of the great effects of that Christianity is that it destroys the barriers which divide. In it there is neither Greek nor Jew, circumcised nor uncircumcised, barbarian, Scythian, slave nor free man. The ancient world was full of barriers. The Greek looked down on the barbarian; and to the Greek any man who did not speak Greek was a barbarian, which literally means a man who says " bar-bar." The Greek was the aristocrat of the ancient world and he knew it. The Jew looked down on every other nation. He belonged to God's chosen people, and the other nations were fit only to be fuel for the fires of hell. The Scythian was notorious as the lowest of the barbarians, more barbarian than the barbarians, the Greeks called him; little short of being a wild beast, Josephus calls him. He was proverbially the savage, who terrorized the civilized world with his bestial atrocities. The slave was not even classified in ancient law as a human being; he was merely a human and a living tool, with no rights of his own at all. His master could thrash or brand or maim or even kill him at his caprice. He had not even the right of marriage. There could be no fellowship in the ancient world between a slave and a free man.

But in Christ all these barriers were broken down. J. B. Lightfoot reminds us that one of the greatest tributes paid to Christianity was paid not by a theologian but by a master linguist. Max Müller was one of the great experts of the science of language. Now, in the ancient world, no one was interested in foreign languages, apart from Greek. There was no learning and no studying of foreign languages. The Greeks were the scholars, and they would never have deigned to study a barbarian tongue. The science of language is a new science, and the desire to know other languages a new desire. And Max Müller wrote: " Not till that word *barbarian* was struck out of the dictionary of mankind, and replaced by *brother*, not till the right of all nations of the world to be classed as members of one genus or kind was recognized, can we look even for the first beginnings of our science of language . . . This change was effected by Christianity." It was Christianity which drew men together sufficiently to wish to know each other's languages.

T. K. Abbott points out how this passage shows in summary fashion the barriers which Christianity destroyed.

(i) It destroyed the barriers which come from birth and from nationality. Different nations, who either despised or hated each other, were all drawn into the one family of the Christian Church. Nations which would have leaped at each other's throats in battle sat in peace beside each other at the Table of the Lord.

(ii) It destroyed the barriers which come from ceremonial and ritual. Circumcised and uncircumcised were drawn together in the one fellowship. While a Jew remained a Jew, to him any man of any other nation was unclean. When he became a Christian, every man of every nation became a brother.

(iii) It destroyed the barriers between the cultured and the uncultured. The Scythian was the ignorant barbarian of the ancient world; the Greek was the aristocrat of learning. The uncultured and the cultured came together in the Christian Church. The greatest scholar in the world and the simplest son of toil in the world can sit in perfect fellowship in the Church of Christ.

(iv) It destroyed the barrier between class and class. The slave and the free man came together in the Church. Nay more, in the early Church it could, and did, happen that the slave was the preacher and the leader of the Church, and the master was the humble member. In the presence of God the social distinctions of the world become irrelevant.

THE GARMENTS OF CHRISTIAN GRACE

Colossians 3: 9b-13 (*continued*)

So Paul moves on to give his list of the great graces with which the Colossians must clothe themselves. Before we begin to study the list in detail, we must note two very significant things.

(i) Paul begins by addressing the Colossians as *chosen of God, dedicated* and *beloved*. The significant thing is that every one of these three words originally belonged, as it were, to the Jews. They were the chosen people; they were the holy, dedicated (*hagios*) nation; they were the beloved of God. So Paul takes these three precious words which had once been the possession of Israel, and gives them to the Gentiles, and thereby he shows that the love and the grace of God have gone out to the ends of the earth, and that there is no "most favoured nation" clause in the economy of God.

(ii) It is most significant to note that every one of the virtues and graces listed has to do with personal relationships between man and man. There is no mention of virtues like efficiency, cleverness, even diligence and industry—not that these things are not important. But the great basic Christian virtues are the virtues which govern and set the tone of human relationships. Christianity is community. Christianity has on its divine side the amazing gift of peace with God, and on its human side, the triumphant solution of the problem of living together.

Paul begins with *a heart of pity*. If there was one thing the ancient world needed it was mercy. The sufferings of animals were nothing to the ancient world. The maimed and the sickly simply went to the wall. There was no provision for the aged. The treatment of the idiot and the simple-minded was unfeeling and inhuman. Christianity brought, and is still bringing, into this world the increasing mercy. It is not too much to say that everything that has been done for the aged, the sick, the weak in body and in mind, the animal, the child, the woman has been done under the inspiration of Christianity.

There is kindness (*chrēstotēs*). Trench calls this a lovely word for a lovely quality. The ancient writers defined *chrēstotēs* as the virtue of the man whose neighbour's good is as dear to him as his own. Josephus uses it as a description of Isaac, the man who digged wells and gave them to others because he would not fight about them (*Genesis* 26: 17-25). It is used of wine which has grown mellow with age, and which has lost its harshness. It is the word which is used of the yoke of Jesus, when Jesus said, " My yoke is *easy*." (*Matthew* 11: 30). Goodness by itself can be stern; but *chrēstotēs* is the goodness which is kind, the goodness which Jesus used to the sinning woman who anointed his feet (*Luke* 7: 37-50). No doubt Simon the Pharisee was a good man; but Jesus was more than good; He was *chrēstos*; He was *kind*. The Rheims version translates it *benignity*. The Christian is marked by a goodness which is a kindly thing.

There is *humility*. It has often been said that humility was a virtue created and introduced by Christianity. It has often been remarked that in classical Greek there is no word for humility which has not some tinge of meanness, of servility and of grovelling. The Christian humility is not a cringing thing. The Christian humility is based on two things. First, on the divine side, it is based on the ever present awareness of the *creatureliness* of humanity. God is the Creator; man is the creature; and in the presence of the Creator the creature cannot feel anything else but humility. Second, on the human side, it is based on the belief that all men are the sons of God; and there is no room for arrogance when we are living among men and women who are all of royal lineage.

There is *gentleness* (*praotēs*). Long ago Aristotle had defined *praotēs* as the happy mean between too much and too little anger. The man who has *praotēs* is the man who is so self-controlled, because he is God-controlled, that he is always angry at the right time and never angry at the wrong time. He has at one and the same time the strength and the sweetness of true gentleness.

There is *patience* (*makrothumia*). This is the spirit which never loses its patience with its fellow-men. Their foolishness and their unteachability never drive it to cynicism or despair; their insults and their ill-treatment never drive it to bitterness or wrath. Human patience is a reflection of the divine patience which bears with all our sinning and which never casts us off.

There is the *forbearing and the forgiving spirit.* The Christian forbears and forgives; and he does so because he never forgets that a forgiven man must always be forgiving. As God forgave him, so he must forgive others, for only the forgiving can be forgiven.

THE PERFECT BOND

Colossians 3: 14-17

> On top of all these things, clothe yourselves with love which is the perfect bond; and let the peace of God be the decider of all things within your hearts, for it is to that peace you were called, so that you might be united in one body. May the word of Christ dwell richly in you with all wisdom. Continue to teach and to admonish each other with psalms and hymns and spiritual songs, singing to God with gratitude in your hearts. And whatever you may be doing in word or in deed, do all things in the name of the Lord Jesus, giving thanks to God the Father through Him.

To the garments of the virtues and the graces Paul adds one more—what he calls *the perfect bond of love.* Love is the binding power which holds the whole Christian body together. The tendency of any body of people is sooner or later to fly apart; and love is the one bond which will hold them together in unbreakable fellowship.

Then Paul uses a vivid picture. " Let the peace of God," he says, " be the decider of all things within your heart." Literally what Paul says is, " Let the peace of God be the umpire in your heart." The verb he uses is a verb from the athletic arena; it is the word that is used of the umpire who settled things with his decision in any matter of dispute. If the peace of Jesus Christ is the umpire in any man's heart, then, when feelings clash, and when we are pulled in two directions at the same time, when Christian charity conflicts in our hearts with unchristian irritation and annoyance, the decision of Christ will keep us in the way of love, and the Church will remain the one body it was meant to be. The way to right action is to appoint Jesus Christ as the arbiter between the conflicting emotions in our hearts; and if we accept His decisions, we cannot go wrong.

It is interesting here to see that from the beginning the Church was a singing Church. The Church inherited that from the Jews, for Philo tells us that often the Jews would spend the whole night in hymns and songs. One of the first descriptions of a Church service which we possess is that of Pliny, the Roman governor of Bithynia, who sent a report of the activities of the Christians to Trajan the Roman Emperor. In that report he said, " They meet at dawn to sing a hymn to Christ as God." The gratitude of the Church has always gone up to God in Christian praise and Christian song.

Finally, in this section, Paul gives the great principle for living that everything we do or say should be done and said in the name of Jesus. One of the best tests of any action is: " Can we do it, calling upon the name of Jesus? Can we do it, asking for His help?" One of the best tests of any word is: " Can we speak it, and can we in the same breath name the name of Jesus? Can we speak it, remembering that He will hear, and asking Him to hear?" If a man brings every word and deed to the test of the presence of Jesus Christ, he will not go wrong.

THE PERSONAL RELATIONSHIPS OF THE CHRISTIAN

Colossians 3: 18-4: 1

Wives, be submissive to your husbands, as is fitting in the Lord. Husbands, love your wives, and do not treat them harshly.

Children, obey your parents in all things, for this is well-pleasing in the Lord. Fathers, do not irritate your children, that they may not lose heart.

Slaves, obey in all things those who are your human masters, not only when you are watched, like those whose only desire is to please men, but in sincerity of heart, reverencing the Lord. Whatever you do, work at it heartily, as if you were doing it for the Lord and not for men; and never forget that you will receive from the Lord your just recompense, even your share in the inheritance. Show yourselves the slaves of the Lord Christ. He who does wrong will be paid back for the wrong that he has done, and there is no respect of persons.

Masters, on your part provide for your slaves treatment which is just and equitable, and remember that you too have a master in heaven.

HERE the ethical part of this letter becomes more and more practical. Here Paul turns to the practical working out of Christianity in the everyday relationships of life and living. Before we begin to study this passage in some detail, we must note two great general principles which lie behind it, and which determine all its demands.

(i) The Christian ethic is an ethic of *reciprocal obligation*. It is never an ethic on which all the duties are on one side. As Paul saw it, husbands have as great an obligation as wives; parents have just as binding a duty as children; masters have their responsibilities as much as slaves.

This was an entirely new thing. Let us take the cases one by one and look at them in the light of this new principle.

Under Jewish law a woman was a thing; she was the possession of her husband, just as much as his house or his flocks or his material goods were. She had no legal rights whatever. For instance, under Jewish law, a husband could divorce his wife for any cause, while a wife had no rights whatever in the initiation of divorce. In Greek society a respectable woman lived a life of entire seclusion. She never appeared on the streets alone, not even to go marketing. She lived in the women's apartments and did not join her menfolk even for meals. From her there was demanded a complete servitude and chastity; but her husband could go out as much as he chose; and could enter into as many relationships outside marriage as he liked, and incur no stigma. Both under Jewish and under Greek laws and custom, all the privileges belonged to the husband, and all the duties to the wife; but here in Christianity we have for the first time an ethic of mutual and reciprocal obligation.

In the ancient world children were very much under the domination of their parents. The supreme example of that was the Roman *Patria Potestas*, the law of the father's power. Under it a parent could do anything he liked with his child. He could even sell him into slavery; he could make him work like a labourer on his farm; he had even the legal right to condemn his child to death, and to carry out the execution. Once again all the privileges and rights belonged to the parent, and all the duties to the child.

Most of all this was the case in slavery. The slave was a thing in the eyes of the law. There was no such thing as a code of working conditions. When the slave was past his work, he could be thrown out to die. The slave had not even the right to marry, and if he did cohabit, and there was a child, the child belonged to the master, as the lambs of the flock belong to the shepherd. The master could scourge, brand, kill his slave and no one could say him nay. Once again all the rights belonged to the master and all the duties to the slave.

The Christian ethic is an ethic of mutual obligation, in which the rights and the obligations fall on every man. Under the Christian ethic no man is without his rights, but equally no man is without his obligations. It is an ethic of mutual responsibility; and, therefore, it becomes an ethic where the idea and the thought of privilege and rights fall into the background. and where the idea and the thought of duty and obligation become paramount. The whole direction of the Christian ethic is not to ask: " What do others owe to me?" but, " What do I owe to others?"

(ii) The really new thing about the Christian ethic of personal relationships is that all relationships are *in the Lord.*

The whole of the Christian life is lived in Christ. In any home the whole tone of personal relationships must be dictated by the awareness that Jesus Christ is always an unseen, but an ever-present guest. He is always the third when two are joined together. In any parent-child relationship the dominating thought is the Fatherhood of God; and we must treat our children as God treats His sons and daughters. The thing which settles any master-servant relationship is that both master and servant are servants of the one Master, Jesus Christ. The new thing about personal relationships as Christianity sees them is that Jesus Christ is introduced into them all as the changing and the re-creating factor.

THE MUTUAL OBLIGATION

Colossians 3: 18-4: 1 (*continued*)

LET us look briefly at each of these three spheres of human relationships.

(i) The wife is to be submissive to her husband; but the husband is to love his wife, and to treat her with all kindness. The practical effect of the marriage laws and customs of ancient times was that the husband became an unquestioned dictator and the wife became little more than a servant to bring up his children and to minister to his needs. The one fundamental effect of this Christian teaching about marriage is that marriage becomes a *co-operation* and a *partnership*. It becomes something which is entered into, not merely for the convenience of the husband, but in order that both husband and wife may find a new joy and a new completeness in life in each other. Any marriage in which everything is done for the comfort and the convenience of one of the partners, and where the other exists simply to gratify the needs and the desires of the first, is not a Christian marriage.

(ii) The Christian ethic quite definitely lays down the

duty of the child to respect the parental relationship. But there is always a problem in the relationship of parent and child. If the parent is too lax and easy-going, the child will grow up indisciplined, and unfit to face life. But there is the other danger. The more conscientious a parent is, the more he or she is likely always to be correcting, admonishing, rebuking and goading the child. Simply because the parent wishes the child to do well, he or she is always, as it were, on top of the child. We remember, for instance, the tragic question of Mary Lamb, whose mind was ultimately unhinged: " Why is it that I never seem to be able to do anything to please my mother?" We remember the poignant statement of John Newton: " I know that my father loved me—but he did not seem to wish me to see it." There is a certain kind of constant criticism which is, in fact, the product of misguided love. The danger of all this is that the child becomes discouraged. Bengel speaks of " the plague of youth, a broken spirit (*Fractus animus pestis iuventutis*). The duty of a parent is not only discipline —it is also *encouragement*; and discipline and encouragement must walk hand in hand. It is one of the tragic facts of religious history that Luther's father was so stern to him that Luther all his days found it difficult to pray: " Our Father." The word *father* in his mind stood for nothing but severity. The duty of the parent is always discipline, but it is also always encouragement. Luther himself said, " Spare the rod and spoil the child. It is true. But beside the rod keep an apple to give him when he does well."

Sir Arnold Lunn, in *Memory to Memory*, quotes an incident about Field-Marshal Montgomery from a book by M. E. Clifton James. Montgomery was famous as a disciplinarian—but there was another side to him. Mr Clifton James was Montgomery's official " double." He was studying Montgomery during a rehearsal for D-Day. " Within a few yards of where I was standing, a very young soldier, still looking sea-sick from his voyage, came struggling along gamely trying to keep up with his comrades in front. I could imagine that, feeling as he did, his rifle and equipment must have been like a ton weight. His heavy boots dragged in the sand, but I could see that he was fighting hard to conceal his distress. Just when he got level with us he tripped up, and fell flat on his face. Half sobbing he heaved himself up and began to march off dazedly in the wrong direction. Monty went straight up to him and with a quick, friendly smile turned him round. ' This way, sonny. You're doing well—very well. But don't lose touch with the chap in front of you.' When the youngster realized who it was that had given him friendly help, his expression of dumb adoration was a study." It was just because Montgomery combined this discipline and encouragement that a private in the Eighth Army felt himself worth a colonel in any other army.

The better a parent is the more he must avoid the danger of discouraging his child, for the parent must give discipline and encouragement in equal parts.

THE CHRISTIAN WORKMAN AND THE CHRISTIAN MASTER

Colossians 3: 18-4: 1 (*continued*)

(iii) Paul then turns to the greatest problem of all—the relationship between slave and master. It will be noted that this section is far longer than the other two; and its length and fulness may well be due to long talks which Paul had with the runaway slave, Onesimus, whom later he was to send back home to his master Philemon.

In it Paul says things which must have amazed both sides to the question.

He insists that the slave must be a conscientious workman. He is in effect saying that a slave's Christianity must make him a better and a more efficient slave. Christianity never in this world offers escape from hard work; it makes a man able to work still harder. Nor does it offer a man escape from a difficult situation; it enables him to meet that situation like a better man.

The slave must not render eye-service. He must not work only when the overseer's eye is upon him. He must not be the kind of servant, who, as C. F. D. Moule puts it, does not dust behind the ornaments or sweep below the wardrobe. He must not put on a show of eager efficiency when his heart has a grudge and a bitterness against the whole business. He must remember that he will receive his inheritance. Here was an amazing thing. Under Roman law a slave could not possess any property whatsoever, and here he is being promised nothing less than the inheritance of God. He must remember that the time will come when the balance is adjusted, and when evil-doing will find its punishment and faithful diligence its reward.

The master must treat the slave, not like a thing, but like a person, with justice, and with the equity which goes beyond justice.

And how is it to be done? The answer is important, for in it there is the whole Christian doctrine of work.

The workman must do everything as if he was doing it for Christ. We do not work for pay; we do not work for ambition; we do not work to satisfy an earthly master. We work so that we can take every task and offer it to Christ. All work is done for God, so that God's world can go on, and so that God's men and women may have the things they need for life and living. All work is work for God.

The master must remember that he too has a Master—Christ in heaven. He is answerable to God, just as his workmen are answerable to Him. No master can say, " This is my business, and I will do what I like with it." He must say, " This is God's business. He has put me in charge of it. I must run it as He would run it. I am responsible to Him." The master, just as much as the servant, works for God. The Christian doctrine of work is that master and man alike are working for God, and that, therefore, the real rewards of work are not assessable in earthly coin, but will some day be given—or withheld—by God.

THE CHRISTIAN'S PRAYER

Colossians 4: 2-4

> Persevere in prayer. Be vigilant in your prayer, and let thanksgiving always be a part of it. And at the same time pray for us, that God may open for us a door for the word, that we may speak the secret of Christ now revealed to His own people, that secret for which I am in bonds, that I may make it manifest to all, as I ought to speak.

Paul would never write a letter without urging the duty and the privilege of prayer on his friends.

He tells them to persevere in prayer. Even for the best of us, there come times when prayer seems to be unavailing, and when our prayers seem to penetrate no farther than the walls of the room in which we pray. At such a time the remedy is not to stop praying, but to go on praying; for in the man who prays spiritual dryness cannot last.

He tells them to be vigilant in prayer. Literally the Greek means to be *wakeful* in prayer. Quite literally the phrase could well mean that Paul is telling them not to go to sleep when they pray. Maybe he was thinking of the time on the Mount of Transfiguration when the disciples fell asleep, and that it was only when they were awake again that they saw the glory (*Luke* 9: 32). Or, maybe he was thinking of that time in the Garden of Gethsemane when Jesus prayed and when His disciples slept (*Matthew* 26: 40). It is true that at the end of a hard day sleep often comes upon us when we try to pray. And even oftener there is in our prayers a kind of listlessness and tiredness. At such a time we should not try to be long in prayer: God will understand the single sentence, when we have to utter it like a child who is too tired to stay awake.

Paul asks their prayers for himself. We must note

carefully that for which Paul does ask. It is not so much that he asks their prayers for himself; he asks their prayers for his work. There were many things for which Paul might have asked them to pray—release from prison, a successful outcome to his coming trial, a little rest and peace at the last. But Paul asks them only to pray that there may be given to him strength and opportunity to do the work which God had sent him into the world to do. When we pray for ourselves, and when we pray for others, we should not ask for them or for ourselves release from any task, but rather strength to complete the task which has been given us to do. Prayer should always be for power, and seldom for release; for not release but conquest must be the keynote of the Christian life.

THE CHRISTIAN AND THE WORLD

Colossians 4: 5, 6

> Behave yourselves wisely to those who are outside the Church.
>
> Buy up every possible opportunity.
>
> Let your speech always be with gracious charm, seasoned with the salt of wit, so that you will know the right answer to give in every case.

HERE are three brief instructions for the life of the Christian in the world.

(i) The Christian must behave himself with wisdom and with tact towards those who are outside the Church. The Christian must of necessity be a missionary. But he must know when and when not to speak to others about his religion and theirs. He must never give the impression of superiority and of censorious criticism. He must remember that there are few people who have ever been argued into Christianity. If that is so, the Christian must remember that, by being what he is, he is either a good or a bad advertisement for the faith which he bears. It is not by his words but by his life that he will attract people to, or repel them from, Christianity. On the Christian there is laid the great responsibility, not of talking about Christ, but of showing men Christ, not in words, but in life.

(ii) The Christian must be a man on the outlook for opportunity. He must buy up every opportunity to work for Christ and to serve men that he possibly can. There are too many people in the world today whose one aim is to evade this kind of opportunity. Daily life and work are continually offering men opportunities to witness for Christ, and to influence people for Christ—and there are so many who avoid the opportunities instead of embracing them. The Church is constantly offering its members the opportunity to teach, to sing, to visit, to work for the good of the Christian congregation—and there are so many who deliberately refuse these opportunities instead of accepting them. Opportunity means work; for opportunity is what we might call the raw material of achievement and of service. The Christian is on the outlook for every opportunity, not to profit himself, but to serve Christ and his fellow-men.

(iii) The Christian must have charm and wit in his speech, that he may know how to give the right answer in every case. Here is an interesting injunction. It is all too true that Christianity in the minds of many is connected with a kind of sanctimonious dullness, and an outlook in which laughter is almost a heresy. As C. F. D. Moule says, this is " a warning not to confuse loyal godliness with graceless insipidity." The Christian must commend his message with the charm and the wit which were in Jesus Himself. There is too much of the Christianity which stodgily depresses a man, and too little of the Christianity which scintillates with life and charm.

THE LETTER TO THE COLOSSIANS

FAITHFUL COMPANIONS

Colossians 4: 7-11

> Tychicus, the beloved brother and faithful servant and
> my fellow-slave in Christ, will inform you all about how
> things are going with me. I send him to you for this
> very purpose, that you may know about what is
> happening to me, and that he may encourage your
> hearts. Along with him I send Onesimus, the faithful
> and beloved brother, who is one of yourselves. They
> will inform you about all that has been happening here.
> Aristarchus, my fellow-prisoner, greets you, and Mark,
> Barnabas' cousin. (I have given you instructions about
> him; if he comes to you, give him a welcome). Jesus,
> who is called Justus, sends you greetings. These were
> all converts from the Jewish faith. These alone are my
> fellow-workers in the work of the Kingdom, men who
> have been a comfort to me.

WHEN we read the list of names at the end of this chapter
we are reading the names of a list of heroes of the faith.
We must remember the circumstances. Paul was in prison
awaiting trial; it is always dangerous to be a prisoner's
friend, for it is easy for the friend of the prisoner to become
involved in the same fate as the prisoner himself. It took
courage to declare oneself a friend of Paul, and to visit him
in his imprisonment and to show that one was on the same
side. Let us collect what we know of these men.

There was *Tychicus*. Tychicus came from the Roman
province of Asia, and he was most likely the representative
of his Church to carry its offering to the poor Christians of
Jerusalem (*Acts* 20: 4). To him also was entrusted the duty
of bearing to its various destinations the letter we know as
the letter to the Ephesians (*Ephesians* 6: 21). There is one
rather interesting thing here. Paul writes that Tychicus will
tell them all about how things are going with him. This
shows how much was left to word of mouth, and how much
was never set down in Paul's letters at all. In the nature of
things the letters could not be very long; and the letters
dealt with the problems of faith and conduct which were
threatening the Churches. The personal details were left

to the bearer of the letter to tell. In the early Church news passed from Church to Church by word of mouth; and the personal details, the very things which we would so much like to know were never written down. Tychicus, then, we can describe as the personal envoy of Paul.

There was *Onesimus*. Paul's way of mentioning Onesimus is full of Paul's lovely courtesy. Onesimus was in fact the runaway slave who had somehow reached Rome. Paul was sending him back to his master Philemon. But he does not call him a runaway slave; he calls him a faithful and a beloved brother. When Paul had anything to say about a man, he always said the best that he could say.

There was *Aristarchus*. He was a Macedonian, from Thessalonica (*Acts* 20: 4). We get only fleeting glimpses of Aristarchus, but from these glimpses one thing emerges— Aristarchus was clearly a good man to have about in a tight corner. He was there when the people of Ephesus rioted in the Temple of Diana, and he was so much to the forefront that he was captured by the mob (*Acts* 19: 29). He was there when Paul set sail a prisoner for Rome (*Acts* 27: 2). It may well be that he had done nothing less than enrol himself as the slave of Paul in order that he might be allowed to make the last journey with him. And now he is here in Rome, Paul's fellow-prisoner. Clearly Aristarchus was a man who was always on the spot when things were at their grimmest. Whenever Paul was in bad trouble Aristarchus was there. Out of the glimpses of Aristarchus there emerges the faint outlines of the picture of a man who was indeed a good companion.

There was *Mark*. Of all characters in the early Church Mark had had the most surprising career. He was so close a friend of Peter that Peter could call him his son (I *Peter* 5: 13). And we know that when Mark wrote his gospel, it was the preaching material of Peter that he was setting down. On the first missionary journey Paul and Barnabas had taken Mark with them to be their secretary (*Acts* 13: 5). but in the middle of the journey, when things got difficult,

Mark quit and went home (*Acts* 13: 13). It was long before
Paul could forgive that. When he was about to set out on
the second missionary journey Barnabas once again wished
to take Mark with them. But Paul refused to take the
quitter again, and on this issue Paul and Barnabas parted
company and never worked together again (*Acts* 15: 36-40).
Tradition says that Mark went as a missionary to Egypt
and founded the Church at Alexandria. What happened in
the interim we do not know; but we do know that Mark is
with Paul in his last imprisonment, and Paul had once
again come to look on Mark as a most useful man to have
about (*Philemon* 24; *2 Timothy* 4: 11). Mark was the man
who redeemed himself. And here in this brief reference to
him there is an echo of the old unhappy story. Paul instructs
the Church at Colosse to receive Mark and to give him a
welcome, if he should come. Why does Paul do that?
Doubtless because Paul's Churches looked with suspicion
on the man whom Paul had once dismissed as useless for
the service of Christ. And now Paul, with his habitual
courtesy and thoughtfulness, is making sure that Mark's
past will not stand in his way, and is giving him full
approval as one of his trusted friends. The end of Mark's
career is a tribute at one and the same time to Mark and to
Paul.

Of *Jesus, who was called Justus*, we know nothing but his
name. These were Paul's helps and comforters. We know
that it was but a cool welcome that the Jews in Rome gave
Paul (*Acts* 28: 17-29); but there were men with him in
Rome whose loyalty must have warmed Paul's heart.

MORE NAMES OF HONOUR

Colossians 4: 12-15

> Epaphras, one of yourselves, the slave of Jesus Christ,
> greets you. He is always wrestling in prayer for you,
> that you may stand mature and fully assured in the
> faith, engaged in doing the will of God. I bear him

witness that he has toiled greatly for you and for those in Laodicaea and in Hierapolis. Luke, the beloved physician, greets you, and so does Demas. Greet the brothers in Laodicaea, and Nymphas, and the Church in their house.

So this honour-roll of Christian workers goes on.

There was *Epaphras*. He must have been the minister of the Church at Colosse (*Colossians* 1: 7). This passage would seem to mean that Epaphras was, in fact, the overseer of the Churches in the group of three towns, Hierapolis, Laodicaea and Colosse. He was a servant of God who prayed and toiled for the people over whom God had set him.

There was *Luke* the beloved physician, who was with Paul to the end (2 *Timothy* 4: 11). Was Luke a doctor, who gave up what might have been a lucrative career, to tend Paul's thorn in the flesh and to preach Christ?

There was *Demas*. It is significant that Demas' name is the only name to which some comment of praise and appreciation is not attached. He is simply Demas and nothing more. There is a story behind the brief references to Demas in the letters of Paul. In *Philemon* 24 he is grouped with the men who are described as Paul's fellow-labourers. Here in Colossians 4: 14 he is simply Demas with no comment at all. And in the last mention of him in 2 *Timothy* 4: 10 he is Demas who has forsaken Paul, because he loved this present world. Surely here we have the faint outlines of a study in degeneration, of the loss of enthusiasm and ideals, of failure in the faith. Here is one of the men who refused to be remade by Christ.

There was *Nymphas* and the Church of the brothers at Laodicaea which met in his house. When we try to think our way back to the early days, we must think of a time when there was no such thing as a Church building. There was no such thing as a special Church building until the third century. Up to that time the Christian congregations met in the houses of those who were the leaders of the Church. There was the Church which met in the house of

Aquila and Prisca in Rome and Ephesus (*Romans* 16: 5; I *Corinthians* 16: 19). There was the Church which met in the house of Philemon (*Philemon* 2). In the early Church, the Church and the home were one and the same thing; and it is still true that every home should also be a Church of Jesus Christ.

THE MYSTERY OF THE LAODICAEAN LETTER

Colossians 4: 16

> When this letter has been read among you, see to it that it is also read in the Church of the Laodicaeans, and see to it that you read the letter, which is on the way to you from Laodicaea.

IN this verse there is one of the mysteries of Paul's correspondence. The letter to Colosse, this letter which we have been studying, has to be sent on to Laodicaea. And, says Paul, a letter is on the way from Laodicaea to Colosse. What was this Laodicaean letter? there are four possibilities

(i) It may have been a special letter to the Church at Laodicaea. If so, it is lost, although, as we shall shortly see, an alleged letter to Laodicaea still exists. It is certain that Paul must have written more letters than we possess. We have thirteen Pauline letters, and these letters cover roughly fifteen years. It is quite certain that Paul did not write only thirteen letters in fifteen years. Many of his letters must have gone lost, and it may be that the letter to Laodicaea was such a one.

(ii) The letter referred to may be the letter which we know as *Ephesians*. As we saw when we were studying *Ephesians* it is well-nigh certain that *Ephesians* was not written to the Church at Ephesus, but was in fact an encyclical letter meant to circulate among all the Churches of Asia. It may be that this encyclical had reached Laodicaea and was now on the way to Colosse.

(iii) The letter referred to may actually be the letter to

Philemon. That is a real possibility, but we shall leave the discussion of it, until we come to study *Philemon*.

(iv) For many centuries there has existed an alleged letter of Paul to the Church at Laodicaea, a letter which, in fact, purports to be the letter referred to here. As we have it, it is in Latin; but the Latin is such that it has every sign of being a literal translation of a Greek original. This letter is actually included in the *Codex Fuldensis* of the Latin New Testament, which belonged to Victor of Capua and which goes back to the sixth century. This alleged Laodicaean letter can be traced even further back. It was mentioned by Jerome in the fifth century, but Jerome himself said that it was a forgery, and that most people agreed that it was not authentic. The letter runs as follows:

> Paul an apostle, not by men neither through any man, but through Jesus Christ, to the brothers who are at Laodicaea. Grace be to you and peace from God the Father, and from our Lord Jesus Christ.

> I thank Christ in every one of my prayers that you remain steadfast in Him, and that you persevere in His works, awaiting His promise on the day of judgment. Let not the empty words of certain men seduce you, words of men who try to persuade you that you should turn away from the truth of the gospel which is preached by me . . . (There follows a verse where the text is uncertain).

> And now my bonds which I suffer in Christ are plain for all to see; in them I delight and joy. And this will result for me in everlasting salvation, a result which will be brought about by your prayers, and by the help of the Holy Spirit, whether by my life or by my death. For to me to live is to be in Christ, and to die is joy. And may He in His mercy bring this very thing to pass in you, that you may have the same love, and that you may be of the one mind.

> Therefore, my best-beloved, as you have heard in my presence, so hold to these things and do them in fear of God, and then there will be to you life for eternity; for it is God who works in you. And do without wavering whatever you do.

As for what remains, best-beloved, rejoice in Christ; beware of those who are sordid in their desire for gain. Let all your prayers be made known before God; and be you firm in the mind of Christ.

Do the things which are pure, and true, and modest, and just, and lovely.

Hold fast what you have heard and received into your heart; and you will have peace.

The saints salute you.

The grace of the Lord Jesus Christ be with your spirit.

Cause that this letter be read to the Colossians, and that the letter of the Colossians be read to you.

Such is the alleged letter of Paul to the Laodicaeans. It is clearly made up mainly of phrases taken from *Philippians* with the opening introduction taken from *Galatians*. There can be little doubt that it was written by some pious writer who read in *Colossians* that there had been a letter to Laodicaea, who knew that it was lost, and who proceeded to compose what he thought that such a letter should be. There are very few people who would accept this ancient letter to the Laodicaeans as a genuine letter of Paul.

We cannot tell the explanation of the mystery of this letter to the Church at Laodicaea; the most commonly accepted explanation is that the reference is to the circular letter which we know as *Ephesians*, but we must wait until we study *Philemon* for an even more romantic and attractive possibility.

THE CLOSING BLESSING

Colossians 4: 17, 18

And say to Archippus, " See that you complete that piece of service which you have received from the Lord to do."

Here is my greeting in the handwriting of myself, Paul.

Remember my bonds.
Grace be with you.

THE letter closes with an urgent spur to Archippus to be true to a special task which has been given to him. It may be that we can never tell what that task was; it may be that when we study the letter to Philemon some light will be thrown upon it. For the moment we must leave it at that.

To write his letters Paul used a secretary. We know, for instance, that the penman who did the writing of *Romans* was called Tertius (*Romans* 16: 22). It was Paul's custom at the end to write his signature and his blessing with his own hand—and here he does so.

" Remember my bonds," he says. Again and again in this series of letters Paul refers to his bonds (*Ephesians* 3: 1; 4: 1; 6: 20; *Philemon* 9). There is no self-pity here; and there is no sentimental plea for sympathy. Paul finishes his letter to the Galatians: " I bear in my body the marks of the Lord Jesus " (*Galatians* 6: 18). Of course, there is pathos here. Alford comments movingly: " When we read of *his chains* we should not forget that they moved over the paper as he wrote (his signature). His hand was chained to the soldier that kept him." But Paul's references to his sufferings are not pleas for sympathy; they are his claims to authority; they are the guarantees of his right to speak. It is as if he said, " This is not a letter from someone who does not know what the service of Christ means. This is not a letter from someone who is asking others to do what he is not prepared to do himself. It is a letter from one who has himself suffered and sacrificed for Christ. My only right to speak is that I too have carried the Cross of Christ."

And so the letter comes to its inevitable end. The end of every letter of Paul is grace; for he always ended by commending others to that grace which he himself had found sufficient for all things.

THE LETTERS TO THE THESSALONIANS

THE LETTERS TO THE THESSALONIANS

INTRODUCTION TO THE LETTERS TO THE THESSALONIANS

Paul comes to Macedonia

For anyone who can read between the lines the story of Paul's coming to Macedonia is one of the most dramatic stories in the book of Acts. Luke, with supreme economy of words, tells it in Acts 16: 6-10. Short as that narrative is, it gives the inescapable impression of a chain of circumstances culminating in one supreme event. Paul had passed through Phrygia and Galatia and ahead of him there lay the Hellespont. To the left there lay the teeming province of Asia; to the right there stretched the great province of Bithynia; but the Spirit would allow him to enter neither of them. There was something driving him relentlessly on to the Aegean Sea. So he came to Alexandrian Troas, still uncertain where he ought to go; and then there came to him the vision in the night of the man who cried, " Come over into Macedonia and help us," and Paul set sail, and for the first time the gospel came to Europe.

One World

But at that very moment Paul must have seen much more than a continent for Christ. It was in Macedonia that he landed; and Macedonia was the kingdom of Alexander the Great, who had conquered the world, and who had wept because there were no more worlds left to conquer. But Alexander was much more than merely a military conqueror. He was almost the first universalist. He was more a missionary than a soldier; and he dreamed of one world dominated and enlightened by the culture of Greece. Even so great a thinker as Aristotle had said that it was a plain duty to treat Greeks as free men and orientals as slaves; but Alexander declared that he had been sent by God " to unite, to pacify and to reconcile the whole world." Deliberately he had said that it was his aim " to marry the East to the West." He had dreamed of an Empire in which there was neither Greek nor Jew, barbarian or Scythian, bond or free. (Colossians 3: 11). Now it is hard to see how Alexander could have failed to be in Paul's thoughts. Paul left from Alexandrian Troas which was called after Alexander; he came to Macedonia which was Alexander's original kingdom; he worked at Philippi which was called after Philip, Alexander's father; he went on to Thessalonica which was called after Alexander's half-sister. The whole territory was saturated with memories of Alexander; and Paul must have thought, not of a country, not of a continent, but of a world for Christ.

Paul comes to Thessalonica

This sense of the wide-stretching arms of Christianity must have been accentuated when Paul came to Thessalonica. It was a great city. Its original name was Thermai, which means The Hot Springs, and it gave its name to the Thermaic Gulf on which it stood. Six hundred years ago Herodotus had described it as a great city. It has always been a famous harbour. It was there that Xerxes the Persian had his naval base when he invaded Europe; and even in Roman times it was one of the world's great dockyards. In 315 B.C. Cassander had rebuilt the city and had renamed it Thessalonica, which was the name of his wife, who was a daughter of Philip of Macedon and a half-sister of Alexander the Great. It was a free city; that is to say it had never suffered the indignity of having Roman troops quartered within it. It had its own popular assembly and its own magistrates. It rose to a population of 200,000 and for a time it was a question whether it or Constantinople would be recognized as the capital of the world. Even to-day, under the name Salonika, it has 70,000 inhabitants. But the supreme importance of Thessalonica lies in this— it lay astride the Via Egnatia, the Egnatian Road, which stretched from Dyrrachium on the Adriatic to Constantinople on the Bosphorus and thence away to Asia Minor and the East. In fact its main street was part of the very road which linked Rome with the East. East and West converged on Thessalonica; it was said to be " in the lap of the Roman Empire." Trade poured into her from East and West, so that it was said, " So long as nature does not change, Thessalonica will remain wealthy and prosperous." It is impossible to overstress the importance of the arrival of Christianity in Thessalonica. If Christianity was settled in Thessalonica it was bound to spread East along the Egnatian Road until all Asia was conquered, and West until it stormed even the city of Rome. The coming of Christianity to Thessalonica was a crucial day in the making of Christianity into a world religion.

Paul's Stay at Thessalonica

The story of Paul's stay at Thessalonica is in Acts 17: 1-10. Now, for Paul, what happened at Thessalonica was of supreme importance. He preached in the Synagogue for three Sabbaths (Acts 17: 2). That is to say his stay there could not have been much more than three weeks in length. He had tremendous success, such success that the Jews were enraged and raised such trouble that Paul had to be smuggled out, in peril of his life, to Beroea; the same thing happened in Beroea (Acts 17: 10-12); and Paul had to leave Timothy and Silas behind him and make his escape to Athens. What exercised Paul's mind was this—he had only been in Thessalonica for three weeks. Was it possible to make such an impression on a place in three weeks' time that Christianity was planted in it in such a way that it could never again be uprooted? If so, it was by no means an idle dream that the Roman

Empire might yet be won for Christ. Or, was it necessary to settle down and to work for months, and even years, before an impression could be made? In that case, no man could even dimly foresee when Christianity would penetrate all over the world. Thessalonica was a test case; and Paul was torn with anxiety to know what would happen.

News from Thessalonica

So anxious was Paul that, when Timothy joined him at Athens, he sent him back to Thessalonica to get the information without which he could not rest. (I Thessalonians 3: 1, 2, 5; 2: 17). What news did Timothy bring back? There was good news. The affection of the Thessalonians for Paul was as strong as ever; and they were standing fast in the faith. (I Thessalonians 2: 14; 3: 4-6; 4: 9, 10). They were indeed " his glory and his joy." (I Thessalonians 2: 20). But there was worrying news. (i) The preaching of the Second Coming had produced an unhealthy situation in which people had stopped working and had abandoned all their ordinary pursuits to await the Second Coming with a kind of hysterical expectancy. So Paul tells them to be quiet and to get on with their ordinary work. (I Thessalonians 4: 11). (ii) They were worried about what was to happen to those who died before the Second Coming arrived. Paul explains that those who fall asleep in Jesus will miss none of the glory. (I Thessalonians 4: 13-18). (iii) There was a tendency to despise all lawful authority; the argumentative Greek was always in danger of producing a democracy run mad (I Thessalonians 5: 12-14). (iv) There was the ever-present danger that they would relapse into immorality. It was hard to unlearn the point of view of generations and to escape the contagion of the heathen world (I Thessalonians 4: 3-8). (v) There was at least a section who slandered Paul. They hinted that he preached the gospel for what he could get out of it (I Thessalonians 2: 5, 9); and that he was something of a dictator (I Thessalonians 2: 6, 7, 11). (vi) There was a certain amount of division in the Church. (I Thessalonians 4: 9; 5: 13). These were the problems with which Paul had to deal; and they show that human nature has not changed so very much in Churches.

Why two Letters?

We must ask why there are two letters. The two letters are very like each other; and they must have been written within weeks, perhaps days of each other. The second letter was written mainly to clear up a misconception about the Second Coming. The first letter insists that the Day of the Lord will come like a thief in the night, and urges watchfulness (I Thessalonians 5: 2; 5: 6). But this had produced the unhealthy situation where men did nothing but watch and wait; and in the second letter Paul explains what signs must come first before the Second Coming should come (2 Thessalonians 2: 3-12). The Thessalonians had got their ideas about the Second Coming out of balance and proportion. As so often happens to a preacher, Paul's preaching had been misunderstood and misinterpreted, and certain phrases had been taken out of their context and over-emphasized; and the second letter seeks to put things back in their proper balance and to correct the thoughts of the excited Thessalonians regarding the Second Coming. Of course, Paul takes occasion in the second letter to repeat and to stress much of the good advice and rebuke he had given in the first, but its main aim is to tell them certain things which will calm their hysteria and make them wait, not in excited idleness, but in patient and diligent attendance to the day's work. Here, in these two letters, we see Paul solving the day to day problems which arose in the growing and expanding Church.

I and II THESSALONIANS

LOVE'S INTRODUCTION

I Thessalonians I

Paul and Silas and Timothy send this letter to the Church of the Thessalonians which is in God the Father and the Lord Jesus Christ. Grace be to you and peace.

——————

Always we thank God for you all, and always we remember you in our prayers. We never cease to remember the work inspired by your faith, the labour prompted by your love and the endurance founded on your hope in our Lord Jesus Christ, before God who is also our Father. For we know, brothers beloved by God, how you were chosen. We know that our good news did not come to you with words only, but with power, and with the Holy Spirit, and with much conviction, just as you know what we showed ourselves to be to you for your sakes. And you became imitators of us and of the Lord, for although you received the word in much affliction, yet you received it with the joy of the Holy Spirit, so that you became an example to all the believers in Macedonia and in Achaea. For the word of the Lord went forth from you like a trumpet, not only in Macedonia and Achaea, but the story of your faith towards God has gone forth in every place, so that we had no need to say anything about it. For the people amongst whom we were could tell us your story, and how we entered into you, and how you turned from idols towards God, to serve the living and true God and to await the coming of His Son from heaven, even Jesus whom He raised from among the dead, and who rescues us from the coming wrath.

PAUL sends this letter to the Church of the Thessalonians *which is in God and the Lord Jesus Christ.* God was the very atmosphere in which the Church lived and moved and had its being. Just as the air is in us, and we are in the air, and we cannot live without the air, so the true Church is in God and God is in the true Church, and there is no true life for the Church without God. Further, the God in whom the Church lives is the God and Father of our Lord Jesus Christ; and, therefore, the Church does not shiver in the icy fear of a God who is a tyrant; it basks in the sunshine of the God who is love.

In this opening chapter we see Paul at his most winsome. In a short time he was going to deal out warning and rebuke; but he begins with unmixed praise. Even when Paul rebuked it was never his aim to discourage, but always to uplift. In every man there is something fine, and often the best way to rid him of the lower things is to praise the higher things. The best way to eradicate his faults is to praise his virtues so that they will flower all the more; for every man reacts better to encouragement than he does to rebuke. It is told that once the Duke of Wellington's cook gave notice and left him. He was asked why he had left so honourable and well-paid a position. His answer was, " When the dinner is good the Duke never praises me, and when it is bad he never blames me; it was just not worth while." Encouragement was lacking, and life was not worth while. Paul, like a good psychologist, and with true Christian tact, begins with praise even when he meant to move on to rebuke.

In verse 3 Paul picks out three great ingredients of the Christian life.

(i) There is *work which is inspired by faith*. There is nothing which tells us more about a man than the way in which he works. He may work in fear of the whip; he may work for hope of gain; he may work from a grim sense of duty; or he may work inspired by faith. His faith is that this is his task given him by God and that he is working, in the last analysis, not for men but for God. Someone has said that the sign of true consecration is when a man can find glory in drudgery. (ii) There is *the labour which is prompted by love*. Bernard Newman tells how once he stayed in a Bulgarian peasant's house. All the time he was there the daughter was stitching away at a dress. He said to her, " Don't you ever get tired of that eternal sewing? " " O no! " she said, " you see this is my wedding dress." Work done for love always has a glory. (iii) There is *the endurance which is founded on hope*. When Alexander the Great was setting out on his campaigns he divided all his possessions among his friends. Someone said, " But you are keeping nothing for yourself." " O yes, I am," he said. " I have kept my hopes." A man can endure anything so long as he has hope, for then he is walking, not to the night, but to the dawn.

In verse 4 Paul speaks of the Thessalonians as *brothers beloved by God*. The phrase *beloved by God* was a phrase which the Jews applied only to supremely great men like Moses and Solomon, and to the nation of Israel itself. Now the greatest privilege of the greatest men of God's chosen people has been extended to the humblest of the Gentiles.

Verse 8 speaks of the faith of the Thessalonians sounding forth like *a trumpet;* the word could also mean crashing out like *a roll of thunder*. There is something tremendous about the sheer defiance of early Christianity. When all prudence and all common-sense would have dictated a way of life that would have escaped notice, and so avoided danger and persecution, the Christians defied their dangers and blazoned forth their faith. They were never ashamed to show whose they were and whom they seeked to serve.

In verses 9 and 10 two words are used which are characteristic of the Christian life. The Thessalonians *served* God and *waited* on the coming of Christ. The Christian is called upon to serve in the world and to wait for glory. The loyal service, the patient waiting, the unconquerable expectation were the necessary preludes to the glory of heaven.

PAUL ON HIS DEFENCE

I *Thessalonians* 2: 1-12

You yourselves know, brothers, that our coming among you was not to no effect; but after we had—as you know—already undergone suffering and ill-treatment at Philippi, we were bold in our God to tell you the good news of God, and a sore struggle we had. Our appeal to you did not proceed from any delusion, nor from impure motives, nor was it calculated to deceive; but as we have been deemed worthy by God to be entrusted with the good news, so we speak, not as if we were seeking to please men, but rather as if we were seeking to please God, who tests our hearts. At no time, as you know, did we use flattering words; at no time did we use our message as a pretext for greed; God is our witness; at no time did we seek reputation from men, either from you or from others, although we might well have claimed a place of weight, as apostles of Christ. But we showed ourselves gentle among you, treating you as a nurse cherishes her children. Yearning for you like this, we wanted to share with you, not only the good news of God, but even our very lives, because you had become very dear to us. For, brothers, you remember our labour and toil. It was while we were working night and day, so as not to be a burden to any of you, that we proclaimed the good news of God to you. You are our witnesses, and so is God. How reverently and righteously and blamelessly we behaved to you who believed. As you know, as a father his children, we exhorted and encouraged and solemnly charged each one of you to walk worthily of God who calls you to His Kingdom and His glory.

BENEATH the surface of this passage there run the slanders which Paul's opponents at Thessalonica attaches to him.

(i) Verse 2 refers to the imprisonment and abuse that he had received at Philippi. (Acts 16: 16-40). There were, no doubt, those in Thessalonica who said that this man Paul had a police record, that he was nothing less than a criminal who was on the run from justice, and that obviously no one could listen to a man like that. A really malignant mind will twist anything into a slander.

(ii) Verse 3 has behind it no fewer than three charges. (a) It was being said that Paul's teaching came from nothing else than sheer delusion. A really original man will always run the risk of being called mad. Festus thought that Paul was mad in later days. (Acts 26: 24). There was a time when Jesus' friends and brethren came and tried to take Him home because they thought that He was mad. (Mark 3: 21). The Christian standards can be so different from the standards of the world that he who follows them with a single mind and a burning enthusiasm can appear to other men to be off his head. (b) It was said that Paul's preaching sprang from impure motives. The word that is used for *impurity* (*akatharsia*) often has to do with sexual impurity and depravity. There was one Christian custom which the heathen often and deliberately misinterpreted; that was the kiss of peace. (I Thessalonians 5: 26). When the Christians spoke of the Love Feast, when they talked of the kiss of peace, it was not difficult for an evil mind to read into these phrases that which was never there. The trouble in life so often is that a mind itself nasty will see nastiness everywhere. (c) It was charged that Paul's preaching was guilefully aimed at deluding others, that, in fact, he was not deluded nearly so much as he was deluding. The propagandists of Hitler Germany discovered that if a lie is repeated often enough and loudly enough it will in the end be accepted as the truth. That was the charge which was levelled at Paul.

(iii) Verse 4 indicates that Paul was accused of seeking to please men rather than to please God. No doubt that charge rose from the fact that Paul preached the glory of the liberty of the gospel and the freedom of grace as against the bondage of the law and the grim slavery of legalism. There are always people who do not think that they are being religious unless they are being unhappy; and any man who preaches a gospel of joy will find his slanderers, for that is exactly what happened to Jesus.

(iv) Verse 5 and verse 9 both indicate that there were

those who said that Paul was in this business of preaching the gospel for what he could get out of it. The word that is used for *flattery* (*kolakeia*) always describes the flattery which flatters in order to get something; it is flattery from motives of gain. The trouble in the early Church was that this kind of thing happened. There were people who did attempt to cash in on their Christianity. The first Christian book of order is called *The Didache, The Teaching of the Twelve Apostles,* and in it there are some illuminating instructions. " Let every apostle that cometh unto you be received as the Lord. And he shall stay one day, and, if need be, the next also, but if he stay three days he is a false prophet. And when the apostle goeth forth, let him take nothing save bread, till he reach his lodging. But if he ask money, he is a false prophet." " No prophet that ordereth a table in the Spirit shall eat of it, else he is a false prophet." " If he that cometh is a passer-by, succour him as far as you can. But he shall not abide with you longer than two or three days unless there be necessity. But if he be minded to settle among you, and be a craftsman, let him work and eat. But if he has no trade, according to your understanding, provide that he shall not live idle among you, being a Christian. But if he will not do this he is a Christmonger: of such men beware." (*Didache,* chapters 11 and 12). The date of *The Didache* is about A.D. 100. Even the early Church knew of the perennial problem of those who traded on charity.

(v) Verse 6 indicates that Paul was accused of seeking personal prestige. It is the preacher's, and the teacher's, constant danger that he or she should seek to display himself or herself and not the message. In I Thessalonians I: 5 there is a suggestive thing. Paul does not say, " I came to you," he says, " *Our gospel* came to you." The man was lost in his message.

(vi) Verse 7 indicates that Paul was charged with being something of a dictator. The gentleness of Paul was the gentleness of a wise father. His was the love which knows

how to be firm. To him Christian love was no easy sentimental thing. He knew that men need discipline, not for
their punishment, but for the good of their souls.

THE SINS OF THE JEWS

I *Thessalonians* 2: 13-16

> And for this, too, we thank God, that, when you
> received the word of God which you heard from us,
> you accepted it, not as the word of men, but—as in
> truth it is—as the word of God, who also works in
> you who believe. For, brothers, you became imitators
> of the Churches of God which are in Judaea in Christ
> Jesus, for you too suffered the same things at the
> hands of your own fellow-countrymen as they did
> at the hands of the Jews; for they killed the Lord Jesus
> and the prophets, and they persecuted us, and they
> do not please God, and they are up against all men,
> and they try to stop us speaking to the Gentiles
> that they may be saved; and all this they keep on
> doing that they may complete the catalogue of their
> sins. But wrath to the uttermost has come upon them.

To the Thessalonians the Christian faith had brought
not peace but trouble. Their new-found loyalty had
involved them in persecution. Paul's method of encouraging
them is very interesting. It is in effect to say to them,

> " Brothers, we are treading
> Where the saints have trod."

Their persecution was a badge of honour which entitled
them to rank with the picked regiments of the army of
Christ.

But the great interest of this passage is that in verses
15 and 16 Paul draws up a kind of catalogue of the errors
and the sins of the Jews.

(i) They killed the Lord Jesus and the prophets. When
God's messengers came to them they eliminated them.

One of the grim things about the gospel narrative is the sheer intensity with which the leaders of the Jews sought to get rid of Jesus before He could do any more damage. But no man ever rendered a message inoperative by slaying the messenger who brought it. Someone tells of a missionary who went to a primitive tribe. He had to use crude and primitive methods to get his message across; so he had a chart painted which showed the progress of the man who accepted Christ to heaven; and the descent of the man who rejected Christ to hell. The whole message disturbed the tribe. They did not want it to be true. So what did they do? *They burned the chart* and, having burned the chart, they thought that all was well! A man may refuse to listen to the message of Jesus Christ, but he cannot eliminate that message from the structure of the universe and of his own life.

(ii) They persecuted the Christians. Even had they refused to accept the message of Christ themselves, they might at least have allowed others to listen to it and to accept it. Let a man always remember that there are more ways to heaven than one; and let him keep himself from intolerance.

(iii) They did not try to please God. The trouble of the Church has so often been that she has clung to a man-made religion instead of a God-given faith. The question men have asked so often is, " What do I think? " and not, " What does God say? " It is not our puny logic that matters; it is God's revelation.

(iv) They were up against all men. In the ancient world the Jews were in fact accused of " hatred of the human race." Their sin was the sin of arrogance. They regarded themselves as the Chosen People, as indeed they were. But they regarded themselves as chosen for *privilege*, and never dreamed that they were chosen for *service*. Their aim was that some day the world should serve them, not that at all times they should serve the world. The man who thinks only of his own rights and his own privileges will always be up against other men—and, what is more serious, he will be up against God.

(v) They wished to keep the offer of the love of God exclusively to themselves. They did not wish the Gentiles to have any share in the grace of God. Someone has summed up the exclusive attitude in four bitter lines of verse,

> " We are God's chosen few;
> All others will be damned.
> There is no room in heaven for you;
> We can't have heaven crammed."

There is something essentially and fundamentally wrong with any religion which shuts a man off from his fellow men. If a man really loves God that love must run over in love for his fellow men. So far from making him hug his privileges to himself, he will be filled with a very passion to share them.

OUR GLORY AND OUR JOY

I *Thessalonians* 2: 17-20

But, brothers, when we had been separated from you—in presence but not in heart—for a short time, we were the more exceedingly eager with a great desire to see your face. So we wished to come to you—I Paul longed for it once and again—but Satan blocked our way. For who is our hope or our joy or the crown in which we boast? Is it not even you, in the presence of the Lord Jesus Christ at His coming? For you are our glory and our joy.

FIRST Thessalonians has been called " a classic of friend-ship," and here is a passage where Paul's deep affection for his friends breathes through his words. Across the centuries we can still feel the throb of love in these sentences.

Paul uses two interesting pictures in this passage.

(i) He speaks of Satan *blocking his way* when he desired

to come to Thessalonica. The word he uses (*egkoptein*) is the technical word for putting up a road-block calculated to stop an expedition on the march. It is Satan's work to throw obstacles into the Christian's way—and it is our work to surmount them, for road-blocks were made to be circumvented.

(ii) He speaks of the Thessalonians being his *crown*. The word is interesting. In Greek there are two words for a *crown*. The one is *diadema*, and it is used almost exclusively for the royal crown. The other is *stephanos*, and it is used almost exclusively for the victor's crown in some contest and especially for the athlete's crown of victory in the games. It is *stephanos* that Paul uses here. The only prize in life that he really valued was to see his converts living well. W. M. Macgregor used to quote the saying of John when he was thinking of the students whom he had taught, " I have no greater joy than to hear that my children walk in the truth." (3 John 4). Paul would have said amen to that. The glory of any teacher lies in his scholars and students; and should the day come when they have left him far behind the glory is still greater. A man's greatest glory lies in those whom he has set or helped on the path to Christ. Anne Ross Cousin turned into verse the thoughts of Samuel Rutherford as he lay in prison in Aberdeen. In one verse she pictures him thinking of his old congregation in Anwoth and she expresses his thoughts like this:

> " Fair Anwoth on the Solway
>   To me thou still art dear;
> Even from the verge of heaven
>   I drop for thee a tear.
> O! if one soul from Anwoth
>   Shall meet me at God's right hand,
> My heaven will be two heavens
>   In Immanuel's land."

Nothing that we can do can bring us credit in the sight of God; but at the last the stars in a man's crown will be those whom he led nearer to Jesus Christ.

THE PASTOR AND HIS FLOCK

I *Thessalonians* 3: 1-10

> So, when we could not stand it any longer, we made up our minds to be left all alone in Athens, and we sent Timothy our brother and God's servant in the good news of Christ, to strengthen you and encourage you about your faith, to see that none of you is beguiled into leaving the faith because of these afflictions, for you yourselves know that that is the very work that God has appointed us to do. For, when we were with you, we told you beforehand that we Christians always suffer for our faith—as indeed it has turned out as you well know. So then, no longer able to stand it, I sent to find out how your faith is doing, in case the tempter had put you to the test and our labour should turn out to be all for nothing. But now that Timothy has come back to us from you, and has brought us the good news of your faith and love, and has told us that you always think kindly of us and that you always yearn to see us—just as we yearn to see you—because of this, we have been encouraged, brothers, by you, through your faith, in all our straits and in all our afflictions, and because now life for us is indeed worth living if you stand fast in the Lord, what thanks can we return to God for you for all the joy with which we rejoice because of you before God, while night and day we keep on praying with all the intensity of our hearts to see your face and to fill up the gaps in your faith?

IN this passage there breathes the very essence of the spirit of the pastor.

(i) There is *affection*. It will always remain true that we can never affect or win people at all unless we begin, quite simply, by liking them. It was Carlyle who said of London, "There are three and a half million people in this city—mostly fools!" The man who begins by despising men or by looking down on them or by disliking them can never go on to save men.

(ii) There is *anxiety*. When a man has put the best of himself into anything, when he has launched anything from a liner to a pamphlet, he is anxious until he knows how the work of his hands and of his brain will weather the storms. If that is true of things, it is still more poignantly true of people. When a parent has trained a child with love and sacrifice he is anxious when that child is launched out on the difficulties and dangers of life in the world. When a teacher has taught a child and has put something of himself into that task of teaching he is anxious to see how that training will stand the test of life. When a minister has received a young person into the Church, after years of training in Sunday School, in Bible Class, in confirmation class, he is anxious to know how that young person will meet and fulfil the duties and the obligations of Church membership. And supremely it is so with Jesus Christ. He staked so much on men and loved men with such a sacrificial love that He anxiously watches and waits to see how men will use that love. A man must stand awed and humbled when he remembers how in earth and in heaven there are those who are bearing him on their hearts and who are watching how he fares.

(iii) There is *help*. When Paul sent Timothy to Thessalonica it was not nearly so much to inspect the Church there as it was to help it. It should be the great aim of every parent, every teacher and every preacher, not so much to criticize and condemn those in his charge for their faults and mistakes, but to save them from these faults and mistakes and, if they have fallen into them, to rescue them from them. The Christian attitude to the sinner and the struggler must never be that of condemnation, but always that of help.

(iv) There is *joy*. Paul was glad that his converts were standing fast. He had the joy of one who had created something which would stand the tests and temptations of time. There is no joy like that of the parent who can point to a child who has done well.

(v) There is *prayer*. Paul carried his people on his heart to God's mercy seat. We will never know from how much sin we have been saved and how much temptation we have conquered because someone has prayed for us. It is told that once a servant-girl became a member of a Church. She was asked what Christian work she did. She said that she had not the opportunity to do much because her duties were so constant, but, she said, " When I go to bed I take the morning newspaper to my bed with me; and I read the notices of the births and I pray for all the little babies; and I read the notices of marriage and I pray that those who have been married may be happy; and I read the announcements of death and I pray that the sorrowing may be comforted." No man can ever tell what tides of grace flowed from that attic bedroom. When we can serve people no other way, when, like Paul, we are unwillingly separated from them, there is one thing we can still do—we can pray for them.

ALL IS OF GOD

I *Thessalonians* 3: 11-13

> May He who is our God and Father and the Lord Jesus Christ direct our way to you. May the Lord increase you and make you to abound in love to each other and to all men, even as we do towards you, in order that he may strengthen your hearts, so that you may be blameless in holiness before the God who is our Father, at the coming of our Lord Jesus with all his saints.

IT is in a simple passage like this that the instinctive turn of the mind of Paul is best seen. For Paul everything was of God.

(i) He prays to God to open a way for him whereby he may come to Thessalonica. It is to God that Paul turned for guidance in the ordinary day to day problems of life. If he contemplated a journey it is to God he turned to open up the way. One of the great and grave mistakes of life is to turn to God only in the great moments and the overpowering emergencies and the shattering crises.

Not long ago I was talking to three young men who had just completed a yachting expedition up the west coast of Scotland. One said to me, " You know, when you are at home you never listen to the weather forecasts, but when we were on that yacht we listened to them with all our ears." It was quite possible to do without the weather forecasts when life was comfortably safe; it was essential to listen to them when life might depend on them. We are apt to try to do the same with God. In ordinary things we disregard Him, thinking that we can manage well enough by ourselves; in the emergency we clutch at Him, knowing that we cannot get through without Him. It was not so with Paul. Even in the ordinary routine thing like a journey from Athens to Thessalonica it is to God that Paul looked for guidance and direction. We use God to try to achieve a God-rescued life; Paul companied with God to achieve a God-directed life.

(ii) He prays to God that God will enable the Thessalonians to fulfil the law of love in their daily lives. We often wonder why the Christian life is so difficult to live, especially in the ordinary everyday relationships of life. The answer may very well be that we are trying to live it by ourselves. The man who goes out in the morning without prayer is, in effect, saying, " I can quite well tackle to-day myself." The man who lays himself to rest without speaking to God, is, in effect, saying, " I can bear whatever consequences to-day has brought myself." John Buchan once described an atheist as " a man who has no invisible means of support." And it may well be that our failure to live the Christian life is due to the fact that we have tried to live it without the help of God — and that is an impossible assignment.

(iii) Paul prays to God for the ultimate safety. At this time his mind was full of thoughts of the Second Coming of Christ, of the day when men would stand before the judgment seat of God. It was his prayer that God would so preserve His people in rectitude and righteousness

229

that on that day they would not be ashamed. No man can ever meet God without God; the only way to prepare to meet God is to live daily with God. The shock of that day will not be for those who have so lived that they have become the friends of God, but for those who meet God as a terrible stranger.

THE SUMMONS TO PURITY

I *Thessalonians* 4: 1-8

Finally then, brothers, we ask and urge you in the Lord Jesus, that, as you have received instructions from us as to how you must behave to please God, even so you do behave, that you may go on from more to more. For you know what orders we gave you through the Lord Jesus; for this is God's will for you, that you should live a consecrated life, I mean, that you should keep yourself from fornication, that each of you should know how to possess his own body in consecration and in honour, not in the passion of lustful desire, like the Gentiles who do not know God, that in this kind of thing you should not transgress against your brother or try to take advantage of him. For of all these things the Lord is the avenger, as we have already told you and testified to you. For God did not call us to impurity but to consecration. Therefore he who rejects this instruction does not reject a man, but rejects the God who gives His holy Spirit to us.

IT may seem strange that Paul should go to such lengths to inculcate sexual purity in a Christian congregation; but two things have to be remembered. First, the Thessalonians had only newly come into the Christian faith; and they had come out of a society in which chastity was an unknown virtue; they were still in the midst of such a society and the infection of it was playing upon them all the time. It would be exceedingly difficult for them to unlearn what they had for all their lives accepted as natural. Second, we must remember that there never was an age in history when marriage vows were so disregarded and divorce so disastrously easy. The phrase which we have translated " that each of you should possess his own body in consecration and in honour " may possibly be translated, " that each of you may possess his own *wife* in consecration and in honour."

Amongst the Jews marriage was theoretically held in the highest esteem. It was said that a Jew must die rather than commit murder, idolatry or adultery. But divorce was tragically easy. The Deuteronomic law laid it down that a man could divorce his wife if he found " some uncleanness," or, " some matter of shame " in her. The difficulty was in defining what was a " matter of shame." The stricter Rabbis confined that to adultery and adultery alone; but the laxer teaching was that it meant if she had spoiled his dinner by putting too much salt in his food; if she went about in public with her head uncovered; if she talked with men in the streets; if she spoke disrespectfully of her husband's parents in his presence; if she was a brawling woman, which was defined as a woman whose voice could be heard in the next house. It was only to be expected that the lower and the laxer view prevailed.

In Rome, for the first five hundred and twenty years of the Republic, there had not been one single divorce; but now, under the Empire, as it has been put, divorce was a matter of caprice. As Seneca said, " Women were married to be divorced and divorced to be married." In Rome the years were identified by the names of the consuls; but it was said that fashionable ladies identified the years by the names of their husbands. Juvenal quotes an instance of a woman who had eight husbands in five years. Morality was dead.

In Greece immorality had always been quite blatant. Long ago Demosthenes had written: " We keep prostitutes for pleasure; we keep mistresses for the day to day needs of the body; we keep wives for the begetting of children and for the faithful guardianship of our homes." So long as a man supported his wife and family there was no shame whatsoever in extra-marital relationships.

It was to men and women who had come out of a society like that that Paul wrote this paragraph. What seems to us the merest commonplace of Christian living was to them startlingly new. One thing Christianity has done—it has laid down a completely new code in regard to the relationship of men and women. Christianity is supremely the champion of purity and the guardian of the home. It may seem superfluous to state things like that to-day, but it is not. In a book entitled *What I Believe*, which is a symposium of the basic beliefs of a selection of well-known men and women, Kingsley Martin writes: " Once women are emancipated and begin to earn their own living and are able to decide for themselves whether or not they have children, their marriage customs are inevitably revised. ' Contraception,' a well-known economist once said to me, ' is the most important event since the discovery of fire.' Basically he was right, for it fundamentally alters the relations of the sexes, on which family life is built. The result in our day is a new sexual code; the old ' morality' which winked at male promiscuity but punished female infidelity with a life-time of disgrace, or even, in some puritanical cultures, with a cruel death, has disappeared. The new code tends to make it the accepted thing that men and women can live together as they will, but to demand marriage of them if they decide to have children." The new morality is only the old immorality brought up to date. There is still a clamant necessity, in Britain as there was in Thessalonica, to place before men and women the uncompromising demands of Christian morality, " for God did not call us to impurity but to consecration."

THE NECESSITY OF THE DAY'S WORK

1 *Thessalonians* 4: 9-12

You do not need that I should write to you about brotherly love; for you yourselves are taught of God to love one another. Indeed you do this very thing to all the brothers who are in the whole of Macedonia. But we do urge you, brothers, to go on to more and more, and to aim at keeping calm and minding your own business. We urge you to work with your hands, as we instructed you to do, so that your behaviour may seem to those outside the Church a lovely thing, and so that you may need no one to support you.

THIS passage begins with praise but it ends in warning; and with the warning we come to the immediate situation behind this letter. Paul urged the Thessalonians to keep calm, to mind their own business and to go on working with their hands. The preaching of the Second Coming had produced an odd and awkward situation in Thessalonica. The result of it had been that many of the Thessalonians had given up their daily work and were standing about in excited groups, upsetting themselves and everybody else, while they waited for the Second Coming to arrive. Ordinary life had been disrupted; the problem of making a living had been abandoned; and they waited excitedly for Christ to come. Paul's advice was preeminently practical.

(i) He told them, in effect, that the best way in which Jesus Christ could come upon them was that He should find them quietly, efficiently and diligently doing their daily job. Principal Rainy used to say, " To-day I must lecture; to-morrow I must attend a committee meeting; on Sunday I must preach; some day I must die. Well then, let us do as well as we can each thing as it comes to us." The thought that Christ will some day come, that life as we know it will end, is not a reason for stopping work; it is a reason for working all the harder and all the more faithfully. It is not hysterical and useless waiting but quiet and useful work which will be a man's passport to the Kingdom.

(ii) He told them that, whatever happened, they must commend Christianity to the outsider, by the diligence and the beauty of their lives. To go on as they were doing, to allow their so-called Christianity to turn them into useless citizens, was simply to bring Christianity into discredit. Paul here touches by implication on a tremendous truth. A tree is known by its fruits; and a religion is known by the kind of men it produces. The only way to demonstrate that Christianity is the best of all faiths is to prove that it produces the best of all men. When we Christians prove that our Christianity makes us better workmen, truer friends, kinder men and women, then and only then are we really preaching. The important thing is not words but deeds, not oratory but life. The outside world never comes into a Church to hear a sermon, but the outside world sees us every day outside the Church; and it is our lives which must be the sermon to win men for Christ.

(iii) He told them that they must aim at independence and must never become spongers on charity. The effect of the conduct of the Thessalonians was that others had to support them. There is a certain paradox in Christianity. It is the Christian duty to help others, for many, through no fault of their own, cannot attain that independence; but it is also the Christian man's duty to help himself. It is his duty not to draw from the community but to put into the community. There will be in the Christian a lovely charity which delights to give and a proud independence which scorns to take, so long as his own two hands can supply his needs.

CONCERNING THOSE WHO ARE ASLEEP

1 *Thessalonians* 4: 13-18

We do not wish you to be ignorant, brothers, about those who are asleep, because we do not wish you to sorrow as the rest of people do because they have no hope. For if we believe that Jesus died and rose again, so also we can be sure that God will bring with Him those who have fallen asleep through Jesus. For we tell you this, not by our own authority but by the word of the Lord, that we who are alive, who survive until the coming of the Lord, will certainly not take precedence over those who have fallen asleep. For the Lord Himself will descend from heaven, with a shout of command, with the voice of an archangel and with the trumpet of God; and the dead who are in Christ will rise first, and then we who are alive, who survive, will be caught up by the clouds together with them to meet the Lord in the air. And so we shall be always with the Lord. So then encourage one another with these words.

THE idea of the Second Coming had brought another problem to the people of Thessalonica. They were expecting it very soon; they fully expected to be themselves alive when it came; but they were worried about those who had died, since becoming Christians, but before the Second Coming. They could not be sure that those who had already died would share the glory of that day which, as they thought, was so soon to come. It is to answer that problem that Paul wrote this passage. His answer is that there will be one glory for those who have died and those who survive.

In this passage he tells them that they must not sorrow as those who have no hope. In face of death the pagan world stood in despair. They met it with grim resignation but with bleak hopelessness. Aeschylus wrote, " Once a man dies there is no resurrection." Theocritus wrote, " There is hope for those who are alive, but those who have died are without hope." Catullus wrote, " When once our brief light sets, there is one perpetual night through which we must sleep." On their tomb-stones grim epitaphs were carved. " I was not; I became; I am not; I care not." One of the most pathetic papyrus letters that has come down to us is a letter of sympathy which runs like this. " Irene to Taonnophris and Philo, good comfort. I was as sorry and wept over the departed one as I wept for Didymas. And all things whatsoever were fitting, I did, and all mine, Epaphroditus and Thermouthion and

Philion and Apollonius and Plantas. But nevertheless against such things one can do nothing. Therefore comfort ye one another." In face of death, for the pagan there was nothing to be done.

Paul's answer lays down a great principle. If a man has lived in Christ and died in Christ, even if he is dead he is still in Christ and he will rise in Christ. This means that between Jesus Christ and the man who loves Him there is a relationship which nothing can break. It is a relationship independent of time; a relationship which overpasses death. Because Jesus Christ lived and died and rose again, so the man who is one with Christ will live and die and rise again. Nothing in life or in death can separate him from Christ.

The picture which Paul draws of the day when Christ will come is poetry. It is an attempt to put into words what is inexpressible and to describe what is indescribable. The picture is this. At the Second Coming Christ will descend from heaven to earth. He will utter the word of command, and thereupon the voice of an archangel and the trumpet of God will waken the dead; and then the dead and the living alike will be caught up in the chariots of the clouds to meet Christ; and thereafter they will be forever with their Lord. We are not meant to take with crude and insensitive literalism that which is a seer's vision. It is not the details which are important. What is important is that in life and in death the Christian is in Christ, and that is a union which nothing can break.

LIKE A THIEF IN THE NIGHT

I *Thessalonians* 5: 1-11

> You have no need, brothers, that anything should be written to you about the times and seasons; for you yourselves well know that, as a thief in the night, so the day of the Lord comes. When they are saying, "All is well; all is safe," then sudden destruction

comes upon them, just as the labour pains come on a woman who is with child, and very certainly they will not escape. But you, brothers, are not in the dark. You are not in a situation in which the day, like a thief, can surprise you. For you are all sons of the light and sons of the day. We do not belong to night or darkness. So then, let us not sleep, as the rest of men do, but let us be watchful and sober. For those who sleep sleep at night; and those who get drunk get drunk at night; but, as for us, because we belong to the day, let us be sober and let us put on the breastplate of faith and love, and let us take for a helmet the hope of salvation, because God did not appoint us for wrath, but to obtain salvation through our Lord Jesus Christ, who died for our sins, so that, whether we wake or whether we sleep, we may live with Him. So then encourage each other, and build up one another —as indeed you are doing.

WE shall not fully understand the New Testament pictures of the Second Coming unless we remember that they have an Old Testament background. In the Old Testament the conception of the Day of the Lord is very common; and all the pictures and the apparatus which belong to the Day of the Lord have been attached to the Second Coming. To the Jew all time was divided into two ages. There was this present age, which was wholly and incurably bad. There was the age to come which would be the golden age of God. But in between there was the Day of the Lord. That day would be a very terrible day. It would be like the birth pangs of a new world; it would be a day in which one world was shattered and another was born. Many of the most terrible pictures in the Old Testament are of the Day of the Lord. (Isaiah 22: 5; 13: 9; Zephaniah I: 14-16; Amos 5: 18; Jeremiah 30: 7; Malachi 4: 1; Joel 2: 31). The main characteristics of the Day of the Lord in the Old Testament were as follows. (i) It would come suddenly and unexpectedly. (ii) It would involve a cosmic upheaval in which the universe was shaken to its very foundations. (iii) It would be a time of judgment. Very naturally the New Testament writers to all intents and purposes identified the Day of the Lord with the day of the Second Coming of Jesus Christ. We will do well to remember that these pictures are what we might call stock pictures. They are not meant to be taken literally. They are pictorial dreams and visions of what would happen when God broke into time.

Very naturally men were anxious to know when that day would come. Jesus Himself had bluntly and definitely said that no man knew when that day or hour would be, that even He did not know, that only God knew. (Mark 13: 32; cp. Matthew 24: 36; Acts 1: 7). But that did not stop people speculating about it, as indeed they still do, although it is surely almost blasphemous that men should seek for knowledge which was denied even to Jesus. To these speculations Paul has two things to say.

He repeats that the coming of the day will be sudden. It will come like a thief in the night. But he also insists that that is no reason why a man should be caught unawares and unprepared. It is only the man who lives in the dark and whose deeds are evil who will be caught unprepared. The Christian lives in the light and no matter when that day comes, if he is watchful and sober, it will find him ready. Waking or sleeping the Christian is living already with Christ and is therefore always prepared.

No man knows when God's call will come for him and there are certain things that cannot be left until the last moment. It is too late to prepare for an examination when the examination paper is before you. It is too late to make the house secure when the storm has burst. Some things have to be done in time. When Queen Mary of Orange was dying her chaplain wished to read to her. She answered, " I have not left this matter till this hour." It was so with an old Scotsman to whom someone offered comforting sayings near the end. The old man's reply was, " Ah theekit (thatched) ma hoose when the weather was warm." If a call comes suddenly it need not necessarily find us unprepared. The man who has lived all his life with Christ is never unprepared to enter the nearer presence of Christ. The man who lives in the light and in the day cannot be caught unawares.

ADVICE TO A CHURCH

I *Thessalonians* 5: 12-22

> We ask you, brothers, to give due recognition to those who labour among you and to those who preside over you in the Lord and admonish you, and to hold them very highly in love because of the work that they are doing.
>
> Be at peace among yourselves.
> We urge you brothers, warn the lazy, comfort the fearful, cling to the weak, be patient with all.
> See that no one pays back evil for evil. Always pursue the good for each other and for all.
> Always rejoice.
> Never stop praying.
> In everything give thanks.
> For this is God's will in Christ Jesus for you.
> Don't quench the gifts of the Spirit, don't make light of manifestations of the gift of prophecy.
> Test everything, hold fast to the fine thing.
> Keep yourselves well away from every kind of evil.

PAUL comes to an end with a chain of jewels of good advice. He sets them out in the most summary way; but every one of them is such that every Christian and every Church member should ponder it.

Respect your leaders, says Paul; and the reason of the respect is the work that they are doing. It is not a question of personal prestige; it is the task which makes a man great, and it is the service that he is doing that is his badge of honour.

Live at peace, says Paul. It is impossible that the gospel of love should be preached in an atmosphere that is poisoned by hate. Better far that a man should quit a congregation in which he is unhappy and in which he makes others unhappy and find one where he may be at peace.

Verse 14 picks out those who need special care and attention. The word which is used for *lazy* originally described a soldier who had left the ranks. It really means " Warn the quitters." The fearful are literally *those whose souls are small.* In every community there is the faint-hearted brother who instinctively fears the worst, but in every community there should be Christians, who, being brave, help others to be brave. " Cling to the weak " is a lovely piece of advice. Instead of letting the weak brother drift away and finally vanish altogether the Christian community should make a deliberate attempt to grapple him to the Church in such a way that he cannot escape. It should forge bonds of fellowship and persuasion to hold on to the man who is temperamentally weak and likely to stray away. To be patient to all is perhaps the hardest of all, for the last lesson that most of us learn is to suffer fools gladly.

Don't take revenge, says Paul. Even if a man seeks our evil we must conquer him by seeking his good.

Verses 16-18 give us three marks of a genuine Church. (i) It is *a happy Church.* There is in it that atmosphere of joy which makes its members feel that they are bathed in sunshine. True Christianity is an exhilarating and not a depressing thing. (ii) It is *a praying Church.* Maybe our Church's prayers would be more effective if we remembered that " they pray best together who also pray alone." (iii) It is *a thankful Church.* There is always something for which to give thanks. Even on the darkest day there are blessings to count. We must always remember that if we face the sun the shadows will fall behind us, but if we turn our backs on the sun all the shadows will be in front.

In verses 19 and 20 Paul warns the Thessalonians not to despise spiritual gifts. The prophets were really the equivalent of our modern preachers. It was they who brought the message of God to the congregation. Paul

is really saying, " If a man has anything to say, don't
stop him saying it."

Verses 21 and 22 describe the constant duty of the
Christian. He must use Christ as touchstone by which to
test all things; and even when it is hard he must keep
on doing the fine thing and must always hold himself
aloof from every kind of evil.

When a Church lives up to Paul's advice it will indeed
shine like a light in a dark place; it will indeed have joy
within itself and power to win others.

THE GRACE OF CHRIST BE WITH YOU

1 *Thessalonians* 5: 23-28

> May the God of peace Himself consecrate you through
> and through; and may your spirit and soul and body
> be kept complete so that you will be blameless at
> the coming of our Lord Jesus Christ. You can rely
> on Him who calls you—and He will do this very thing.
>
> > Brothers, pray for us.
> > Greet all the brothers with a holy kiss.
> > I adjure you by the Lord that this letter should
> > be read to all the brothers.
> > The grace of our Lord Jesus Christ be with you.

So at the end of his letter Paul commends his friends to
God in body, soul and spirit. But there is one very lovely
saying here. " Brothers," said Paul, " pray for us." Surely
it is a wonderful thing that the greatest saint of them all
should feel that he was strengthened by the prayer of the
humblest Christian. Once his friends came to congratulate
a great statesman who had been elected to the highest
office which this country could offer him. His answer was,
" Don't give me your congratulations, but give me your
prayers." For Paul prayer was a golden chain in which he
prayed for others and others prayed for him.

LIFT UP YOUR HEARTS

2 *Thessalonians* I

Paul and Silas and Timothy send this letter to the Church of the Thessalonians which is in God our Father and the Lord Jesus Christ.

Brothers, we ought always to thank God for you, as it is fitting, because your faith is on the increase, and because the love of each one of you all for each other grows ever greater, so that we ourselves are telling proudly about you in the Churches of God, about your constancy and faith amidst all the persecutions and afflictions which you endure—which indeed is proof positive that the judgment of God was right that you should be deemed worthy of the Kingdom of God, for the sake of which you are suffering. And just that judgment is, if indeed it is right in God's sight, as it is, to recompense affliction to those who afflict you, and relief with us to you who are afflicted, when the Lord Jesus shall be revealed from heaven, with the power of His angels, in a flame of fire, when He renders a just recompense to those who do not recognize God and who do not obey the good news of our Lord Jesus. These are such men that they will pay the penalty of eternal destruction which will banish them forever from the face of the Lord, and from the glory of His strength, when He shall come to be glorified in His saints and admired in all those who believed—because our testimony to you was believed—on that day. To this end we also always pray for you, that our God may deem you worthy of the call that came to you, and that He may by His power bring to completion every resolve after goodness and every work that faith inspires, so that the name of our Lord Jesus may be glorified in you, and you in it, according to the grace of our God and of the Lord Jesus Christ.

THERE is all the wisdom of the wise leader in this opening passage. It seems that the Thessalonians had written, or sent a message, to Paul, which had been full of self-doubtings and self-distrustings. They had been timorously afraid that they were not good enough, that their faith was not going to stand the test, that—in the expressive modern phrase—they were not going to make the grade. Paul's answer was not to push them further into the slough of despond by pessimistically agreeing with them; it was to pick out their virtues and their achievements, in such a way, that these despondent, frightened Christians would square their shoulders and fling back their heads and say, " Well, if Paul thinks that of us we'll make a fight of it yet." " Blessed are those," said Mark Rutherford, " who heal us of our self-despisings," and Paul did just that for the Thessalonian Church. He knew that often judicious praise can do what indiscriminate criticism cannot do; he knew that the praise of those we love does not make us proud; it makes us humble; he knew that wise praise never makes a man rest upon his laurels but fills him with the desire to do still better and to deserve it.

There are three things which Paul picked out as being the marks of a vital Church. (i) *A faith which was strong.* It is the mark of the advancing Christian that he grows surer and surer of Jesus Christ every day. The faith which may begin as an hypothesis ends as an absolute certainty. James Agate once said, " My mind is not like a bed which has to be made and remade. There are some things of which I am absolutely sure." The Christian comes to that stage; and he comes to it when, to the thrill of Christian experience, he adds the discipline of Christian thought, when both in life and in thought he tests everything and then holds fast to that which stands the test. (ii) *A love which is increasing.* A growing Church is a Church which grows greater and greater in service. That is well-nigh inevitable. A man may begin serving his fellow men as a duty which his Christian faith lays upon him; he will end by doing it because in it he finds his greatest joy. The selfish life is never the happy life. The life of service opens up the great discovery that unselfishness and happiness go hand in hand. (iii) *A constancy which endures.* The word which Paul uses is a magnificent word. It is the word *hupomone*; it is usually translated *endurance*; but it does not mean the ability passively to bear anything that may descend upon us; it has been described as " a masculine constancy under trial." It describes the spirit which does not only patiently endure the circumstances in which it finds itself; but which masters them and uses them to strengthen its own nerve and sinew. It accepts the blows of life, but in accepting them it transforms them into stepping stones to new achievement.

Paul's uplifting message ends with the most uplifting vision of all. It ends with what we might call *the reciprocal glory.* When Christ comes He will be glorified *in His saints* and *admired in those who have believed.* Here we have the breath-taking truth that our glory is Christ, and that Christ's glory is ourselves. The glory of Christ is in those who through Him have learned to endure and to suffer and to conquer, to shine like lights in a dark place, to become radiant with goodness and loveliness. A teacher's glory lies in the scholars he produces; a parent's glory lies in the children whom he has begotten not only for living but for life; a master's glory lies in his disciples; and to us there is given the tremendous privilege and responsibility that Christ's glory can lie in us. We can be such that we can bring discredit or we can bring glory to the Master whose we are and whom we seek to serve. Can there be any privilege and can there be any responsibility greater than that?

THE LAWLESS ONE

2 *Thessalonians* 2: 1-12

Brothers, in regard to the coming of our Lord Jesus Christ, and in regard to our being gathered to Him, we ask you not to be readily shaken in your mind and not to get into a state of nervous excitement because of any statement purporting to come from us either in the Spirit or by word of mouth or by a letter and alleging that the Day of the Lord is here. Let no one deceive you in any way. The Day of the Lord will not come unless there comes first The Rebellion against God, and unless there be revealed The Man of Sin, The Son of Perdition, the one who opposes himself to and exalts himself against everyone who is called God or made an object of worship, so that he attempts to take his seat in the very temple of God and proclaims that he himself is God. Don't you remember that when I was still with you I told you these things? As for the present, you know the power which restrains him, so that he may be revealed in his own time. For the secret of lawlessness is even now in operation. But The Man of Sin will only appear when the one who restrains him is removed from the scene. And then The Lawless One will be revealed and the Lord Jesus will destroy him with the breath of His mouth and will render him ineffective by His appearance and His coming. The coming of The Lawless One is for those who are doomed. He will come according to the working of Satan with all power and signs and wonders which issue from falsehood, and with all wicked deceit. They are doomed because they did not receive the love of truth that they might be saved. For this cause God sends them a deceiving energy, so that they might believe in a lie, so that all who have not believed but who have consented to that principle of unrighteousness may be judged.

This is undoubtedly one of the most difficult passages in the whole New Testament; and it is so because it is using terms and thinking in pictures which were perfectly familiar to those to whom Paul was speaking but which are utterly strange to us. To those who read and heard it for the first time it required no explanation at all, but to us, who have not their local knowledge, it is obscure.

The general picture is this. Paul was telling the Thessalonians that they must give up their nervous, hysterical waiting for the Second Coming. He denied that he had ever said that the Day of the Lord had come. That was a misinterpretation of his words which must not be attributed to him; and he told them that before the Day of the Lord could come much had still to happen. The events which had to happen were like this. First there would come an age of rebellion against God; into this world there had already come a secret evil power which was working in the world and on men to bring this time of rebellion. Somewhere there was being kept one who was as much the incarnation of evil as Jesus was the incarnation of God. He was The Man of Sin, The Son of Perdition, The Lawless One. In time the power which was restraining him would be removed from the scene; and then this devil incarnate would come. When he came he would gather his own people to him just as Jesus Christ had gathered His. Those who had refused to accept Christ were waiting to accept him. Then there would come a last and final battle in which Christ would utterly destroy The Lawless One; and then Christ's people would be gathered to Him and the wicked men who had accepted The Lawless One as their master would be destroyed. It would be a kind of cosmic battle in which evil incarnate would make its final assault and receive its final defeat.

Now we have to remember one thing. Almost all the Eastern faiths believed in a power of evil as they believed in a power of good. They believed in a kind of battle between God and this power of evil. For instance the Babylonians had a story that Tiamat, the dragon, had rebelled against Marduk, the creator, and had in the final battle been destroyed. Paul was dealing in a set of ideas which were common property when he lived. The Jews too had that idea. They called the Satanic power *Belial*, or more correctly, *Beliar*. When the Jews wished to describe a man as utterly bad they called him *a son of Beliar*. (Deuteronomy 13: 13; I Kings 21: 10, 13; 2 Samuel 22: 5). In I Corinthians 16: 15 Paul uses this term as the opposite of God. This evil incarnate, this humanized devil, was the antithesis of God. The Christians took this over, later than Paul, under the title *Antichrist*. (I John 2: 18, 22; 4: 3). Obviously such a power cannot go on existing for ever in the universe; and there was a widespread belief in one final battle in which God would triumph and this force of anti-God would be finally destroyed. That is the picture with which Paul is working.

What is the restraining force which at the moment was still keeping The Lawless One under control? No one can really answer that question with certainty. Most likely Paul meant the Roman Empire. Time and again he himself was to be saved from the fury of the mob by the justice of the Roman magistrate. Rome was the restraining power which kept the world from insane anarchy. But the day would come when the Roman power would be removed—and after that the chaos.

So then Paul pictures a growing rebellion against God, the emergence of one who was the devil incarnate of Christ had been God incarnate, one final struggle, and then the full and ultimate triumph of God.

Now when this incarnate evil came into the world there would be some who would accept him as master. Those who had refused Christ would accept him; and they, the evil ones with their evil master, would find their final defeat and their terrible judgment.

However remote these pictures may be from us they nevertheless have certain permanent truth in them.

(i) There is a force of evil in the world. Even if he could not logically prove that there was a devil many a man would say, " I know there is because I have met him." We but hide our heads in the sand if we deny that there is an evil power at work amongst men.

(ii) God is in control. Things may seem to be crashing to chaos, but the chaos is a plan. In some strange way even evil is in control by God.

(iii) The ultimate triumph of God is sure. In the end, and in the final battle, nothing can stand against God. The Lawless One may have his day, but there comes a time when God says, " Thus far and no farther." And so the great question for us is, " On what side are you? In the struggle which is at the heart of the universe are you for God—or Satan? "

GOD'S DEMAND AND OUR EFFORT

2 Thessalonians 2: 13-17

We ought always to give thanks for you, brothers beloved by the Lord, because God chose you from the beginning to be saved by the consecration of the Holy Spirit and by faith in the truth. For this he called you by the good news which we brought, that you might obtain the glory of our Lord Jesus Christ. So then, brothers, stand fast and hold on to the traditions which you were taught either by word of mouth or through our letter.

May the Lord Jesus Christ Himself, and God our Father, who loved us, and who gave us, by His grace, eternal encouragement and good hope, encourage your hearts and make you strong in every good deed and word.

IN this passage there is a kind of synopsis of the Christian life.

(i) The Christian life begins with God's call. No man ever chose himself. We could never even begin to seek God unless God had already found us. The whole initiative is with God; the ground and the moving cause of the whole matter is the seeking love of God.

(ii) It develops in our effort. The Christian is not called to dream, but to fight; he is not called to stand still, but to climb. He is called not only to the greatest privilege in the world, but also to the greatest task in the world.

(iii) This effort is helped continually by two things. (a) It is helped by the teaching, the guidance and the example of good and godly men. God speaks to us through those to whom He has already spoken. " A saint," as someone has said, " is a person who makes it easier for others to believe in God." And there are others who help us, not by anything they say or write, but simply by being what they are, men whom to meet is to meet God. (b) It is helped by God Himself. We are never left to fight and struggle and toil alone. He who gives us the task also gives us the strength to do it; more, He actually does it with us. We are not thrown into the battle and the struggle of life to meet them with the puny resources which we can bring to them. At the back of us and beside us there is God. When Paul was up against things in Corinth, he had a vision by night, and in it the Lord said to him, " Be not afraid . . . for I am with Thee." (Acts 18: 9, 10). They that are for us are always more than they that be against us.

(iv) This call and this effort are all designed to produce two things. (a) They are designed to produce *consecration on earth*. Literally, in Greek, a thing which is consecrated is *set apart for God*. It is meant to set us apart in such a way that God can use us for his service. The result of it is that a man's life no longer belongs to him to do with it as he likes; it belongs to God, for God to use it as He likes. (b) They are designed to produce *salvation in heaven*. The Christian life does not end with time; its goal is eternity. Its end is the purity which will see God. The Christian is the man who can regard his present struggle and affliction as a light thing in comparison with the glory that shall be. As Christina Rosetti wrote:

" ' Does the road wind up-hill all the way? '
    ' Yes, to the very end.'
' Will the day's journey take the whole long day? '
    ' From morn to night my friend.'

' But is there for night a resting-place? '
    ' A roof for when the slow dark hours begin.'
' May not the darkness hide it from my face? '
    ' You cannot miss that inn.'

' Shall I meet other wayfarers at night? '
    ' Those who have gone before.'
' Then must I knock, or call when just in sight? '
    ' They will not keep you standing at that door.'

' Shall I find comfort, travel-sore and weak? '
    ' Of labour you will find the sum.'
' Will there be beds for me and all who seek? '
    ' Yes, beds for all who come.' "

A FINAL WORD

2 Thessalonians 3: 1-5

> Finally, brothers, keep on praying for us, that the word of God may run its race and receive its crown of glory—as it does in your case—and that we may be saved from these wicked and evil men, for the faith is not for everyone. You can rely on the Lord who will make you steady and who will guard you from the evil one. We have confidence in the Lord that you both do and will do what we command you to do. May the Lord direct your hearts so that you may feel the love of God and display the endurance which Christ can give.

ONCE again Paul comes to the end of a letter with the request that his people should pray for him. (cp. I Thessalonians 5: 25; Romans 15: 30 ff; Philemon 22). There is something deeply moving in the thought of this giant among men asking for the prayers of the Thessalonians who so well recognized their own weakness. Nowhere is Paul's humility more clear to see. And the fact that he, as it were, threw himself on their hearts, must have done much to bind even his opponents to him, because it is very difficult to dislike a man who asks you to pray for him.

But in spite of his love for and trust in men Paul was a realist. The faith, he said, is not for everyone. We can be certain that he said it not cynically but sorrowfully. Once again we see the tremendous responsibility of free-will. We can use it to open our hearts and we can use it to shut them. Faith's appeal is not selective; it goes out to every man, but the heart of man can refuse its response.

In the last verse of this passage we see what we might call the inward and the outward characteristic of the Christian. The inward characteristic is the awareness, the realization of the love of God. It is the deep awareness that we cannot drift beyond that love and care, the sense that the everlasting arms are underneath and about us. One of the basic needs of life is the need of security and we find that need met in the consciousness of the unchanging love of God.

The outward characteristic of the Christian is the endurance which Christ can give. We live in a world where there are more nervous break-downs than at any time in history. It is simply a sign that more and more people have the feeling that they cannot cope with life. We live in a world where men are afraid to look ahead. The outward characteristic of the Christian is that when others break he stands erect, and when others collapse he shoulders his burden and goes on. With the love of God in his heart and the strength of Christ in his life a man can face anything.

DISCIPLINE IN BROTHERLY LOVE

2 *Thessalonians* 3: 6-18

> Brothers, we command you in the name of our Lord Jesus Christ, keep yourselves from every brother who behaves like a truant from duty and who does not conduct himself in accordance with the teaching which they received from us, for you yourselves know that you must imitate us, because we never played the truant from work when we were among you, nor did we eat bread which we had received from you without paying for it, but in labour and toil, we kept on working night and day so that we would not be a burden to any of you. It is not that we had not the right to claim support from you, but we kept at work that we might give ourselves to you as an example for you to imitate, for when we were with you we used to give you this order, " If a man refuses to work, neither let him eat." For we hear that there are some amongst you whose behaviour is that of truants from work, who are busy in nothing except in being busy-bodies. To such we give orders and exhort them in the Lord Jesus Christ that they should quietly go on working and so eat their bread. Brothers, don't grow tired of doing the fine thing. If anyone does not obey the word we send to you through this letter, mark him; don't associate with him that he may be shamed. Don't reckon him as an enemy, but give him advice as a brother.
>
> May the Lord of peace himself give you peace always and everywhere. The Lord be with you all.

> Here is the greeting of me Paul in my own hand-
> writing, which is the sign of genuineness in every
> letter. This is how I write. The grace of our Lord
> Jesus Christ be with you all.

HERE Paul is dealing, as he had to deal in the previous
letter, with the situation produced by those who took the
wrong attitude to the Second Coming. There were those
in Thessalonica who had given up their work and who had
abandoned the routine claims of everyday to wait about in
excited idleness for Christ to come. Paul uses a vivid
word to describe them. Twice he uses the adverb *ataktos*
and once the verb *ataktein*. The word means *to play truant*.
It occurs, for instance, in the papyri, in an apprentice's
contract in which the father agrees that his son must
make good any days on which he absents himself from
duty or plays truant. The Thessalonians in their excited
idleness were truants from duty and from work.

To bring them to their senses Paul quotes his own example.
All his life Paul was a workman and a man who worked with
his hands. The Jew glorified work. " He who does not teach
his son a trade," they said, " teaches him to steal." Paul
was a trained Rabbi; but the Jewish law laid it down that
a Rabbi must take no pay for teaching. He must have a
trade and must satisfy his daily needs with the work of his
hands. So we find Rabbis who were bakers, barbers,
carpenters, masons and who followed all kinds of trades.
The Jew believed in the dignity of honest toil; and they
were sure that a scholar lost something when he became so
academic and so withdrawn from life that he forgot how
to work with his hands. Paul quotes a saying, " If a man
refuses to work, neither let him eat." It is the *refusal* to
work that is important. This has nothing to do with the
unfortunate man who, through no fault of his own, can
find no work to do. This has been called " the golden rule
of work." Deissmann has the happy thought that, when
Paul said this, " he was probably borrowing a bit of good
old workshop morality, a maxim coined perhaps by some

industrious workman as he forbade his lazy apprentice to sit down to dinner." After all in this we have the example of Jesus Himself. Jesus was the carpenter of Nazareth, and legend has it that He was so good a carpenter that He made the best ox-yokes in all Palestine and that men came from all over the country to buy the yokes that He made so well. A tree is known by its fruits and a man is known by his work. Once a man was negotiating to buy a house; he bought it without even seeing it; he was asked why he took such a risk; his answer was, " I know the man who built that house and he builds his Christianity in with the bricks." The Christian, just because he is a Christian, should be a better workman than anyone else.

Paul disliked the busybody intensely. There may be greater sins than gossip, but there is no sin which does more damage in the Church. A man who is doing his own work with his whole strength will have enough to do without being maliciously and pryingly interested in the affairs of other people.

It is Paul's instruction that those who disregard his instructions must be dealt with by the community; but they are to be dealt with not as enemies; they are to be advised as brothers. The discipline which is given by a man who stands above the sinner and who contemptuously looks down upon him, and who speaks to hurt, may terrify and wound, but it seldom amends. It is more likely to produce resentment than reformation. When Christian discipline is necessary it is to be given as by a brother to a brother. It is to be given not in anger, still less in contempt; it is always to be given in love.

So Paul draws to an end; and at the end he adds his autograph to authenticate his letter. " Look," he says, " this is what my handwriting is like. Mark it, so that you will know it again." And then, with the truth expounded, with praise and rebuke lovingly intermingled, he commends the Thessalonian Church to the grace of Jesus Christ.